FATHERING

Promoting Positive Father Involvement

Edited by Annie Devault, Gilles Forget, and Diane Dubeau

Over the past few decades, researchers and practitioners have moved towards a more diverse, inclusive concept of fatherhood. As well, they have developed valuable new strategies for cultivating the positive involvement of fathers in the lives of their children, even with such challenging populations as fathers livings in poverty or in prison.

This volume draws on the innovative work of Prospère, a Quebec organization that brought together fathers, health and social service practitioners, and university researchers. The contributors provide numerous examples of strategies and interventions with fathers, lessons learned from these practices on how to better support vulnerable fathers and families, and in-depth information on ways of designing, implementing, evaluating, and disseminating the results of participatory action research (PAR) – all with the goal of making fathers active partners in decision-making.

ANNIE DEVAULT is a professor in the Department of Social Work at l'Université du Québec en Outaouais.

GILLES FORGET is a PhD candidate in the School of Public Health and Social Work at the Queensland University of Technology. He was a health promotion officer in Montreal's Public Health Department for more than twenty years.

DIANE DUBEAU is a professor in the Department of Psychoeducation and Psychology at l'Université du Québec en Outaouais.

FATHERING

Promoting Positive Father Involvement

Edited by Annie Devault, Gilles Forget,
and Diane Dubeau

UNIVERSITY OF TORONTO PRESS
Toronto Buffalo London

© University of Toronto Press 2015
Toronto Buffalo London
www.utppublishing.com

ISBN 978-1-4426-3713-9 (cloth)
ISBN 978-1-4426-2876-2 (paper)

___

Library and Archives Canada Cataloguing in Publication

Fathering : promoting positive father involvement / edited by Annie Devault, Gilles Forget, and Diane Dubeau.

Includes some material previously published in French under title: La paternité au XXIe siècle. Québec: Presses de l'Université Laval, 2009.
Includes bibliographical references.
ISBN 978-1-4426-3713-9 (bound).–ISBN 978-1-4426-2876-2 (paperback)

1. Fatherhood. 2. Father and child. 3. Fathers. 4. Parenting.
I. Devault, Annie, 1963–, editor II. Forget, Gilles, 1952–, editor
III. Dubeau, Diane, 1961–, editor

HQ756.F3822 2015   306.874'2   C2015-904446-4

___

This book has been published with the help of a grant from the Federation for the Humanities and Social Sciences, through the Awards to Scholarly Publications Program, using funds provided by the Social Sciences and Humanities Research Council of Canada.

University of Toronto Press acknowledges the financial assistance to its publishing program of the Canada Council for the Arts and the Ontario Arts Council, an agency of the Government of Ontario.

Canada Council for the Arts
Conseil des Arts du Canada

ONTARIO ARTS COUNCIL
CONSEIL DES ARTS DE L'ONTARIO
an Ontario government agency
un organisme du gouvernement de l'Ontario

Funded by the Government of Canada   Financé par le gouvernement du Canada

To our sons and daughters.

Father involvement is built around multiple experiences and reflections. This volume is a mirror of both our professional and personal experiences. The authors and the many contributors to this work have expressed their heartfelt concern for the welfare of children. We hope this volume will be the first step towards discovering a renewed concept of fatherhood and finding new ways of designing services for fathers. We also hope this will lead to a supportive environment for our sons and daughters, enabling them to fulfil their own future roles as fathers and mothers concerned with the health and wellness of their children.

Contents

List of Figures ix

List of Tables x

Foreword by Kerry Daly xi

Introduction 3
ANNIE DEVAULT, GILLES FORGET, AND DIANE DUBEAU

1 Traditions, Tensions, and Trends in Participatory Action Research 13
SANDRINA DE FINNEY AND JESSICA BALL

2 Father Involvement: A Multifaceted Concept 47
DIANE DUBEAU, ANNIE DEVAULT, AND DANIEL PAQUETTE

3 Mobilizing Actors in Participatory Action Research: Promoting Father Involvement in Two Vulnerable Communities in Quebec 71
GENEVIÈVE TURCOTTE AND FRANCINE OUELLET

4 The Challenging Evaluation of Complex Interventions 93
DIANE DUBEAU, GENEVIÈVE TURCOTTE, FRANCINE OUELLET, AND SYLVAIN COUTU

5 A Retrospective Look at the Partnership between Researchers and Actors 122
GILLES FORGET AND DOMINIC BIZOT

viii   Contents

6   Support for Father Involvement in a Socio-professional Integration Context   133
    ANNIE DEVAULT, GILLES FORGET, FRANCINE OUELLET,
    AND MARIE-PIERRE MILCENT, WITH JEANNE DORÉ

7   Fathers behind Bars: A Participatory Action Research Project to Support Father Involvement following Incarceration   160
    DIANE DUBEAU, MARTINE BARRETTE, AND DENIS LAFORTUNE

8   An Outreach and Support Program for Socio-economically Vulnerable Fathers   187
    GENEVIÈVE TURCOTTE, GILLES FORGET, FRANCINE OUELLET,
    AND ISABELLE SANCHEZ

9   Knowledge Transfer: Moving Evidence into Practice   213
    GILLES FORGET

    Conclusion: Fathering: New Paths, Future Possibilities   243
    ANNIE DEVAULT, GILLES FORGET, AND DIANE DUBEAU

Appendix A: The Father Involvement Questionnaire   256

Appendix B: Methodological Parameters of the Effects of the Evaluation   262

Contributors   269

Figures

1.1 The PAR Praxis-Making Cycle   22
4.1 A Conceptual Framework for the Implementation Evaluation   100
4.2 The Process of the Production of Effects in the Prospère Project   101
4.3 Prospère's Community Impacts Evaluation Model   107
6.1 Conceptual Model of the Life-Story Study   140
8.1 Relaying Fathers: The Analysis Framework for Evaluating the Project   191
9.1 Knowledge Transfer, an Analytical Perspective   216

Tables

2.1 Fathers' Profiles, as Compiled by Fournier and Quéniart (1994) 60
2.2 Fathers' Profiles, as Compiled by Dufour (2001) 64
3.1 Activities Carried Out within the Four Principal Action Strategies at Both Sites 84
4.1 Measurement Synthesis 110
7.1 Workshops of the Father-Child Intervention Program 172
7.2 Practitioners' Guide for Working with Young People Facing Parental Incarceration 175
8.1 Characteristics of Fathers Outreached by the Relaying Fathers Program 203
9.1 Summary of the Evaluation of Changing Fathers, Evolving Practices 226
B.1 Measurement Method and Instruments Used to Evaluate the Ultimate Results 263
B.2 Expected Effects, Methods, and Respondents in the Post-test Research Design, with Comparisons 267

Foreword

The degree to which fathering has changed continues to be a focus of debate. On the one hand, we have a new language of fathering activity that focuses on the "new father," who carries out the work of parenting in a way that reflects a significant departure from previous generations of fathers. This new dad works alongside mom or his gay partner to be engaged with and attentive to the kids, takes his share of responsibility for planning activities, and, when the opportunity arises, takes parental leave or becomes a stay-at-home dad so that his partner can take advantage of the higher income that she or he can earn. And, if there is a separation or divorce, there is a growing expectation that men will be granted their fair share of custody. On the other hand, we live in a culture where the perception of fathers suggests that little has changed. For example, studies indicate that men have increased the time they devote to child care – but only incrementally and still disproportionately compared to women. As a result, there is still talk about women's "double day" rooted in their responsibility for the "second shift," along with an implicit charge of men's parenting deficiency and failure to step up to the plate. Television images of fathers continue to reinforce the stereotype of the incapable and bumbling father (Mr. Mom) who is fully dependent on his partner for direction. And from the perspective of those who advocate for fathers after separation and divorce, there are ongoing calls to revamp a justice system that continues to favour mothers in custody decisions.

Of course, the question is not about which of these perspectives best reflects reality, but how to make sense of these tensions and diverse perspectives on father involvement. There is nothing static about these competing perspectives; instead, they create a strong voltage that reflects the dynamic and political process of change. Indeed, many forms shape the landscape of fathering, where we have deeply committed fathers serving as the primary parent living next to fathers who work excessively and who resemble what we think of as fathers from the previous generation. We have fathers who, despite their employer's ridicule and discouragement, argue for flexibility and parental leave. These fathers work alongside other fathers who defer to their partner's preference to take on the primary responsibility of parenting. We see young, vulnerable fathers who persist in their efforts to be a good provider for their children, as well as fathers who drop out of their children's lives after separation or divorce. Change is occurring, and the diverse forms of father involvement are an indication of the movement we have witnessed away from monolithic, stereotypical views of father involvement.

This book plays an important role in not simply helping us to understand the process of change in father involvement, but also in serving as a catalyst for change. Although an appreciation of "diversity" and the identification of underlying tensions help us to understand a spectrum of father involvement possibilities in the here and now, they do not serve us well in thinking about how to move towards the preferred future of father involvement. Specifically, how can we build on our understandings of the ways fathers contribute to healthy child development outcomes? How can we use emerging research literature that highlights the beneficial features of father involvement for men's own emotional and social growth? How do we move forward with a research-informed agenda of change that is attentive to principles of fairness and equity for both men and women? How do we ensure that we hear a wide range of men's voices that inform us about parenting success, preferences, and dreams for a better future?

With a focus on building and sharing knowledge through participatory action research, this volume goes a long way to helping us see the transformative power of research that both listens to men's voices and engages them in processes of learning, advocacy, and social change. In these chapters, the reader will see an expansive view of the types of research that are subsumed in this transformation. This includes research that is rooted in singular and multidisciplinary perspectives and in quantitative and qualitative methodologies, as well as research that emphasizes a range of units of analysis, from individual fathers' perspectives to couples' relationships and negotiations to systemic dynamics and properties.

Behind this catalytic research is Prospère, one of Canada's pioneering father involvement organizations. With a mandate to support father involvement among fathers of vulnerable, young children, Prospère was established in Quebec in 1993 and continued until 2010, when its funding came to an end. Over that time Prospère brought together university researchers and health and social services practitioners to explore how to support father involvement, ensure protection for vulnerable children, optimize healthy developmental outcomes, and develop successful programs to enhance family well-being overall. In this regard, Prospère has been a catalytic force for change in Quebec and Canada at all levels, including those of individual fathers, social and health services, and social policy. The chapters in this book provide many examples of the ways Prospère has been an instrument of change. Most important, Prospère has played a key role in the articulation and implementation of action plans for fathers and families that are carried out in shopping malls, arenas, community halls, and parks. These action plans are designed to encourage the personal empowerment of men as fathers, to mobilize neighbourhood resources, and to create appropriate and meaningful services for fathers.

This book represents an important chapter in the development of father involvement research and practice in Canada. From a research perspective, it provides tremendous insight into the experiences and challenges all fathers face – but most particularly young fathers, fathers living in precarious economic circumstances, and incarcerated fathers. Furthermore, the research reported here not only outlines in detail the methodological approaches used to understand these experiences; it also provides direction on how to conduct research in a way that is respectful and inclusive of fathers' voices and that builds on these understandings to bring about much needed social change. There are also excellent examples of how to evaluate the outcomes of research efforts, and to ensure that knowledge transfer successfully moves the evidence gained from the research into strategies for clinical and educational practice.

The research described in this volume provides many excellent examples of how inquiry, learning, and advocacy come together to create change in the delivery of community services and in the broader policies that govern the types and modes of services that are available. Although we might continue to debate the degree to which fathers have changed, the message from this important book is that change in father involvement is not only possible, but desirable, and is already happening in many different ways with vulnerable fathers. Most important, this book provides guidance on how we all can play a more effective role, through research and advocacy, in cultivating positive father involvement in Canada and beyond.

Kerry Daly
University of Guelph

FATHERING

Promoting Positive Father Involvement

Introduction

ANNIE DEVAULT, GILLES FORGET,
AND DIANE DUBEAU

In 1991 an advisory committee headed by senior lecturer Camil Bouchard submitted a report entitled *Un Québec fou de ses enfants* (A Quebec Crazy about Its Kids) to the health and social services minister of the province of Quebec. The report highlighted the numerous challenges that infants, children, and teenagers face, and proposed that all sectors of society mobilize to evaluate and implement practices to build a healthier and brighter future for the next generation, so that children could grow and develop in conditions that ensure their health and well-being. One of the practices urged was that of promoting father involvement. At the same time the Conseil québécois de la recherche sociale (Quebec Council of Social Research) reviewed its funding policies and instituted a new program offering medium-term funding around key issues to teams of researchers from universities and public and community agencies. These two events led to the birth in 1993 of research and actions aimed at instilling, supporting, and reinforcing father involvement as a means to reduce child victimization. This book relates the work of the research team known as Prospère, whose name is a play on words in French alluding to the prosperity that comes from having many children (*prospère*) and to a commitment to fathering (pro, as in proactive or in favour of, and *pères*, as in fathers). The team was formed within the Groupe de recherche et d'action sur la victimisation des enfants (GRAVE, or Action and Research Group on Child Victimization). Prospère has since been recognized as "a pioneering organization in Canada that combined research, advocacy, clearing house, and training of practitioners in agencies, services and community-based programs" (Ball & Daly, 2012, p. 19).

Building on studies conducted in Quebec and elsewhere, the Prospère team first focused on developing a common understanding of father involvement to discover its impact on the health and well-being of children. These discussions led to the following definition of father involvement: *the continuous participation and preoccupation of the father, or his substitute, towards the physical, psychological, and social development of his child.* Over the next twenty years, the team explored the complexity of father involvement with various clientele using different research methods, from conceptualization to knowledge transfer, and from different methodological and theoretical perspectives. During this long-term undertaking, the team chose to contribute to discussions on fathering and the promotion of father involvement by sharing its main participatory action research (PAR) projects, which focused on fathers in contexts of vulnerability.

This book offers innovations in the field of fathering studies in several ways. First, it presents a PAR framework with a view to encouraging its use in building understanding and instigating social change in relation to father involvement in Canada. We see PAR as a means by which to engender transformative engagement for and by fathers, and as a relational praxis, as the process by which theoretical knowledge is enacted to bring about concrete outcomes on the ground. Second, the volume is addressed to several important groups: to the scientific community, by providing in-depth information on challenges and ways to design, implement, evaluate, and disseminate the results of PAR; to practitioners, by offering numerous examples of strategies and interventions with fathers; and to policy-makers, by detailing the lessons learned from these practices to better support fathers and their families. Third, the book sheds light on the lives of men who often have not had the opportunity to share their inner experiences of fatherhood or to express their understanding of father involvement and their hopes for their children's future, as they have been excluded from the social debate around fathering due to their age, poverty, employment status, low level of education, or seclusion. Fourth, the volume offers an in-depth assessment of knowledge transfer, as well as examples of innovative ways to disseminate research results at local, provincial, national, and international levels. Finally, the team members' different disciplines (sociology, psychology, social work, and public health) provide a multidisciplinary look at father involvement, the actions to put in place to promote it, and the social policies that define the outlines of today's and tomorrow's fathering practices.

What More Is There to Say on Fathering?

Some forty years ago Michael Lamb, a respected figure in the field of fatherhood studies, stated that "fathers are the most forgotten actors of the scientific community" (Lamb, 1975, p. 245). He emphasized that studies on child development and families had always been approached from the mother's perspective, as she was considered the main caregiver and the one who knew best what was good for the child. Things have changed, however, to the extent that some audiences now say that too much attention is given to fathers. In recent years magazines, television shows, and advertisements have used images of fathers depicted in various family-related circumstances. In libraries it is now easier to find books on fatherhood than it was in the 1980s. But does this mean there is no need to say more? This book attempts to show that this is not the case. Its specific contribution relies on the two choices guiding Prospère's work over the years. First, father involvement is studied from the child's perspective – that is, on how father involvement can best support the child's health and well-being. Because the main objective of this work is the prevention of child abuse and neglect, however, the different PAR projects referred to in this book do not address father involvement from a gender-specific angle or as imbedded in the social construct of gender relations. The second aspect governing this work, as elaborated by other researchers (Dienhart, 1998; Featherstone, 2009; Hawkins & Dollahite, 1997; Pratt, Lawford, & Allen, 2012), is a generative perspective that emphasizes the father's strengths and competencies. This perspective brings us to direct our actions promoting father involvement within the different settings that shape its specificity on a theoretical, methodological, and practical basis.

An Ecological Perspective to Father Involvement

The team's research studies are situated within the evolution of the meaning of fatherhood, the profound changes affecting the composition of families, the changes in social relations between genders, and the concept of fatherhood as redefined by the globalization of our economy. As such the angle we have chosen in addressing these different studies is a constructivist, ecological perspective. The ecological perspective of human development (Bronfenbrenner, 1979, 1986) considers the complex relations between fathers and their global environment. The development of the field of community psychology in the early 1980s led to the progressive adoption of this perspective in other fields, such as social work and public health in the planning of programs and the mobilization of communities. This process was added to the already existing will to describe how this knowledge of the evolving understanding of father involvement was built through the years. Knowledge construction relies on praxis, or a synthesis of theory and practice, using research, practice, and the use of knowledge to drive changes in the representation and the actions of parents and practitioners regarding fatherhood. From the researcher's point of view, approaching fatherhood from a constructivist, ecological perspective means dedicating oneself to considering the complexity of an issue, refusing to consider only individual factors, and taking into account the impact of action on the social environment (Allen, Daly, & Ball, 2012; Ball & Daly, 2012). It also means linking the individual to this environment by reinforcing his social connectedness; bringing resources to collective action to change these environments; and, finally, acknowledging the capacity of each individual to act upon these environments.

The Structure of the Book and the Topics Discussed

This book is built around four main sections. The first section (Chapter 1) situates the PAR framework that has inspired Prospère's work throughout the years. The second section (Chapters 2, 3, 4, and 5) is dedicated to the description of the first major PAR realized by the team. It describes the team's reflection on the concept of father involvement and its definition, and the design of a measurement scale, the Father Involvement Questionnaire, that helped evaluate the impact of a health promotion program aimed at increasing father involvement in two vulnerable communities. The section then outlines the context of the emergence of the project, its model, the sites in which it was implemented, the mobilization of stakeholders and the population, and the numerous activities carried out in both communities during the five years that the social innovation project lasted. This section presents the evaluation of the outcome of this initiative, and concludes with an interview with community representatives. The third section of the book (Chapters 6, 7, and 8) presents further studies carried out by Prospère. A common characteristic of these PAR projects was the desire to reach vulnerable fathers and to support their involvement with their children. The final section (Chapter 9) proposes a conceptual framework for understanding and designing knowledge transfer strategies intended to reach the scientific community, practitioners, policy-makers, and the population at large. In this last section, numerous devices and evaluation tools are described to give a fuller picture of the work undertaken by Prospère.

In Chapter 1, Sandrina de Finney and Jessica Ball offer a comprehensive look at participatory action research and its challenges. After reminding readers of the conditions that exclude many fathers from support – mother-centric images of family, social barriers, and a monolithic view of fathers – the authors outline the growing interest in father involvement and the need for a more differentiated analysis of father involvement in Canada. To meet these challenges, the authors present participatory action research as a promising praxis through which to engage groups of fathers in sharing fatherhood experiences, highlighting opportunities, and eliminating barriers to their social inclusion. After describing the roots of the PAR approach to social investigation, challenging the artificial borders between theory, research and action, the authors present the ideologies and principles guiding PAR projects. Imbedded in a desire to influence the distribution of power, PAR is a cyclical and fluid process that aims to bring about change grounded in the experiences of the participants. To be in line with these principles, the procedures of PAR must be built upon strong partnerships and developed on a relational praxis that questions the more traditional boundaries that delineate researchers' roles. Ethics, data sources, and collection and analysis procedures can also reflect the PAR position. As an illustration of this, the authors refer to the various innovative methodologies used by PAR researchers and the analytical strategies incorporated in PAR. After reviewing the challenges associated with data collection and the implementation of analytical strategies, the authors discuss some of the tensions and dilemmas in PAR. They also discuss the usefulness of this approach in bringing fathers, families, and community organizations together to collaborate with researchers, and in deepening and broadening the understanding of fathers' experiences, needs, and goals.

Chapter 2 introduces the description and evaluation of the first PAR implemented by Prospère and its partners to instil, reinforce, and maintain father involvement. It describes the thought process and the various studies done over the years to better circumscribe the different dimensions of fathering. The chapter first recalls the main ways researchers have defined father involvement. Father involvement was first considered using a quantitative approach based on the number of minutes that fathers interacted with their children. Other researchers then used a comparative approach to delineate the respective contributions of parents according to their direct interaction with the child and their availability and accessibility, and the implication of these factors for parental responsibilities. These findings and the discussion they raised led the members of Prospère to work out a multidimensional vision of father involvement and to reach a consensus. This definition was then operationalized in a measurement scale, the Father Involvement Questionnaire. If much effort was deployed to bring an innovative and rigorous way of measuring father involvement, Prospère also realized studies using a qualitative approach to arrive at the first phenomenological description of the situation as it is experienced and felt by the actors. These studies brought nuances to the definition of father involvement and characterized the impact of different conditions on the ways fathers interact with and care for their children.

Chapters 3 and 4 describe the complete research cycle in detail, from the conceptualization of a health promotion program and the building of partnerships to the implementation and process of the impact evaluation developed by the members of Prospère, a cycle that took more than seven years. Aiming at reducing child victimization by promoting father involvement, Prospère relied on a strategy of community immersion that took into account the complexity of the needs and roles of fathers and families and the influence of both close and distant environments. This strategy was characterized by simultaneously putting in place a number of complementary activities to reach the father, his partner, practitioners, and local policy-makers. The activities were grouped within local annual action plans built and agreed upon by the researchers and their partners.

Chapter 4 describes how the Prospère project ended with a major effort to evaluate the program implementation and its impact. The authors present the three successive evaluations of this PAR project carried out over the years. First, the needs analysis allowed the researchers and their partners to assess the openness of the various services in the communities and the perceptions of father involvement among mothers, fathers, and practitioners. This analysis helped researchers to define more precisely the activities that needed to be developed. The second evaluation was an implementation analysis, which helped the steering committees of the two communities in their decision-making, in order to build knowledge about the program's model and to identify the process that brought about the outcome. Finally, the third evaluation, the impact evaluation, aimed to bring out the results of the PAR project on father involvement. Based on a quasi-experimental design with pre- and post-intervention measures, this evaluation showed how the model proposed by the researchers and adapted by the communities influenced the ways fathers interacted and cared for their children and families.

Chapter 5 concludes this section with an interview with community representatives who were associated with the PAR project from its beginning and who are still promoting father involvement after fifteen years.

Prospère's first PAR research targeted communities where many families were economically disadvantaged and socially excluded, and where children were victimized more often than in other communities. Its ultimate goals were to protect children, prevent victimization, and promote father involvement. The same goals directed the research, targeting vulnerable fathers in other settings, as described in the third section of the book.

The concept of vulnerability is used in various ways. Prospère members decided to look at the context of vulnerability, more than at fathers on an individual level, to take into account the life situations that restrict, or place barriers on, their involvement. When describing these contexts, authors use different terms, such as social exclusion, disaffiliation, marginalization, or disqualification, but they agree on considering vulnerability as a dynamic process rather than as a static situation (Fitzgerald & London Bocknek, 2013). For the French author Robert Castel, marginalization represents the end of a "double drop-out process, with respect to work and with respect to relational integration" (Castel, 1994, p. 13). According to Castel, the overlapping of these two domains can produce an *integration zone*, where work transition and relational integration are stable; a *vulnerability zone (or assistance)*, where work is unsettled and interpersonal relations are tenuous; and a *disaffiliation zone*, where dropping out is imminent at both the work and relational support levels.

Fathers targeted by the research presented in Chapter 6 would be included in the zones of vulnerability or disaffiliation because of their work situation and their lack of a social network. The description of this study follows the steps described previously, starting with a needs assessment among young fathers and practitioners, observation of practices in the settings where the program was implemented in socio-professional integration program organizations in the Montreal area, and the implementation of an annual action plan and its evaluation. The PAR project offers an in-depth view of the ways young men envision and experience their fatherhood, the barriers to their involvement with their children, and the support they receive to fulfil their desire to be "good fathers." Finally, this chapter describes a group experience that young fathers qualified as very positive, and from which they emerged stronger and better equipped.

Chapter 7 offers a rare look at some of the most forgotten fathers: those who are incarcerated. It outlines the efforts the researchers made to build partnerships with associate partners, practitioners, and fathers, as was done in previous Prospère PAR projects. This chapter also discusses the challenges, barriers, and opportunities to make the program sustainable. Throughout this chapter, the reader, like the researcher, will have in mind the question: Why and how should we reinforce father involvement for men who, quantitatively, are physically absent, sometimes for a prolonged period of time, and qualitatively, whose behaviour is considered delinquent? Even if this PAR project does not fully answer this question, it gives us a new understanding of fathers who have been incarcerated and the impact of that situation on their families, as well as a clearer idea of the parameters that should guide intervention in such cases.

Chapter 8 describes another study by Prospère that targeted vulnerable fathers. For this study, instead of working in specific communities or settings such as socio-professional programs or halfway houses, the researchers focused on an innovative practice in the field of father support. Building on partnerships and relationships established during previous PAR projects, members of Prospère put in place a practice in which home visitors or street workers supported men in their involvement as fathers and in the realization of their professional and social goals. The chapter describes the implementation process and the results of this intervention as described by the workers and the fathers themselves. It identifies the main factors that contributed to the changes seen in the fathers and the particular components of this innovative practice.

Finally, Chapter 9 describes several of the team's knowledge transfer experiences. Although the use of research results has gained importance in the past couple of decades (McQueen & Anderson, 2000; Wilson, Petticrew, Calnan, & Nazareth, 2010), there is still a gap between the available knowledge and its use for planning or practice purposes (Kramer Holmes, Cowan, Pape Cowan, & Hawkins, 2013). Various factors explain this underuse of knowledge. Practitioners might not value research results, have views that differ from those of the researchers, or lack access to the knowledge. Other factors are related to researchers, who might delay the production or dissemination of results, have difficulty in translating knowledge into meaningful content for practitioners, or lack support from funding agencies for knowledge transfer. The description of multiple knowledge transfer experiences provides the reader with an original reflection on this last, but essential, step of participatory action research. These activities are presented according to the targeted clientele, the scientific community, practitioners, policy-makers, and the general population. The chapter not only describes these activities; it also presents a reflection on the determinants and processes that can improve knowledge transfer.

Father-Friendly Environments

This synthesis of studies and actions promoting father involvement suggests that there is still much more to do to understand and support fathers better. The book also shows that father involvement is inscribed within the evolution of the family in Western society. Laws and rules must be revised to take these changes into account to support the willingness of fathers to be more than providers (Coltrane & Behnke, 2013). They should also evolve to acknowledge that couples and families are diverse and that society must be inclusive. Finally, this book reminds us that fathering is also the responsibility of men towards their children. All too often, men do not participate in the programs and activities offered by practitioners and community agencies. Opening up avenues for sharing experiences is another way to get closer to fathers and to their unique experience of a complex phenomenon, and to build with them a friendly environment for them and for their families.

REFERENCES

Allen, S., Daly, K., & Ball, J. (2012). Fathers make a difference in their children's lives: A review of the research evidence. In J. Ball & K. Daly (Eds.), *Father involvement in Canada: Diversity, renewal, and transformation* (pp. 50–88). Vancouver, BC: UBC Press.

Ball, J., & Daly, K. (2012). Father involvement in Canada: A transformative approach. In J. Ball & K. Daly (Eds.), *Father involvement in Canada: Diversity, renewal, and transformation* (pp. 1–25). Vancouver, BC: UBC Press.

Bronfenbrenner, U. (1979). *The ecology of human development: Experiments by nature and design.* Cambridge, MA: Harvard University Press.

Bronfenbrenner, U. (1986). Ecology of the family as a context for human development: Research perspectives. *Developmental Psychology, 22*(6), 723–742. http://dx.doi.org/10.1037/0012-1649.22.6.723

Castel, R. (1994). La dynamique des processus de marginalisation: de la vulnérabilité à la désaffiliation. *Cahiers de Recherche Sociologique, 22*(22), 11–25. http://dx.doi.org/10.7202/1002206ar

Coltrane, S., & Behnke, A. (2013). Fatherhood and family policies. In N.J. Cabrera & C.S. Tamis-LeMonda (Eds.), *Handbook of father involvement: Multidisciplinary perspectives* (pp. 419–437). New York, NY: Routledge.

Dienhart, A. (1998). *Reshaping fatherhood: The social construction of shared parenting*. Thousand Oaks, CA: Sage. http://dx.doi.org/10.4135/9781483345482.

Featherstone, B. (2009). *Contemporary fathering: Theory, policy and practice*. Bristol, UK: Policy Press.

Fitzgerald, H.E., & London Bocknek, E. (2013). Fathers, children, and the risk-resilience continuum. In N.J. Cabrera & C.S. Tamis-LeMonda (Eds.), *Handbook of father involvement: Multidisciplinary perspectives* (pp. 168–185). New York, NY: Routledge.

Hawkins, A.J., & Dollahite, D. (1997). *Generative Fathering*. Thousand Oaks, CA: Sage.

Kramer Holmes, E., Cowan, P.A., Pape Cowan, C., & Hawkins, A.J. (2013). Marriage, fatherhood, and parenting programming. In N.J. Cabrera & C.S. Tamis-LeMonda (Eds.), *Handbook of father involvement: Multidisciplinary perspectives* (pp. 438–454). New York, NY: Routledge.

Lamb, M.E. (1975). Fathers: Forgotten contributors to child development. *Human Development, 18*, 254–266.

McQueen, D.V., & Anderson, L. (2000). What counts as evidence? Issues and debates on evidence, relevance to the evaluation of community health promotion programs. In I. Rootman, M. Goodstadt, L. Potvin, B. Hyndman, D.V. McQueen, J. Springett, & E. Ziglio (Eds.), *Evaluation in health promotion: Principles and perspectives* (pp. 63–81). Copenhagen, Denmark: WHO Regional Office for Europe.

Pratt, M.W., Lawford, H.L., & Allen, J.W. (2012). Young fatherhood, generativity, and men's development: Travelling a two-way street to maturity. In J. Ball & K. Daly (Eds.), *Father involvement in Canada: Diversity, renewal, and transformation* (pp. 107–25). Vancouver, BC: UBC Press.

Wilson, P.A., Petticrew, M., Calnan, M.W., & Nazareth, I. (2010). Disseminating research findings: what should researchers do? A systematic scoping review of conceptual frameworks. *Implementation Science; IS, 5*(1), 91. http://dx.doi.org/10.1186/1748-5908-5-91

1 Traditions, Tensions, and Trends in Participatory Action Research

SANDRINA DE FINNEY AND JESSICA BALL

Introduction

Rooted in popular education, community development, and social change movements, participatory action research (PAR) is a research approach well suited to support the emerging father involvement movement in Canada. The needs, goals, and effects of fathers on children's growth and development, and on family life more broadly, have often been overlooked in health and social policy and programs, as well as in the media. Many programs that claim to reach out to and support "parents" are actually mostly mother-centred and involve only mothers. Similarly, much of the research literature about parenting fails to differentiate data collected from mothers and fathers, as if they were indistinguishable. PAR offers an approach that directly involves fathers in explorations of experiences and issues, and places them at the centre of decision-making in the areas of service provision, research, and policy that directly affect them. Thus the umbrella methodology of PAR has guided the studies described in this book, and framed the community development, knowledge transfer, and social change strategies elaborated by chapter authors. Fathers can and often do play important roles in the lives of children and youth (Allen, Daly, & Ball, 2012; Tamis-LeMonda & Cabrera, 2002). Calls for policy reform and program investments to support father involvement arise primarily from community-based organizations that meet children, youth, and families in direct service capacities within health care, education, child welfare, recreation, newcomer services, and Aboriginal programs (Kishcuk, 2001). Given these grassroots origins, and in the absence of a robust and differentiated knowledge base of the diverse conditions and experiences of father involvement, PAR's commitment to relationship building, peer support, community building, and theoretical flexibility makes it a particularly promising research framework (Doherty, 2000). Underlying this approach is the conviction that fathers are producers both of learning for and about themselves, and of support, growth, and social changes within their families and communities.

This chapter presents an overview of PAR's histories, applications, promises, and problematics, with a view to using it to develop understanding and instigate meaningful participation and action relating to father involvement in Canada. The chapter lays the foundation for a pivotal assertion that underpins the work described by authors in this edited collection – namely, that PAR can engender transformative engagement for and by fathers, father activists, service providers, advocates, and theorists. We describe procedures typically used in PAR praxis, involving iterative cycles of community building, exploration, reflection, analysis, evaluation, and action. We explore some of the tensions and gaps in PAR, especially concerning community members' access to research participation and modes of knowledge creation and the difficulty of moving from engagement to social action. We address interpretation dilemmas in PAR related to knowledge production and ownership, ethics, research outcomes, validity, and participation. Finally, we identify the promise that PAR holds as a relational praxis of knowledge co-generation and a springboard for social action (Cahill, 2007), which is to engage fathers in processes of personal and social transformation.

Priorities of the Father Involvement Movement in Canada

Despite their increasing visibility in Canadian policy and discussions of paternity leave and child custody, the diversity of fathers' experiences across varied and dynamic family structures and wide-ranging and changing circumstances remains poorly engaged in policy debates, theoretical understandings, and parent- and family-serving programs (Lero, Ashbourne, & Whitehead, 2006). Monolithic discourses of fatherhood and father rights do not account for the complex ways in which fathers engage with their children as caregivers, providers, role models, and teachers (Palkovitz, 1997). Many fathers are bewildered about how to be directly involved in caring for their children given that mothers tend to be the primary caregivers, especially when children are young, and given that social services are dominated by mother-centric parenting education and support programs and the use of exclusionary terms such as "maternal and child health," "mom and tot" playgroups, and Mother Goose library time (Broughton & Rogers, 2007).

Although mother-centric images of family life reinforce the stereotype of the absent or invisible father, some fathers are excluded even further, not only from mother-centred discourses, but also from exclusive representations of fatherhood. Outreach and intervention service systems are sustained by research that studies and reproduces dominant cultural and gendered images of fatherhood and understandings of family life in Canada, as if fathers were a homogeneous population with a common history, sociocultural context, needs, and goals. The social sciences have tended to develop theoretical conceptualizations of fatherhood that are assumed to be universally valid, and service agencies often promote "best practice" programs and policies based on these undifferentiated and underverified assumptions (Coltrane, 2007; Lupton & Barclay, 1997). As a result, fathers who fall outside dominant constructions of white, able, heterosexual fatherhood face additional barriers to their social inclusion related to their citizenship-immigration-refugee status, language, religion, socio-economic status, ethnicity, ability, and sexual orientation, among other factors (Bell, 2009; Epstein, 2009; Este & Tachble, 2009). These barriers affect their visibility in debates about fatherhood and their level of engagement in the care of their children. Meanwhile, institutional and policy structures that promote dominant narrow views of what it means to be positively involved as a father remain unexamined, and structural gaps sustain the social exclusion of some groups of fathers (Devault, Gaudet, Bolte, & St-Denis, 2005). These gaps include, for example, a lack of support to enable immigrant fathers to find meaningful employment (Este & Tachble, 2009), programs and resources that reproduce the problematic heteronormative binary of mother/father (Bell, 2009; Epstein, 2009; Pendleton Jiménez, 2009; Stafford, 2009), health care policies that tend to exclude consideration of fathers of children with a chronic illness and/or disability (Beaton, Nicholas, McNeill, & Wenger, 2012; Nicholas, 2003; O'Brien, Hunt, & Hart, 2005), and a lack of effective poverty reduction measures for Indigenous fathers (Ball & George, 2007).

Over the past decade, some movement has occurred in Canada towards recognizing the important and diverse roles that fathers can and often do play as parents, along with some acknowledgment of serious gaps in knowledge about the experiences of Canadian fathers. The impetus for this movement has come in part from public alarm, as the number of children being raised in lone-mother-headed households continues to rise, while mothers' labour force participation increases and shortages of affordable, quality child care persist. As Canada's demographic and social composition continues to change, fathers' local realities and engagement with fatherhood are also changing; correspondingly, dominant Euro-Western, mother-centric, and heteronormative models and discourses must be expanded to encompass multiple experiences of fatherhood in diverse families and contexts. A more differentiated analysis of father involvement would examine men's experiences of the transition to fatherhood, forms of providing and caring for children and youth and sustaining relationships with adult children, and the barriers fathers face in developing and sustaining positive involvement with their children across transitions in family relationships, socio-economic circumstances, geographic location, child welfare interventions, incarceration, and other conditions.

PAR as a Promising Praxis

Given gaps in Canadian images of the family, policy supports, and family-focused practice, critical tools are needed to excavate and engage with the intersecting political and social forces that shape father involvement. PAR can contribute to the growing field of father involvement research with praxis that engages groups of fathers in sharing their fatherhood experiences, which, in the process, will illuminate opportunities and barriers to their positive involvement and social inclusion in various contexts of child bearing and child rearing. How do fathers, especially those who tend to be socially excluded, negotiate a sense of belonging and engagement in caring for their child when the options available to them are determined by social forces inscribed with dominant social dictates, norms, and views of families, sexuality, masculinity, and gender roles? PAR offers avenues to get beyond the decontextualized, material measures of father involvement that have predominated research in this area (Allen, Daly, & Ball, 2012), shedding light on the ways fathers themselves conceive of and gauge their multilayered involvement. Engaging with fathers to understand how they see the world in relation to their father role can highlight structural as well as psycho-social barriers to their meaningful involvement, enhance their visibility in research about parenting, and support the contributions they can make to children's development, mothers' wellness, and family life.

PAR's emphasis on understanding the perspectives of participants in social interactions is particularly relevant to expanding discourses, policies, and practices of social inclusion. Insights yielded by PAR can have important implications for transforming the landscape of family life in Canada through policy reform, program development, and practice in diverse disciplines, including child health, child welfare, men's health, family services, parent education, and related fields. The explicitly action-oriented stance of PAR on knowledge production and its focus on community involvement make it ideologically compatible with investigators and practitioners whose interest in examining fathers' experiences is motivated by a desire to enhance fathers' visibility and meaningful participation in decision-making about policy and service provisions for children and families.

Men's Inclusion in Parent and Family Policy, Services, and Research

Debates about social inclusion and exclusion are an increasingly prevalent focus of social policy and research in Canada, and a prominent theme in the field of fatherhood research. In the context of this chapter, a tension relating to the historical roots of PAR, and its ideology, is that it has been used most often to include the most "voiceless" or marginalized populations, such as racialized women, poor communities, and sexual minorities. Many middle-class men aligned with dominant cultures do not face the kinds of social exclusions that PAR was originally created to address. Nevertheless, PAR can be a useful approach for studying diverse groups of men, because even white, middle-class fathers tend to be excluded from parenting policy, research, and programming. Unless challenged, their social exclusion in the domain of fatherhood will serve to maintain polarizing gender norms and the status quo that structures men's roles as being "outside the home," or men as "absent parents"; these all serve to maintain the construction of women as "natural" primary caregivers.

Research on social exclusion reiterates the critical role that context plays in shaping family life, underscoring a need to enhance social systems that normalize, embrace, and reflect the experiences of all people, including marginalized peoples, such as the young, racialized, and incarcerated fathers discussed in this volume. Characteristics of social exclusion include: residence in substandard housing; inequitable access to employment, social, and health services; stigmatization; spatial and social isolation; disconnection from civil society; and everyday experiences of discrimination, racism, and violence (Galabuzi, 2004). These conditions intersect and tend to be mutually reinforcing, erecting barriers to access to various forms of social capital (Kaspar & Noh, 2001). For instance, due to the ongoing effects of colonial policies, Indigenous communities often deal with housing and health deficits and dismantled social and cultural institutions, resulting in reduced access to family support services, life skills training, education, employment, child care, health care services, and recreational opportunities (de Finney & Saraceno, 2015; Trocmé, Knoke, & Blackstock, 2004).

One sharpening focus within social inclusion debates is how men learn fathering and engage in caring and providing for their children (Doucet, 2006; Hobson, 2002). Another focus asks the extent to which their involvement and skills development as parents not only promote optimal child health and development outcomes (Ball, Moselle, & Pedersen, 2007) and build social capital for the family unit (Ravanera, 2007), but also promote fathers' visibility and participation in social and health policy and programs for children and families (Long, 2008). Socio-cultural capital grants fathers access to institutional and social networks, gives them "insider" knowledge of family life, and enhances their ability to participate fully in civic life. One of PAR's strengths is its inherent flexibility, which provides a diversity of avenues by which fathers can engage in collaborative, community-based, participatory research with peers and key stakeholders (such as policy-makers and service providers), as well as engage with their own children, families, and communities. Participation in a PAR project actually might be one way fathers – acting as participant-researchers – can build social capital through solidarity with other fathers, as well as engage in shaping more positive images of fatherhood, and use combined actions to increase the visibility and cogency of their needs and goals for policy and program reform.

Methodological Strategies in Participatory Action Research

No single history or unified set of explanatory concepts defines PAR practice. Rather than being a unitary method, PAR is a broad and constantly evolving methodological framework covering a spectrum of approaches and procedures (see, for example, Chambers, 2002; Fals Borda, 1987, 1996; Gaventa, 1988; Gayfer, 1981, 1992; Israel, Eng, Schulz, & Parker, 2012; Kesby, Kindon, & Pain, 2009; Park, Brydon-Miller, Hall, & Jackson, 1993; Tandon, 2002; Tolman & Brydon-Miller, 1997, 2001;

Weis & Fine, 2004). A framework for participatory action research in diverse locations and contexts across the world has grown out of the work of community researchers who perceived a schism between the philosophies of participatory education and development and the positivist research practices still prevalent in their fields (Gayfer, 1981; Martín-Baró, 1994; Tandon, 2002). The principles of popular education and, in particular, the work of grassroots Latin American intellectuals Orlando Fals Borda (1987, 1996) and Paulo Freire (1971, 1973, 1975) have greatly influenced PAR's focus on critical consciousness, the democratization of knowledge production, anti-oppressive practice, and social justice. In a groundbreaking 1975 issue of the journal *Convergence*, Budd Hall, a Canadian academic, social activist, and early innovator of PAR, articulated the value of an approach to social investigation that would challenge the artificial borders between theory, research, and action. His conceptualization of PAR holds participant knowledge to be integral to validity, and democratic and participatory knowledge production as foundational to social change. PAR is part of a groundswell against the assertive seizure of epistemic space by academic researchers, wherein the lives and knowledge of vulnerable, often colonized communities have served as "data plantations" (Ladson-Billings, 2000) for research done ostensibly on their behalf. Hall (1975, 1981, 1993, 2000a, 2000b) highlights commonalities that run through the many iterations of PAR – namely, an engagement with three fundamental issues: (1) the meaningful and consequential participation of marginalized communities; (2) the production of critical knowledge through participatory inquiry; and (3) the implementation of social change for and by communities themselves. Interaction of these elements provides the ideological impetus behind a research process that empowers participants to transform their social reality by becoming critical participants in knowledge production, community development, and social change.

Today PAR's influence extends to a broad spectrum of ideological, political, intellectual, and methodological streams applied in diverse international settings and disciplines and across academic and applied fields. These include, for example, participatory research in community development, action research in organizations and educational settings, practitioner action research, rural participatory research, feminist action research, Indigenous community-based research, and child- and youth-centred PAR (Cahill, Rios-Moore, & Threatts, 2008; Greenwood & Levin, 1998; Herr & Anderson, 2005; Torre, Fine, Stoudt, & Fox, 2012). Researchers have developed iterations that fall under the broader banner of community-based research, including collective action research (Leonard, 2002), research for development (Chambers, 2002), and community action research (Reitsma-Street, 2002; Reitsma-Street & Brown, 2003). Many of these streams informed the development of our own PAR praxis (Ball & Havassy, 1984; Ball & Janyst, 2008; de Finney, 2007; de Finney, Green, & Brown, 2009; de Finney & Lee, 2008; Lee & de Finney, 2005). PAR's diverse methodological iterations offer a wealth of options for university and community partners interested in innovative father-centred and father-engaged research.

PAR Ideologies and Principles

Given its interdisciplinarity, heterogeneity, and highly contextualized nature, PAR cannot be reduced to a single formula or fixed set of principles. It is better understood as a cyclical, emerging process out of which underlying principles evolve from the discussions and debates that arise as it is enacted in specific contexts. PAR researchers nonetheless share a deep concern about the ethics of conventional research practices, in which university-based investigators frequently mine population groups or communities for knowledge without confirming the validity of their interpretations with research participants or engaging with them in the pursuit of their own research goals. PAR processes subvert the role of the outside "expert" researcher, thereby aiming to flatten the traditionally hierarchical researcher-researched relationship. In PAR, researchers and community members collaborate, pooling their varying expertise and cultural knowledge in a generative process that, ideally, results in socially meaningful analysis and engagement, action plans, and social action that are grounded in the needs and goals of community members. The definition and operationalization of PAR principles is a source of much debate within and outside the field. Nonetheless, PAR researchers have written extensively about commonalities within the PAR spectrum (Fals Borda, 1996; Gayfer, 1981, 1992; Hall, 1975, 1981, 1993; Maguire, 1987, 2001; McTaggart, 1991, 1997; Park et al., 1993; Smith, Willms, & Johnson, 1997). Five features common to many PAR initiatives are worth highlighting.

(1) PAR involves a collective process and seeks a more horizontal distribution of power. PAR is explicitly politicized and eschews modernist claims to objectivity and value-free theorizing. It seeks to redefine the privileged relationship between researchers and knowledge production by positioning participants as agents at the centre of their own process of knowledge generation. In contrast to traditional research relationships, PAR works towards a redistribution of resources and power, as reflected, for instance, in the use of such terms as *participant-researchers, co-researchers, community researchers, research team,* and *research partners.*

(2) PAR is grounded in the experiences and participation of communities. PAR is concerned with supporting local knowledge, working across borders of insiders and outsiders, and ensuring that research works *with* rather than *for* (Hall, 1993). Although PAR's organic and contextualized nature accounts for multiple potential pathways and iterations, at its root PAR originates with, and is owned by, the community. Ideally, participants are involved in all stages of the research process, from the conceptualization of the research agenda and design, to the collection and analysis of data, to the evaluation of outcomes, to their dissemination and potential implementation (Smith et al., 1997). The use of diverse methods (for example, theatre, video-ethnography, mapping, narrative interviews, focus groups, community surveys, evaluation, textual analysis, and so on) that reflect diverse participant experiences, backgrounds, and capacities, and that are embedded in participants' cultural contexts, positions participants to articulate their own theories about issues they identify.

(3) The cyclical process of PAR generates new praxis. PAR is deeply critical of linear thinking; it considers causality as circular or spiral in nature, with multiple determinants, rather than singular, predictable antecedents (Fine et al., 2001). As illustrated in Figure 1.1, PAR evolves through a cycle of reflection, analysis, action, and evaluation that recurs throughout the research process, allowing participants to draw increasingly complex implications for praxis, and apply these to social action.

Budd Hall (1975, 1981), Ignacio Martín-Baró (1994), Rajesh Tandon (2002), and Francisco Vio Grossi (1981) have been instrumental in theorizing approaches to the implementation of the reflection-analysis-action-praxis cycle in PAR. Praxis is a synthesis of theory and practice; it avoids exclusive academic claims to knowledge production by giving community members tools to translate theoretical knowledge into concrete outcomes on the ground. To develop praxis, participants undertake many iterations of the PAR cycle. To initiate a PAR cycle, a research team typically develops a process or framework for working in partnership, in order to outline common themes and goals. Next, a research problematic originating within the community is defined, refined, and elaborated, drawing out initial themes and strategies that

Figure 1.1. The PAR Praxis-Making Cycle

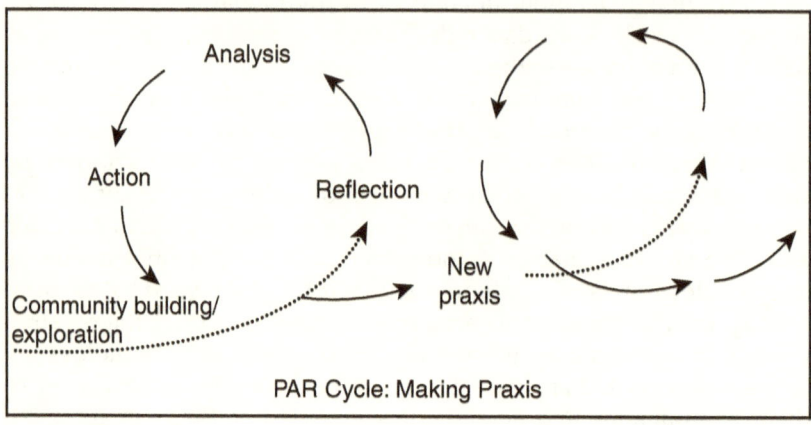

participant-researchers will use to describe and explore the issues they face and their ideas for effective interventions. By coding information about experiences and comparing and linking information, they slowly move from a micro- to a macro-analysis and, in the process, make theoretical and practical sense of the challenges they have identified. At this stage the goal is to peel back the layers to uncover and develop critical consciousness and analytical thinking – in other words, to develop a critical understanding of the underlying forces that shape those everyday issues, typically rendered invisible by dominant social constructions and forms of interaction. A cycle of critical analysis, involving the identification, problematization, and politicization of the participants' individual experiences, is used to deepen understanding of the issues. Through a process of collective consciousness raising or "conscientization" (Freire, 1971, 1997), "people develop their power to perceive critically the *way they exist* in the world *with which* and *in which* they find themselves; they come to see the world not as a static reality, but as a reality in process, in transformation" (Freire, 1997, p. 64; emphasis added).

Over time, participatory research strategies, such as consultations, focus groups, expressive arts, journaling, community meetings, and other methods, help participants to link their individual experiences to the broader context, thereby promoting critical consciousness and collective education about the systemic or structural nature of their personal experiences. At multiple points throughout this cyclical process, participants can initiate actions and change strategies that speak to their emerging findings.

(4) PAR is emergent, fluid, context specific, and open ended. As the PAR cycle demonstrates, PAR sets in motion an iterative, open-ended, highly contextualized process that cannot be prescribed; consultation and ongoing participation emerge in an organic and layered manner. Such a fluid process is necessary to shape the goals and process of any given PAR project. The stages in a cycle of PAR are rarely sequential or distinct, and they might receive different emphasis according to the research context. Training, data collection, consultations, analysis, evaluation, dissemination, and action can overlap and occur at any point during the process, depending in part on the group's membership, goals, available resources, timelines, identified issues, and desired outcomes.

(5) PAR is focused on action and change. Concerned as it is with the relationships between research, knowledge production, social control, and social inequity, PAR aspires to move beyond the promotion of critical consciousness and new knowledge to mobilize social change strategies for and through groups who often, though not always, experience some form of marginalization or exclusion. In this respect the success of PAR projects is typically contested and partial, due to complex ethical considerations related to representation and participation, collaborative research and knowledge ownership, and team-based dissemination and action, among others. Although the PAR cycle promotes critical awareness of inequitable power relations, the actual transformation of social conditions is inevitably the greater – and more elusive – challenge. The schism between ideologies of social change and their implementation highlights the gap that can occur between PAR's promise and its practice, as discussed later in this chapter.

Procedures in PAR

PAR procedures are rooted in the strength of partnerships among research team members. Although they typically involve researchers and community members acting as co-researchers, PAR partnerships are incredibly diverse in constitution and scope. Different partners might be engaged during all or some parts of the process, and partners can include community members, students, researchers and other university representatives, agencies, community groups, institutions, and stakeholders such as funders, policy-makers, and government representatives. The important issue to consider in terms of partnerships that bring together diverse participants is that these groups cannot be thought of as essential and mutually exclusive. Categories such as "researchers" and "fathers" can become tokenized and deeply problematic when they are represented as monolithic, naturally aligned, or unproblematically representative. In reality, partnership building involves constant negotiation of different voices, histories, and agendas within and across any presumed category. Further, partners' roles (community member, student, advocate, researcher, and so on) might overlap, which raises important ethical and procedural issues for the conduct of partnership-based research. Successful PAR requires that research teams address the inevitable tensions that arise when they try to create and sustain a process for collective analysis, action, and solidarity.

Relational Praxis

In PAR, conscientization, networking, and empowerment depend greatly on the quality of the relationships and the processes of partnership and trust building within the research team. Investing in resilient relationships is neither a methodological indulgence nor a by-product of the research design; rather, it is the driving force in the PAR process. Relationships are the medium through which other aspects of research – power, knowledge production, benefit sharing, and social action – become discussed, challenged, implemented, and evaluated. The visceral power of relationships can often be more evocative of transformation than can critical analysis guided by theories alone. As such, effective PAR requires a deliberate praxis of relational engagement and reciprocity. Working relationships among participant researchers often sustain projects through the many challenges encountered in doing PAR. For many research teams, relationships continue years after a research project concludes.

This is why, compared to more traditional research approaches that clearly delineate research roles and boundaries, PAR methodologies typically provide much deeper and therefore messier entry points into collaboration, engagement, action, knowledge creation, and transformation. The relational stakes are always high in research projects that address complex social problems and difficult social action. Thus, although collaborative, purposeful, mutually supportive, and reciprocal relationships are foundational to PAR, sustaining positive partnerships can also be its greatest stumbling block. All iterations of PAR hold critical tensions about voice and participation (who gets to participate, whose perspective is incorporated, who owns the knowledge, who is accountable to whom), what sort of analysis is superimposed onto the participatory process, and who controls and implements recommendations for social advocacy and change. Debates about participation and representation raise important issues about who speaks and participates on behalf of a certain group, agency, community, or stakeholder.

Unfortunately PAR researchers are often challenged by how to conceptualize and facilitate issues of access, participation, and representation as they are shaped by relational dilemmas, since these are always underwritten by multiple layers of interdisciplinarity and the personal, community, and political politics that are central to PAR. In much of the literature on PAR, this "messiness" is often taken for granted or glossed over. PAR investigators and participant-research teams rightly want to celebrate their successes, but at the same time, are often reluctant to make salient the struggles they faced in implementing complex partnerships and methodologies. These relational complexities nonetheless must be placed on the table, facilitated thoughtfully and skilfully, and supported with sufficient time and resources. Safe spaces, time, and interpersonal processes must be planned and respectfully facilitated to allow grievances to be heard, problems to be resolved, and successes in stabilizing and consolidating relationships among team members to be celebrated. A critical issue in building and sustaining purposeful partnerships in PAR is to establish the open-ended, questioning, knowledge-creating goal of the research, and to prevent, as much as possible, efforts by research team members to insert potentially divisive, exploitive, and pre-emptive ideological standpoints into the research process.

Research Ethics and Protocols

Effective PAR involves multiple cycles of consultation, collective discussion, data gathering, analysis, evaluation, dissemination, and action. This iterative process requires rethinking traditional ethical guidelines and protocols for conducting research. Research partners engaged in PAR typically invest a substantial amount of time and energy in developing agreements that protect the rights and knowledge of partners and their communities. These agreements might address the storage, ownership, and dissemination of collectively produced data and findings, in addition to the participation of diverse partners at different stages of the project. The emerging nature of ethics in PAR places new demands on researchers; they must be willing to locate themselves critically, to make time for community-paced processes (Ball, 2005), and to put themselves on the line in ways that go well beyond the legal rhetoric of traditional, university-centric research ethics and protocols. In this context, ethics and protocols are always emerging and must be revisited and evaluated at each step, as well as woven through every aspect of project planning and coordination. Community-based processes related to ethics and protocols cannot be prescribed or rushed without destroying the integrity of the PAR process. PAR is, therefore, both a highly challenging and a rewarding methodology. It demands tremendous commitment to process and partnership, a great deal of the research team's energy, time, and resources, a high tolerance of ambiguity, and a willingness to be accountable to a range of expectations from diverse community and academic partners. Research team members must be willing to trust this process and to negotiate compromises through sustained and meaningful power sharing. For example, PAR projects often set aside funds for community members to be involved as co-presenters at conferences and as co-authors of publications, even years after the conclusion of the project.

Data Sources, Collection, and Analysis Procedures

Investigators who use PAR need to be prepared to use a variety of data collection procedures, analytical methods, interpretive frameworks, and reporting and evaluative strategies, and these must be contextually relevant and accessible to research partners. Data collection and analytical methods used in PAR originate from a variety of disciplines; common methods include appreciative inquiry, surveys, case studies, ethnography, narrative inquiry, and creative participatory methods, such as video ethnography, popular theatre, photovoice, and community mapping, among others. As seen in Figure 1.1, the methodological design of many PAR projects allows for continuous data generation, gathering, interpretation, and theorizing through iterative cycles of ongoing collaborative processes.

The choice of PAR as an approach to investigation and social action does not constrain or prescribe any particular data-collection procedures or the use of qualitative or quantitative data. What counts as relevant data (such as survey responses, process, stories, analytical conversations, art, scripts) is varied and context specific. Although non-numerical data are more commonly collected than numerical data in PAR, a research team might decide that, for the purposes of the topic and the population involved, it is more appropriate to collect numerical data by means of a survey questionnaire or even a set of tests. Survey topics, questions, and procedures would be developed and analysed in a participatory process. Also, if verbal data are obtained via interviews, a decision might be made to reduce those data through a coding scheme – such as frequency distributions of key themes that recur in interview data – that yields quantifiable representations. Thus data sources might include open-ended questionnaires, structured surveys, conversational interviews, narrative storytelling, videotapes, photojournalism, drawings and other art work, journals, emails, field notes, participant observations, administrative documents, program media, other documents such as program planning, budget, and evaluation records, and secondary data sources such as archives, statistical data sets, and individual records, among many other possibilities. PAR research teams often pursue the goal of working towards more critical and complex self-representations than are found in existing theory or in the social status quo by using methodologies for counter-storytelling, including expressive arts, documentaries, popular theatre, ceremony, community organizing, social and policy advocacy, popular education, and political action (Brown & Rodriguez, 2009; Etherton, 2004; Lee & de Finney, 2005; Lykes, 2001a, 2001b; Tolman & Brydon-Miller, 2001; Tuck, 2009).

Analytical Strategies

The iterative nature of PAR incorporates a multiplicity of processes and contributions that lead to a wide array of possible data, interpretations, and actions (Creswell, 2002; Gaventa, 1988; Leonard, 2002). PAR's transformative power is made manifest through its unique analytical lens, as it requires a critical analysis that challenges participants to question the social, political, and economic conditions that underlie the data collected. Otherwise PAR would remain a surface methodology – another form of storytelling that would reify the participants' experiences as objects of study (Stoudt, Fox, & Fine, 2012). Without the use of comprehensive analytical strategies that expose historical lines of power, PAR could indeed further entrench silences and reinstate itself as an objectifying research tool (Bennett, 2004; Tuck, 2009). In the case of PAR involving fathers, seeking to represent fathers as a homogenous group with a united voice and agenda would be counter to the principles of

PAR; rather, the aim is to deploy critical analytical tools to challenge normative, essentialized categories that maintain social inequities among different groups of fathers, as well as prevailing stereotypes and assumptions about normative fatherhood. PAR has the potential to redress often-taken-for-granted categories thought of as unproblematic and natural, and to politicize the discursive and material construction of fatherhood.

PAR requires facilitative and analytical tools that take into account the participant-researchers' particular social locations, as well as the nature and level of their engagement with inquiry and social action. The research team must evaluate which analytic tools will help to sharpen the collaborative analysis of interlocking social formations, and move emergent understandings beyond one-dimensional representations of the lives of the research participants and their communities. This aspect of a PAR project is both aided and complicated by the multitude of data sources that are often brought into play. The mixed methods of data collection in many PAR projects call for the research team to create a hybrid analytic strategy that engages multiple layers of data. Some investigators innovate fluid, multimethod analytical tools to aid in critical and collaborative data interpretation (see, for example, Weis & Fine, 2004). Others borrow approaches from hermeneutic inquiry, grounded theory, phenomenology, appreciative inquiry, discourse analysis, thematic analysis, and other qualitative analysis approaches that aim to organize copious textual or visual data and that represent them in ways that capture participants' meanings and intentions, thereby laying the groundwork for recommendations for education and action.

As co-researchers and co-participants, university investigators are accountable not only to their own goals for data interpretation and dissemination, but also to other team members, to the constituents whose interests the research is intended to represent and support, and to the community members with whom the research team has worked (Hagey, 1997; Naples, 2003). The interwoven layers of "answerability" in PAR studies create significant ethical and conceptual dilemmas, particularly for academic researchers. The requirement in academe to make individualized knowledge claims collides with the deeply held belief of many PAR investigators in the communal ownership of knowledge. These dilemmas might become particularly salient when academic researchers who engage in PAR are considered for peer review, tenure, and promotion on the basis of collaboratively developed and co-authored research products.

In addition to making these tensions visible to their research teams, university investigators must reconcile for themselves debates on data analysis within PAR, particularly those that relate to the validity of knowledge claims within community-university co-generated projects. Unfortunately, due to their diverse nature, PAR frameworks offer few explicit guidelines for navigating the challenging inner workings of collective knowledge making. In fact, PAR methodologies provide a rather thin analytical structure for systematic and comprehensive data interpretation (Bradbury & Reason, 2003; Cook & Campbell, 1976; Kock, McQueen, & Scott, 2003; Ladson-Billings, 2000; Maguire, 2001). Since PAR researchers are committed to "opening up the private lives of participants to the public," it is ironic, as Constas (1992) argues, that PAR investigators' own methods of analysis "often remain private and unavailable for public inspection" (p. 254).

Because PAR outcomes are shaped by communal knowledge and the co-construction of praxis, prescriptive analytical procedures that objectify data as separate from the collaborative process fail to capture the most integral aspects of PAR (Guba & Lincoln, 1994; Morawski, 2001; Park et al., 1993). As a result, PAR researchers are often criticized for overemphasizing the positive aspects of collective praxis making, while undertheorizing and obscuring salient dilemmas in data interpretation and the production of research-based knowledge. A research team must therefore ask itself: How do we reconcile and adequately represent multiple interpretations within a research system that promotes individual claims to knowledge? What interpretive methods will reflect the coherence achieved between the research design and methodology, the research team's diverse epistemological and ontological locations, and our ideologies about social change? And what kinds of interpretive processes have the capacity to produce concrete, relevant tools for the research partners and the development of their communities?

Verification and Accountability

To make data-interpretation procedures more transparent in PAR, traditional notions of reliability and validity must be rethought, and transparency and trustworthiness must be established through ongoing and flexible verification strategies. This requires a dynamic and recursive interpretive dialogue among many sources in an "interpretive community" (Fish, 1980; Tappan & Brown, 1992). In many PAR projects, reliability, trustworthiness, and authenticity of findings are established through a multipronged strategy that goes beyond the typical "data triangulation" of more traditional approaches. First, the collaborative analytical process is evaluated through persistent and rigorous member/community checking and consultation; responsiveness to emerging questions and tensions; adoption of a participatory and active analytical stance; and methodological coherence. Second, the process and outcomes themselves are transparently evaluated, including the level, quality, and impact of participants' engagement, and benefits to and effects on the community's capacity to address and act on identified social issues (Pretty & Chambers, 1995).

These measures, focusing as they do on both content and process, are intended to ensure that data analysis is multifaceted – that is, based on multiple perspectives – grounded in intersubjectivity, and shared transparently. Because PAR involves transformational praxis, data analysis focuses not only on what is, but also on "what is not ... and what ought to be" (Martín-Baró, 1994, p. 29). In stark contrast to the positivism that typifies traditional social science and health research, these qualities take precedence over the need to "control" the research process, thus destabilizing hegemonic constructions of validity and ownership of scientific knowledge.

The deliberately dynamic and generative nature of the interpretive phase of a PAR project is in stark contrast to the dominant tendency to freeze analyses as a means through which to objectify research findings and make declarative truth claims. This tentative hold on knowledge is, perhaps, congruent with the positioning of many investigators, like ourselves, who are attracted to PAR – interdisciplinary, "in-between" knowers, shaping knowledge by engaging with various sources of data and documentation, fields of study, interpretive communities, sociopolitical issues, and contexts of research and practice.

From Micro- to Macro-analysis

As discussed earlier, although PAR often takes participants' personal experiences as a starting point, the research does not remain in the personal realm. Herr and Anderson (2005) note that PAR "challenges many of the premises of more traditional models of action research ... [which tend] to concentrate on an individual or group level analysis of problems, whereas participatory research, with its more emancipatory emphasis, tends to focus on a broader societal analysis" (p. 16).

At some point in the cycle of PAR praxis, participants move from exploring their individual circumstances and stories to a critical collective analysis that sets the stage for action. At this juncture participants develop their own theories and solutions to identified problems (Hall, 1975), thus moving beyond knowledge generation to concrete social transformation and praxis making. Taking on the roles of advocates and activists, PAR participants select and decide on actions. Outcomes reported for PAR projects are incredibly diverse, and can include community forums, training opportunities, workshops, conferences, public media, resources for community members or service providers, documentaries, arts-based projects, meetings with policy-makers, advocacy and educational campaigns, political lobbying, innovative policy or program development, proposals for follow-up research, or the creation of a community or political organization.

Creating and mobilizing such strategies requires the research team to move beyond the boundaries of the project participants and their own political communities and into public consciousness. Most PAR projects aim to link the micro-experiences of participants and their communities to an evolving macro-analysis that typically, and importantly, involves critical reflection on the socio-political, economic, and historical contexts of social inequity. To avoid the homogenizing and universalizing flatness and erasures that are frequently disappointing outcomes of traditional social science research, PAR teams must incorporate an analysis of the relations of power that exist within any community and provide strategic alternatives for change. In this regard PAR projects often suffer limitations due to their insufficient attention to the intersecting effects of ethnicity, race, language, sexuality, ability, class, gender, nationality, and age, among other factors, that shape not only the social conditions under investigation, but also power dynamics within research teams themselves (Torre et al., 2012).

The capacity of a PAR project to produce useful and transformative knowledge ultimately depends on the much more elusive development of strategies for social change. It is in meeting this challenge that many PAR projects struggle and even collapse. The partnership-building, knowledge-generation, and collaborative-analysis stages of PAR projects often drain participants of energy, time, and commitment, and exhaust project resources in terms of time, funds, and institutional support. Ideally, however, PAR results in a continuum of meaningful interventions and action achieved for and by participants. These benefits, however, are neither immediate nor guaranteed.

Tensions and Dilemmas in PAR

Although PAR is a promising approach for research on issues such as the experiences, needs, and goals of diverse populations of fathers, there are gaps and tensions in PAR as well. Conceptual, theoretical, and practical dilemmas almost always complicate easy assumptions about the applications and benefits of transformative, community-based PAR. These complexities are due, in part, to tensions between the core principles and practices of PAR and a social group's highly contextual history and concerns (Hall, 1992). For instance, many PAR projects encounter difficulties negotiating engaged action research with an under-resourced community network. Further, PAR is not an inherently transformative medium dissociated from existing power dynamics embedded in modes of research production. Indigenous, feminist, queer, and youth-centred theorists, among others, have rightly questioned claims to empowerment, democratic research, community participation, and equal access in studies that have employed PAR (Bennett, 2004; Smith, 1999; Tolman & Brydon-Miller, 2001). Strategies are thus needed for critical analysis that resonates with the participants' own goals for personal and social change, and offers them creative, flexible tools to foster engagement and action. For some academic investigators, their desire to bolster communities of interest and to make participatory claims might conflict with the onus to make visible their own collusion with dynamics of power in the practice of social research. Academic researchers' roles, and the ways in which they benefit from the knowledge and funding produced, often remain unquestioned, while few returns accrue to research participants.

Questions also must be raised about establishing equity in collaboration and in building solidarity. Many PAR projects are founded on the implicit assumption that privileged, educated members of the dominant culture can, through the equalizing tenets of PAR, uncritically operate in solidarity with a vulnerable community. Some academic researchers influenced by PAR have addressed the conundrum of participation by developing research models that straightforwardly acknowledge the elusiveness of building fully participatory community-university collaborations involving vulnerable populations. For instance, Reitsma-Street (2002) has developed a model for community action research that provides a framework for undertaking action-oriented community-based research partnerships without making claims of comprehensive or sustainable participation by community members. Rather than glossing over these complexities and accepting the limitations of participation as inevitable, much can be learned from making them explicit and engaging as a research team to work through them (Fuentes, 2009; Ravitch, 1998; Sabo Flores, 2008). Indeed, efforts to address debates about appropriation, power, and participation are critical to the integrity of implementation of a PAR project and to creating the enabling conditions for the participatory research to have its intended effect of increasing civic engagement and achieving social transformation.

Exclusions from PAR

One important concern for father-related PAR is the lack of engagement of children and youth in PAR scholarship and practice. Because of its strong roots in adult education, PAR historically has focused on adults. The prevalence of adult-based research, education, and development programs in PAR has obscured the needs and realities of children and youth, who have often been seen as secondary, de facto beneficiaries of effective adult education and PAR, rather than as primary, decision-making participants.

Recently, however, child and youth participation has become a more important policy focus, resulting in a proliferation of PAR projects involving child/youth-adult partnerships (Cammarota & Fine, 2008; Sabo Flores, 2008). Many of these initiatives engage young people to use diverse PAR principles and practices in order to document social issues and intervene in social problems that touch their lives (Berg, Owens, & Schensul, 2002; Cahill, Arenas, Contreras, Na, Rios-Moore, & Threatts, 2004; Fine, Torre, Burns, & Payne, 2007; Morgan et al., 2004; Sydlo et al., 2000). Some PAR projects with youth focus primarily on understanding the experiences of youth (Strack, Magill, & McDonagh, 2004; Zeller-Berkman, 2007). Unfortunately, multiple barriers can impede implementation of these partnerships, and young participants frequently debate the extent to which PAR methods and practices that involve them are wholly participatory or collaborative. In many research projects that tout a participatory approach, homogeneous notions of "child participation" and "youth leadership" obscure age, gender, class, and racialized dynamics. Legal and social issues about informed consent, full participation, and access to funding and research resources add to these barriers.

In the field of father involvement research, the perspectives of boys on topics such as sexuality, contraception, anticipation of fatherhood, and, for some, becoming a teen father are sorely lacking (Ball, 2008). Also lacking are studies involving children and youth discussing their constructions of gender roles in relation to parenting, their experiences of their own fathers and mothers, the meaning and significance of father involvement in their own lives, and their needs and goals for understanding fatherhood. Several well-documented PAR projects carried out across the world have illustrated the potential of PAR for engaging young people using creative research methods (Backett & Alexander, 1991; Barker & Weller, 2003; Cammarota & Fine, 2008; Loiselle, de Finney, Khanna, & Corcoran, 2012). For example, children in Lahore and Nepal used video projections of street life as a backdrop to their theatre production about street children, which they then used to lobby local government (Etherton, 2004). Turner (1982) documents a Zimbabwean project where children transformed art and natural materials such as stones and sand to map a project for child-focused social change in their communities. An educational PAR project in a US school engaged boys in exploring constructions of violence and masculinity (Stoudt, 2007). In Canada, Sanford and Madill (2008) responded to boys' insistence on playing more active roles by including them in their research on the use of video game playing as an alternative literacy activity, creative enterprise, and elaboration of masculine identities through virtual social engagement. These examples suggest various ways that young people might be engaged in exploring father-related issues through methods that are age and context appropriate. Child- and youth-friendly PAR methodologies also provide rich opportunities for intergenerational PAR projects, where children and youth might work with fathers and perhaps other family members to explore fatherhood-related topics from their unique perspectives. Such intergenerational participatory studies might provide useful models for generational programming and policy innovations involving fathers and their children.

Tokenism and Appropriation in PAR

Limitations related to funding, scope and depth of analysis, structural constraints, and sustainability are important considerations for projects employing PAR (Israel et al., 2012; Kesby et al., 2009). When a PAR process fails to engage fully with structural and material barriers, abstract and potentially tokenistic notions of participation and transformation become problematic. Hall recognized early on the potentially manipulative role that third parties (for example, funding and sponsoring agencies, government officials) can play in influencing research goals, processes, and outcomes: "It would be an error to assume that naive or uncontrolled use of participatory research results in strengthening the power of the powerless, for experience has shown that power [under PAR methods] can easily accrue in those already in control" (Hall, 1981, in Bennett, 2004, p. 22).

Many researchers impose an institutionally sanctioned model of PAR that does not necessarily represent research participants' models of knowledge production or social change, thus making research an imperialistic tool (Lykes, 2001b; Smith, 1999). Potentially manipulative or exploitative research partnerships might be instituted under the tokenistic guise of the "best interest" of communities. Ostensibly participatory community research projects might actually impose and expand a hidden agenda of government objectives, policies, and procedures that serve to regulate social groups – especially marginalized and vulnerable groups (McTaggart, 1997). PAR then becomes a coercive instrument used to promote predetermined outcomes, rather than one that engages with the self-identified needs and goals of the research participants (Bennett, 2004; Hall, 1981; Hondagneu-Sotelo, 1993).

Under such conditions, PAR concepts and terminologies become entwined in exploitative research practices, particularly when oft-used concepts such as "vulnerable," "leadership," "voice," and "community" collapse important hierarchies of age, gender, sexuality, ethnicity, religion, language, class, citizenship, and ability. The presumed homogeneity of a population, such as "fathers," or a "community," such as "gay fathers," "Indigenous fathers," or "incarcerated fathers," minimizes the power differences that exist within any group, and thus limits opportunities to explore how PAR itself can reproduce lines of power, essentialism, and exclusion within and across communities. PAR researchers must seriously consider critical questions about the degree, quality, and nature of participation in a PAR project – namely, who is included and excluded, who becomes engaged and takes on leadership positions and how, who leaves the project, who will be involved in evaluating the project, and what concrete outcomes stem from these processes. Given that economic and political power typically flow outside the realms of influence of populations living in contexts of social exclusion, it is important to consider the extent to which they can become empowered and/or transformed by a research process – and to what extent critical awareness and politicization in and of themselves can transform structural and material conditions.

For community members to be truly involved in PAR, they must be directly involved in translating their experiences into meaningful knowledge – inside and outside academic contexts – and there must be concrete implications for multiple levels of change, from solidarity, community building, and innovative storytelling, to policy, programming, and institutional change. These are methodological issues that must be carefully considered in order to harness the potential of PAR findings to facilitate, support, and reinforce positive social change. When co-researchers are engaged fully in research that is motivated by their self-identified needs for action and change and carried out in ways that they perceive as congruent and potentially effective for achieving the transformations they envision, then a PAR project finds its stride. Conscientization, networking, empowerment, and critical socio-political analyses of the web of factors creating both barriers and opportunities to achieving desired personal and social transformations are, in themselves, enabling conditions for the production of new knowledge and for an emerging social agency and informed social change agenda. Partnerships and solidarity among participant-researchers and their constituent social and political communities can provide the momentum needed to enter the social arena with plans for meaningful action for social transformation.

Conclusion

Participatory action research is a broad methodological framework that can inform theoretical, policy, and practice debates in child and youth care, parenting education and support, child welfare, child health, family services, and understandings of men, masculinities, gender norms and roles, and fatherhood. PAR's flexibility and emergent quality value engagement as a way to build social capital, consolidate social movements, and advocate for policy, research, programming, and social change. Despite its gaps and tensions, PAR's overarching principles – collaboration between university and community partners, meaningful participation of low-visibility or marginalized groups, critical consciousness about social, economic, and political problems, and community-driven social change – provide a framework within which the enabling conditions for social transformation can be nurtured.

As growing numbers of children in Canada are being raised in lone-mother-headed households, several federal and provincial agencies, community organizations, and fathers' groups have acknowledged fathers' relative invisibility in public policies and programs intended to support child and family well-being. Calls for research as a first step in identifying the social and policy reforms needed to support father engagement have led to a growing literature on the effects of positive father involvement on children, families, communities, and fathers themselves. PAR can be a useful way for fathers, family members, parenting groups, and community organizations to collaborate with researchers in order to deepen and broaden understandings of fathers' experiences, needs, and goals in regard to developing and sustaining positive involvement with their children across varied conditions and changing circumstances. PAR's methods of raising awareness, strengthening communities of praxis, and building solidarity to stimulate social transformation offer a set of strategies for engaging diverse voices, including those of boys and men, to make their experiences more visible, address dilemmas they face as fathers and prospective fathers, and work towards civic actions to redress the status quo and create awareness about their needs for policy, knowledge, and practice reforms.

REFERENCES

Allen, S., Daly, K., & Ball, J. (2012). Fathers make a difference in their children's lives: A review of the research evidence. In J. Ball & K. Daly (Eds.), *Father involvement in Canada: Diversity, renewal, and transformation* (pp. 50–88). Vancouver, BC: UBC Press.

Backett, K., & Alexander, H. (1991). Talking to young children about health: Methods and findings. *Health Education Journal, 50*(1), 34–38. http://dx.doi.org/10.1177/001789699105000110

Ball, J. (2005). "*Nothing about us without us*": Restorative research partnerships involving Indigenous children and communities in Canada. In A. Farrell (Ed.), *Exploring ethical research with children* (pp. 81–96). Maidenhead, UK: Open University Press/McGraw-Hill Education.

Ball, J. (2008). Policies and practice reforms to promote positive transitions to fatherhood among Aboriginal young men. *Horizons, 10*(1), 52–56.

Ball, J., & George, R. (2007). Policies and practices affecting Aboriginal fathers' involvement with their children. In J. White, S. Wingert, D. Beavon, & P. Maxim (Eds.), *Aboriginal policy research: Moving forward, making a difference* (pp. 123–144). Ottawa, ON: Thompson Educational.

Ball, J., & Havassy, B. E. (1984). A survey of the problems and needs of homeless consumers of acute psychiatric services. *Hospital and Community Psychiatry, 35*(9), 917–921.

Ball, J., & Janyst, P. (2008). Enacting research ethics in partnerships with Indigenous communities in Canada: "Do it in a good way. *Journal of Empirical Research on Human Research Ethics*, 3(2), 33–51. http://dx.doi.org/10.1525/jer.2008.3.2.33

Ball, J., Moselle, K., & Pedersen, S. (2007). *Father's involvement as a determinant of child health*. Ottawa, ON: Public Health Agency of Canada, Population Health Branch. Retrieved from http://www.ecdip.org/reports

Barker, J., & Weller, S. (2003). "Is it fun?": Developing children centred research methods. *International Journal of Sociology and Social Policy*, 23(1/2), 33–58. http://dx.doi.org/10.1108/01443330310790435

Beaton, J., Nicholas, D., McNeill, T., & Wenger, L. (2012). The experiences of fathers of a child with a chronic health condition: Caregiving experiences and potential support interventions. In J. Ball & K. Daly (Eds.), *Father involvement in Canada: Diversity, renewal, and transformation* (pp. 190–204). Vancouver, BC: UBC Press.

Bell, L. (2009). Who's your daddy? Reflections on masculinity in butch-parented sons. In R. Epstein (Ed.), *Who's your daddy? And other writings on queer parenting* (pp. 360–362). Toronto, ON: Sumach Press.

Bennett, M. (2004). A review of literature on the benefits and drawbacks of participatory action research. *First Peoples Child & Family Review*, 1(1), 19–32.

Berg, M., Owens, D. C., & Schensul, J.J. (2002). Participatory action research, service-learning and community youth development. *Community Youth Development*, 3(2), 20–25.

Bradbury, H., & Reason, P. (2003). Issues and choice points for improving the quality of action research. In M. Minkler & N. Wallerstein (Eds.), *Community-based participatory research for health* (pp. 121–132). San Francisco, CA: Jossey-Bass.

Broughton, T. L., & Rogers, H. (2007). Introduction: The empire of the father. In T. L. Broughton & H. Rogers (Eds.), *Gender and fatherhood in the nineteenth century* (pp. 1–42). New York, NY: Palgrave Macmillan.

Brown, T., & Rodriguez, L. (2009). *New directions for youth developments: Youth in participatory action research*. San Francisco, CA: Jossey-Bass.

Cahill, C. (2007). Repositioning ethical commitments: Participatory action research as relational praxis of social change. *ACME: An International E-Journal for Critical Geographies*, 6(3), 360–373.

Cahill, C., Arenas, E., Contreras, J., Na, J., Rios-Moore, I., & Threatts, T. (2004). Speaking back: Voices of young urban womyn of color using participatory action research to challenge and complicate representations of young women. In A. Harris (Ed.), *All about the girl: Culture, power, and identity* (pp. 231–242). New York, NY: Routledge.

Cahill, C., Rios-Moore, I., & Threatts, T. (2008). Different eyes/open eyes: Community-based participatory action research. In J. Cammarota & M. Fine (Eds.), *Revolutionizing education: Youth participatory action research in motion* (pp. 89–124). New York, NY: Routledge.

Cammarota, J. & Fine, M. (Eds.). (2008). *Revolutionizing education: Youth participatory action research in motion.* New York, NY: Routledge.

Chambers, R. (2002). *Participatory workshops: A sourcebook of 21 sets of ideas and activities.* London: Earthscan.

Coltrane, S. (2007). Fathering: Paradoxes, contradictions, and dilemmas. In M. Kimmel & M. Messner (Eds.), *Men's lives,* (7th ed., pp. 448–465). Boston, MA: Pearson.

Constas, M. (1992). Qualitative analysis as a public event: The documentation category development procedures. *American Educational Research Journal, 29*(2), 253–266. http://dx.doi.org/10.3102/00028312029002253

Cook, T. D., & Campbell, D. T. (1976). Four kinds of validity. In M. D. Dunnette (Ed.), *Handbook of industrial organizational psychology* (pp. 224–246). Chicago, IL: Rand McNally.

Creswell, J. (2002). *Educational research: Planning, conducting and evaluating qualitative and quantitative research.* Trenton, NJ: Pearson Education.

de Finney, S. (2007). "It's about us!": Racialized minority girls' transformative engagement in feminist participatory action research. Retrieved from http://amicus.collectionscanada.gc.ca/ (34432263)

de Finney, S., Green, J., & Brown, L. (2009). Towards transformational research for and with Indigenous communities: The new British Columbia Indigenous Child Welfare Research Network. *First Peoples Child and Family Review, 4*(2), 161–164. Retrieved from http://journals.sfu.ca/fpcfr/index.php/FPCFR/article/view/170/127

de Finney, S., & Lee, J. A. (2008). *Spaces of encounter: Racialized minority and Indigenous girls and women negotiate mediated solidarities.* Proceedings of the 2008 International Community-University Exposition, University of Victoria.

de Finney, S., & Saraceno, J. (2015). Warrior girl and the searching tribe: Indigenous girls' everyday negotiations of racialization under neocolonialism. In C. Bradford & M. Reimer (Eds.), *Girls, texts, cultures.* Waterloo, ON: Wilfrid Laurier University Press.

Devault, A., Gaudet, J., Bolte, C., & St-Denis, M. (2005). A survey and description of projects that support and promote fathering in Canada: Still work to do to reach fathers in their real-life settings. *Canadian Journal of Community Mental Health, 24*(1), 5–17. http://dx.doi.org/10.7870/cjcmh-2005-0001

Doherty, W. J. (2000). Family science and family citizenship: Towards a model of community partnership with families. *Family Relations, 49*(3), 319–325. http://dx.doi.org/10.1111/j.1741-3729.2000.00319.x

Doucet, A. (2006). *Do men mother? Fathering, care, and domestic responsibility.* Toronto, ON: University of Toronto Press.

Epstein, R. (2009). *"Who's your daddy" And other writings on queer parenting.* Toronto, ON: Sumach Press.

Este, D., & Tachble, A. (2009). The perceptions and experiences of Russian immigrant and Sudanese refugee men as fathers in an urban centre in Canada. *Annals of the American Academy of Political and Social Science, 624*(1), 139–155. http://dx.doi.org/10.1177/0002716209334470

Etherton, M. (2004). South Asia's child rights. Theatre for development: The empowerment of children who are marginalized, disadvantaged and excluded. In R. Boon & J. Plastow (Eds.), *Theatre and empowerment: Community drama on the world stage* (pp. 188–219). Cambridge, UK: Cambridge University Press.

Fals Borda, O. (1987). The application of participatory action research in Latin America. *International Sociology, 2*(4), 329–347. http://dx.doi.org/10.1177/026858098700200401

Fals Borda, O. (1996). A north-south convergence on the quest for meaning. *Qualitative Inquiry, 2*(1), 76–87. http://dx.doi.org/10.1177/107780049600200111

Fine, M., et al. (2001). *Participatory action research: From within and beyond prison bars. Bridging the gap: Feminisms and participatory action research conference.* Conference papers. Retrieved from http://www.wnmu.org/gap/fine.htm

Fine, M., Torre, M. E., Burns, A., & Payne, Y. A. (2007). Youth research/participatory methods for reform. In D. Thiessen & A. Cook-Sather (Eds.), *International handbook of student experience in elementary and secondary school* (pp. 805–828). New York, NY: Springer. http://dx.doi.org/10.1007/1-4020-3367-2_32

Fish, S. (1980). *Is there a text in this class? The authority of interpretive communities.* Cambridge, MA: Harvard University Press.

Freire, P. (1971). *Pedagogy of the oppressed.* New York, NY: Seabury Press.

Freire, P. (1973). *Education for critical consciousness.* New York, NY: Seabury Press.

Freire, P. (1975). *Cultural action for freedom.* Boston, MA: Harvard Educational Review.

Freire, P. (1997). *Pedagogy of the heart* (2nd ed.). New York, NY: Continuum Press.

Fuentes, E. (2009). Learning power and building community: Parent-initiated participatory action research as a tool for organizing community. *Social Justice, 36*(4), 69–83.

Galabuzi, G.-E. (2004). Social exclusion. In D. Raphael (Ed.), *Social determinants of health* (pp. 235–252). Toronto, ON: Canadian Scholars Press.

Gaventa, J. (1988). Participatory research in North America. *Convergence: An International Journal of Adult Education, 24*(2–3), 19–28.

Gayfer, M. (Ed.) (1981). Participatory research: Developments and issues. *Convergence: An International Journal of Adult Education, 14*(3), 5.

Gayfer, M. (1992). The sound of people learning and organizing for change. *Convergence: An International Journal of Adult Education, 25*(4), 17–25.

Greenwood, D., & Levin, M. (1998). *Introduction to action research: Social research for social change*. Thousand Oaks, CA: Sage.

Guba, E. G., & Lincoln, Y. S. (1994). Competing paradigms in qualitative research. In N. K. Denzin & Y. S. Lincoln (Eds.), *Handbook of qualitative research* (pp. 105–117). Newbury Park, CA: Sage.

Hagey, R. (1997). The use and abuse of participatory action research. *Chronic Diseases in Canada, 18*(1), 1–4.

Hall, B. (1975). Participatory research: An approach for change. *Convergence: An International Journal of Adult Education, 8*(2), 24–31.

Hall, B. (1981). Participatory research, popular knowledge and power: A personal reflection. *Convergence: An International Journal of Adult Education, 14*(3), 5–17.

Hall, B. (1992). From margins to center? The development and purpose of participatory research. *American Sociologist, 23*(4), 15–28. http://dx.doi.org/10.1007/BF02691928

Hall, B. (1993). Introduction. In P. Park, M. Brydon-Miller, B. Hall, & T. Jackson (Eds.), *Voices of change: Participatory research in the United States and Canada* (pp. xiii–xxii). Toronto, ON: OISE Press.

Hall, B. (2000a). Global civil society: Theorizing a changing world. *Convergence: An International Journal of Adult Education, 33*(2), 10–32.

Hall, B. (2000b). Breaking the educational silence: For seven generations, an information legacy of the Royal Commission on Aboriginal Peoples. In G. J. Sefa Dei, B. L. Hall, & D. Golden Rosenberg (Eds.), *Indigenous knowledges in global context: Multiple readings of our world* (pp. 202–214). Toronto, ON: OISE in association with University of Toronto Press.

Herr, K., & Anderson, G. L. (2005). *The action research dissertation: A guide for students and faculty*. Thousand Oaks, CA: Sage.

Hobson, B. (2002) (Ed.). *Making men into fathers: Men, masculinities and the social politics of fatherhood*. Cambridge, UK: Cambridge University Press. http://dx.doi.org/10.1017/CBO9780511489440

Hondagneu-Sotelo, P. (1993). Why advocacy research? Reflections on research and activism with immigrant women. *American Sociologist*, 24(1), 56–68. http://dx.doi.org/10.1007/BF02691945

Israel, B., Eng, E., Schulz, A., & Parker, E. (2012). *Methods for community-based participatory research for health*. San Jose, CA: Jossey-Bass.

Kaspar, V., & Noh, S. (2001). *Discrimination and identity: An overview of theoretical and empirical research*. Paper commissioned by the Department of Canadian Heritage for the ethnocultural, racial, religious, and linguistic diversity and identity seminar, Halifax, NS, 1–2 November.

Kesby, M., Kindon, S., & Pain, R. (2009). *Participatory action research approaches and methods: Connecting people, participation and place*. New York, NY: Routledge.

Kishcuk, N. (2001). *Case studies of the regional mobilization of population health: Final report*. Ottawa, ON: Health Canada, Population and Public Health Branch.

Kock, N., McQueen, R., & Scott, J. (2003). *Can action research be made more rigorous in a positivist sense? The contributions of an iterative approach*. Action Research International-Online Journal. Retrieved from http://www.scu.edu.au/schools/gcm/ar/arr/arow/kms.html

Ladson-Billings, G. (2000). Racialized discourses and ethnic epistemologies. In N. K. Denzin & Y. S. Lincoln (Eds.), *Handbook of qualitative research* (2nd ed., pp. 398–432). Thousand Oaks, CA: Sage.

Lee, J. A., & de Finney, S. (2005). Using popular theatre for engaging racialized minority girls in exploring questions of identity and belonging. *Child and Youth Services*, 26(2), 95–118. http://dx.doi.org/10.1300/J024v26n02_06

Leonard, J. (Ed.). (2002). *Participatory community research: Theories and methods in action*. Washington, DC: American Psychological Association.

Lero, D. S., Ashbourne, L. M., & Whitehead, D. L. (2006). *Inventory of policies and policy areas affecting father involvement*. Guelph, ON: Father Involvement Research Alliance. Retrieved from http://www.fira.ca/cms/documents/176/April7.Long.PDF

Loiselle, E., de Finney, S., Khanna, N., & Corcoran, R. (2012). "We need to talk about it!": Doing CYC as politicized praxis. *Child and Youth Services*, 33(3-4), 178–205. http://dx.doi.org/10.1080/0145935X.2012.745778

Long, D. (2008, December). *All dads matter: Towards an inclusive vision of father involvement initiatives in Canada*. Guelph, ON: Father Involvement Research Alliance. Retrieved from http://www.fira.ca/cms/documents/176/April7.Long.PDF

Lupton, D., & Barclay, L. (1997). *Constructing fatherhood: Discourses and experiences*. London: Sage.

Lykes, M. B. (2001a). Creative arts and photography in participatory action research in Guatemala. In P. Reason & H. Bradbury (Eds.), *Handbook of action research: Participative inquiry and practice* (pp. 363–371). London: Sage.

Lykes, M. B. (2001b). Activist participatory research and the arts with rural Maya women: Interculturality and situated meaning-making. In D. L. Tolman & M. Brydon-Miller (Eds.), *From subjects to subjectivities: A handbook of interpretive and participatory methods* (pp. 183–199). New York, NY: New York University Press.

Maguire, P. (1987). *Doing participatory research: A feminist approach*. Amherst, MA: University of Massachusetts, Center for International Education.

Maguire, P. (2001). The congruency thing: Transformation psychological research and pedagogy. In D. Tolman & M. Brydon-Miller (Eds.), *From subjects to subjectivities: A handbook of interpretive and participatory methods* (pp. 276–290). New York, NY: New York University Press.

Martín-Baró, I. (1994). *Writing for a liberation psychology*. Cambridge, MA: Harvard University Press.

McTaggart, R. (1991). Principles for action research. *Adult Education Quarterly*, 41(3), 168–187. http://dx.doi.org/10.1177/0001848191041003003

McTaggart, R. (Ed.). (1997). *Participatory action research: International contexts and consequences*. New York, NY: State University of New York Press.

Morawski, J. (2001). Feminist research methods: Bringing cultural to science. In D. Tolman & M. Brydon-Miller (Eds.), *From subjects to subjectivities: A handbook of interpretive and participatory methods* (pp. 57–76). New York, NY: New York University Press.

Morgan, D., et al. (2004). Youth participatory action research on hustling and its consequences: A report from the field. *Children, Youth and Environments*, 14(2), 201–228.

Naples, N. (2003). *Feminism and method: Ethnography, discourse analysis, and activist research*. London: Routledge.

Nicholas, D. B. (2003). Participant perceptions of online groupwork with fathers of children with spina bifida. In N. Sullivan, E. S. Mesbur, N. C. Lang, D. Goodman, & L. Mitchell (Eds.), *Social work with groups: Social justice through personal, community and societal change* (pp. 227–240). Binghamton, NY: Haworth Press.

O'Brien, R., Hunt, K., & Hart, G. (2005). "It's caveman stuff, but that is to a certain extent how guys still operate": Men's accounts of masculinity and help-seeking. *Social Science & Medicine, 61*(3), 503–516. http://dx.doi.org/10.1016/j.socscimed.2004.12.008

Palkovitz, R. (1997). Reconstructing "involvement": Expanding conceptualizations of men's caring. In A. J. Hawkins & D. C. Dollahite (Eds.), *Generative fathering: Beyond deficit perspectives* (pp. 201–216). Thousand Oaks, CA: Sage.

Park, P., Brydon-Miller, M., Hall, B., & Jackson, T. (Eds.). (1993). *Voices of change: Participatory research in the United States and Canada*. Toronto, ON: OISE Press.

Pendleton Jiménez, K. P. (2009). Little white children: Notes from a Chicana dyke dad. In R. Epstein (Ed.), *Who's your daddy? And other writings on queer parenting* (pp. 242–250). Toronto, ON: Sumach Press.

Pretty, J., & Chambers, R. (1995). *A trainer's guide for the participatory learning and action*. London: International Institute for Environment and Development.

Ravanera, Z. (2007). Informal networks social capital of fathers: What does the social engagement survey tell us? *Social Indicators Research, 83*(2), 351–373. http://dx.doi.org/10.1007/s11205-006-9053-7

Ravitch, S. (1998). Becoming uncomfortable: Transforming my praxis. In M. Nakkula & S. Ravitch (Eds.), *Matters of interpretation: Reciprocal transformation in therapeutic and developmental relationships with youth* (pp. 105–121). San Francisco, CA: Jossey-Bass.

Reitsma-Street, M. (2002). Processes of community action research: Putting poverty on the policy agenda of a rich region. In W. K. Carroll (Ed.), *Critical strategies for social research* (pp. 303–319). Toronto, ON: Canadian Scholars Press.

Reitsma-Street, M., & Brown, L. (2003). The values of community action research. *Canadian Social Work Review, 20*(1), 61–78.

Sabo Flores, K. (2008). *Youth participatory evaluation: Strategies for engaging young people*. San Francisco, CA: Jossey-Bass.

Sanford, K., & Madill, L. (2008). Adolescents teaching video-game making– Who is the expert here? In R. Ferdig (Ed.), *Handbook of research on electronic gaming in education* (pp. 345–356). New York, NY: Information Science Reference. http://dx.doi.org/10.4018/978-1-59904-808-6.ch020

Smith, L. T. (1999). *Decolonizing methodologies: Research and indigenous peoples*. London: Zed Books.

Smith, S. E., Willms, D. G., & Johnson, N. A. (Eds.). (1997). *Nurtured by knowledge: Learning to do participatory action-research*. New York, NY: Apex Press.

Stafford, A. (2009). Beyond normalization: An analysis of heteronormativity in children's picture books. In R. Epstein (Ed.), *Who's your daddy? And other writings on queer parenting* (pp. 160–179). Toronto, ON: Sumach Press.

Stoudt, B. (2007). The co-construction of knowledge in "safe spaces": Reflecting on politics and power in participatory action research. *Children, Youth and Environments, 17*(2), 280–297.

Stoudt, B., Fox, M., & Fine, M. (2012). Contesting privilege with critical participatory action research. *Journal of Social Issues, 68*(1), 178–193. http://dx.doi.org/10.1111/j.1540-4560.2011.01743.x

Strack, R. W., Magill, C., & McDonagh, K. (2004). Engaging youth through photovoice. *Health Promotion Practice, 5*(1), 49–58. http://dx.doi.org/10.1177/1524839903258015

Sydlo, S. J., et al. (2000). *Participatory action research curriculum for empowering youth*. Hartford, CT: Institute for Community Research.

Tamis-LeMonda, C. S., & Cabrera, N. (2002). Multidisciplinary perspectives on father involvement: An introduction. In C. S. Tamis-LeMonda & N. Cabrera (Eds.), *Handbook of father involvement: Multidisciplinary perspectives* (pp. xi–xviii). Mahwah, NJ: Lawrence Erlbaum.

Tandon, R. (2002). *Participatory research: Revisiting the roots*. New Delhi, India: Mosaic.

Tappan, M., & Brown, L. (1992). Hermeneutics and developmental psychology: Towards an ethic of interpretation. In W. Kurtines, M. Azmitia, & J. Gewirtz (Eds.), *The role of values in psychology and human development* (pp. 105–130). New York, NY: John Wiley.

Tolman, D., & Brydon-Miller, M. (1997). *Transforming psychology: Interpretive and participatory research methods*. Malden, MA: Blackwell.

Tolman, D. & Brydon-Miller, M. (Eds.). (2001). *From subjects to subjectivities: A handbook of interpretive and participatory methods*. New York, NY: New York University Press.

Torre, M. E., Fine, M., Stoudt, B., & Fox, M. (2012). Critical participatory action research as public science. In H. Cooper et al. (Eds.), *APA handbook of research methods in psychology: Vol. 2. Research designs: Quantitative, qualitative, neuropsychological, and biological* (pp. 171–184). Washington, DC: American Psychological Association. http://dx.doi.org/10.1037/13620-011

Trocmé, N., Knoke, D., & Blackstock, C. (2004). Pathways to the overrepresentation of Aboriginal children in Canada's child welfare system. *Social Service Review, 78*(4), 577–600. http://dx.doi.org/10.1086/424545

Tuck, E. (2009). Re-visioning action: Participatory action research and Indigenous theories of change. *Urban Review, 41*(1), 47–65. http://dx.doi.org/10.1007/s11256-008-0094-x

Turner, V. (1982). *From ritual to theatre: The human seriousness of play*. New York, NY: PAJ Publications.

Vio Grossi, F. (1981). Socio-political implications of participatory research. *Convergence: An International Journal of Adult Education, 3*, 43–51.

Weis, L., & Fine, M. (2004). *Working method: Research and social justice*. New York, NY: Routledge. http://dx.doi.org/10.4324/9780203342435

Zeller-Berkman, S. (2007). Peering in: A look into reflective practices in youth participation action research. *Children, Youth and Environments, 17*(2), 315–328.

2 Father Involvement: A Multifaceted Concept

DIANE DUBEAU, ANNIE DEVAULT,
AND DANIEL PAQUETTE

Despite its apparent simplicity, the concept of father involvement is an evolving one, and therefore readers interested in this area of knowledge might raise questions about its meaning. In contrast to most research topics, the study of father involvement is situated at the confluence of several disciplines (the principal ones being sociology, psychology, history, anthropology, and education) and subdisciplines (such as psycho-dynamic and behavioural approaches in child psychology). The richness of this disciplinary diversity is clear; however, it complicates efforts to arrive at a coherent synthesis of knowledge in this area of study. Mastering the theoretical and conceptual frameworks of these several disciplinary fields, together with their different terminologies, is not an easy task. Thus, the multidisciplinary nature of the Prospère research team was an asset in reviewing the literature on father involvement, and it also inevitably influences the content of this chapter. In addition, the research approach chosen (quantitative/ deductive or qualitative/inductive) and, consequently, the knowledge obtained will differ according to the discipline. We wish, therefore, to clarify the concept of father involvement by looking at a number of contributions that researchers with different perspectives have made at both the methodological and disciplinary levels.

Research methodology is characterized by two main approaches, the ultimate objective of which is the advancement of knowledge (Goertz & Mahoney, 2012). The quantitative, or deductive, approach aims to confirm or infirm the researcher's hypotheses. For this approach the researcher must rely on the body of existing knowledge to propose and test theoretically plausible links among relevant variables. In the qualitative, or inductive, approach, the researcher often takes an active part in the process, playing the role of facilitator to extract knowledge from the discourse of the principal actors concerned with the study subject. These two approaches have made complementary contributions to the concept of father involvement, and both inspired the studies the Prospère team carried out. Their respective contributions are presented in the two main sections of this chapter.

The Quantitative View of Father Involvement

First, let us look at the evolution of the definition and the measurement of father involvement based on research studies that have adopted the quantitative or deductive approach. This approach often confuses readers, who might associate it with the nature of the data collected. In this research paradigm, however, the data make up only one element of the whole. The researcher's role (objectivity) and goals (to confirm or infirm the research hypotheses), the methodology used (maximum control of the variables), and the utility of the study (the advancement of knowledge) constitute other important parameters of the paradigm (Goertz & Mahoney, 2012).

It might seem strange that the quantitative approach was the principal approach guiding the first research studies on father involvement, since it is usually the preferred choice in the first exploration of a phenomenon. In the early days of the study of father involvement, however, the researchers' first reflex was to validate among fathers the findings of studies that had been carried out among mothers for many years. The results of these quantitative studies broke new ground at three consecutive moments, contributing to the advancement of knowledge in this domain by establishing important conceptual tools: (1) a definition of father involvement based on various measurement techniques; (2) a comprehensive vision of father involvement in relation to its effects on children's developmental outcomes; and (3) the integration of father involvement within a systemic perspective of the family.

An Initial Preoccupation with Measuring Father Involvement

The concept of parental involvement is relatively recent, initially introduced in the framework of fatherhood studies. Pre-1970s literature on the parental role, which essentially centred on mothers, barely mentioned fathers. The traditional division of parental roles, in which mothers' child care and child-rearing expertise was recognized and emphasized, made the concept of maternal involvement superfluous, since it was largely taken for granted. Social changes over the past thirty years, however, have affected family functioning due, among other things, to the more active role assumed by fathers. This new distribution of parental roles opened the way to a conceptualization of the involvement of both parents.

The development of a model of parental involvement that included both maternal and paternal realities required a definition of this concept. The literature provided only a limited definition of father involvement when operationalizing the concept for measurement purposes. Whether in terms of absolute or relative frequency or of duration, the dimension researchers most often evaluated – through interviews, questionnaires, or time diaries – concerned basic caregiving tasks such as feeding, bathing, and changing diapers (Pleck & Masciadrelli, 2004).[1] In a few cases fathers' participation in child care was given a broader scope through measuring the disciplining of children, leisure activities, game playing, communication skills, accompanying the child to appointments, religious instruction, and help with homework (Fagan & Cabrera, 2012; Schoppe-Sullivan, Kotila, Jia, Lang, & Bower, 2012). Despite the wide range of parental behaviour evaluated, researchers adopted a rather one-dimensional view of the concept of involvement by calculating global scores based on the sum of interactions with the child. This view assumed that quantity meant quality (Grimm-Thomas & Perry-Jenkins, 1994).

Over the years these studies contributed to the recognition that fathers were becoming more involved with their children (Pleck & Masciadrelli, 2004). This finding inspired several researchers to investigate the factors associated with father involvement, with a view to identifying the personal, family, and social characteristics that led some fathers to be more involved than others. At the methodological level most of these studies investigated the determinants of father involvement by comparing groups of fathers distinguished by certain characteristics – for example, fathers in dual-earner and single-earner families. Other researchers adopted a comparative approach that focused on the differences between maternal and paternal measurements. Little insight was gained, due to the reporting of higher levels of involvement among mothers, but these studies did incite researchers to broaden the operationalization of the concept of involvement. The definition proposed by Lamb, Pleck, Charnov, and Levine (1987) reflects the broader view of parental involvement used in fatherhood studies by numerous researchers (Jacobs & Kelley, 2006; McBride et al., 2005; Schoppe-Sullivan, McBride, & Ringo Ho, 2004). This definition includes three principal components of parental involvement: (1) the parent's direct interactions with the child (time dedicated to various activities with the child); (2) availability and accessibility (the time the parent is present and accessible to the child without interacting directly with the child); and (3) parental responsibilities (child care tasks organized by the parent without interacting with the child – for example, arranging a dental appointment for the child). Such studies showed that, overall, father involvement was increasing in terms of availability and time spent in direct interaction with the child, although fathers still assumed fewer parental responsibilities than mothers.

Another consequence of the broadening of the involvement concept was the development of measurement tools that allowed a differential evaluation of the interactions of each parent with the child (Palkovitz, 1997). In contrast to a unitary construct of father involvement (the one-dimensional view), operationalized by adding up interactions, researchers sought to quantify father involvement within specific parenting activities. This multidimensional vision was the one preferred by the Prospère team, and is reflected in our definition of father involvement, below.

Prospère's Definition of Father Involvement

> Father involvement consists of the continuous participation and preoccupation of the father, or his substitute, towards the physical and psychological development and wellbeing of his child. This involvement is manifested in various dimensions, and develops step by step, and in its own way, according to the individual.
>
> - An interacting father is a direct or indirect presence for the child
> - A care-giving father shares child-rearing tasks
> - An affectionate father soothes and encourages by words and gestures
> - A responsible father works toward the child's development and well-being
> - A providing father provides financial support to meet the child's needs
> - An evocative father thinks of the child when the child is not with him.
>
> (Dubeau, Devault, & Forget, 2009, translation by authors)

This multidimensional view of father involvement allowed, among other things, a more in-depth analysis of the differences, not only between fathers, but also between mothers and fathers in the various dimensions of involvement. The tools developed, however, were still essentially inspired by instruments that had been validated among mothers, then adapted to varying degrees to take fathers' realities into account. To bridge the remaining gaps, Prospère drew up its own father involvement questionnaire (FIQ), which was validated among more than 800 fathers.

The Father Involvement Questionnaire

The Prospère researchers' first project concerned the implementation and evaluation of a community-based intervention initiative promoting father involvement (see Chapter 3 for details). Evaluation in this PAR project with respect to its expected outcome (an increase in father involvement) required an instrument with psychometric qualities that could measure the different dimensions identified in the definition of father involvement proposed at the two pilot sites.

Realizing that no single instrument concerning parental involvement could measure all the components identified in our definition, we created a new instrument inspired by existing assessment tools, notably the Parental Involvement in Child Care Index (Radin, 1981a, 1981b), which has since been used in many studies to evaluate father involvement.

The full version of Prospère's instrument appears in Appendix A. Briefly described, it comprises fifty-two items grouped according to six dimensions considered in our definition of father involvement, with an additional scale that measures participation in domestic chores:

- affective support (12 items);
- discipline (4 items);
- openness to the outside world (9 items);
- physical care (9 items);
- physical play (7 items);
- evocation (6 items); and
- domestic chores (5 items).

We used two rating scales. Whenever possible we used an absolute scale with the following choice of answers:

1	2	3	4	5	6
Never	Once a month	2 or 3 times a month	Once a week	A few times a week	Every day

For less frequent activities and those that were difficult to quantify, we adopted the following relative scale:

1	2	3	4	5
Never	Seldom	Regularly	Often	Very often

CONTRIBUTIONS OF THE FIQ

The FIQ was essential to our research as it allowed us to confirm that fathers and mothers differed in their levels of parental involvement. It was possible for us to verify the structural validity of the questionnaire using statistical techniques, such as factorial analysis. After carrying out this analysis separately for maternal and paternal evaluations, we found that the instrument was less effective in evaluating mother involvement. This finding – to our knowledge the first concerning instruments for fathers – is in itself an important contribution that justifies the adaptation of measurement instruments to the specific realities experienced differently by mothers and fathers. It is pertinent to recall in this respect that studies carried out among fathers still tend to use instruments drawn up and validated based on mother samples.

The multidimensional view of father involvement operationalized by the FIQ also proved relevant. As shown in Chapter 4, the results obtained in the community impacts evaluation of the Prospère project were differentiated by the FIQ. Results for certain dimensions of father involvement were more salient, showing influence by the intervention activities carried out at the two pilot sites. On the other hand, a total score (the sum of the activities evaluated) allowed little possibility of differentiating between the sites that benefited from the intervention.

LIMITATIONS OF THE FIQ

The FIQ's principal limitation concerns its insufficiency in the context of non-traditional family structures, including those in which the parents are separated or divorced. For such family situations, the rating scales used in the questionnaire became irrelevant when child custody arrangements affected the frequencies identified. Furthermore, the instrument elicited little information on the father's indirect contributions, principally those associated with his provider role; hence, we combined these data using information on the income and employment status of each parent. We should also point out that the FIQ focused principally on the father's behaviour towards his child, which in itself represents an important dimension of father involvement. However, the chosen items did not allow us to evaluate adequately the availability and responsibility components, as defined by Lamb et al. (1987). Any evaluation of father involvement should also take into account the contextual elements associated with the father's access to the child, as well as the meaning he gives to fatherhood, which might vary according to cultural background and other factors.

Studies that evaluate parental involvement based on the types of activities in which parents interact with their children are interesting in that they occasionally uncover significant differences between mothers and fathers. One example is the greater participation of mothers in domestic chores. The scientific community is divided on whether to include such activities when measuring parental involvement (Deutsch, Lussier, & Servis, 1993). Some authors include them, from the perspective that they contribute to the child's well-being (Dubeau, Coutu, & Lavigueur, 2013); others consider domestic chores to influence the child only indirectly. Therefore, it is not surprising that some instruments include questions to evaluate such activities, while others exclude it.

Mothers also participate more than fathers in caregiving activities, whereas fathers participate more in play activities (Lamb, 2010). The importance attributed to this difference requires us to go further and investigate the effects of mothers' and fathers' relative degrees of involvement on children's developmental outcomes (Coyl-Shepherd & Newland, 2012). These limitations must be resolved if we want to arrive at a broadened conceptualization of parental involvement that integrates the involvement characteristics of both mothers and fathers in differentiated and non-differentiated models of parental roles.

From Measurements to Effects

Following advances in the measurement of parental involvement, researchers directed their attention to the effects of different forms of involvement on the child's development (Allen, Daly, & Ball, 2012; Lamb & Lewis, 2013; Pleck, 2007).[2] Most of these numerous studies were carried out during the 1980s and 1990s, and the great majority of them issued from the discipline of psychology.

Diversified disciplinary perspectives are rich at the conceptual level, but differences in terminology can lead to confusion. For instance, when discussing fathers, the terms "role" and "function" are often closely linked to the concept of involvement. These same terms refer to specific contents that might possess significant distinctions according to the particular disciplinary field and socio-cultural context in which they are used. Without discussing these distinctions in detail, some clarification is pertinent. Overall, the more general concept of *role* (parental role) falls within a sociological perspective (such as the role of provider, educator, and so on). The concept of *function*, on the other hand, is more specific, and is associated with a psychological perspective (such as the function of security, separation, and so on). The studies of the effects of father involvement on child development we refer to here generally use the concept of function rather than role. To avoid confusion with the term "father's function" by the proponents of the psycho-analytical approach, which looks at the father's symbolic involvement, some authors have adopted the expression "father's contribution" to qualify the father's concrete involvement with his children (Le Camus, 1997). These differences of use and the respective meanings of terms underscore the need to be vigilant when consulting the literature.

On the whole, studies on parental involvement reveal positive effects of father involvement on different aspects of children's developmental outcomes. They also shed light on contributions specific to fathers, distinguishing them from those attributed to mothers (Dubeau et al., 2013; Feldman & Klein, 2003). In this context, we should mention the studies by Paquette (2004) and Paquette and Dumont (2013) on the correlation between father involvement in physical play and the child's development of self-control.

Inconsistencies in some of the results, however, have given rise to harsh criticism of the methodological approaches used. More specifically, researchers have questioned the relevance of using instruments designed and validated to measure mothers' situations while fathers' realities are not taken into account. Studies on attachment are a good example of this (Hoffman, 2011; Newland & Coyl, 2010; Youngblade, Park, & Belsky, 1993). Results obtained in this area show that maternal measurements are more frequently and more strongly associated with child development than those of fathers (a higher number of statistically significant links are observed for mothers, and the intensity of these links is stronger) (Grossmann et al., 2002). Moreover, some studies actually obtained results that are contrary to the theoretical predictions issuing from the attachment model. To give one example, Cox, Owen, Henderson, and Margand (1992) show that the more time a father spends interacting with his child, the less likely the child is to develop a secure attachment relationship. The ensuing peer criticism inevitably challenged the conceptual framework that was used, according to which the knowledge acquired about mothers can be applied to fathers and thus also adequately represents fathers' reality.

In a similar vein, several researchers in the 1990s decried the paradigm of the inadequate father (Dienhart, 1998; Dollahite, Hawkins, & Brotherson, 1997), or "toxic father" (Dulac, 1997), which emerged following the publication of certain studies that compared mothers and fathers. These researchers emphasized the importance of moving away from a maternal model in which the attributes of sensitivity, affection, and communication are given a preponderant value, to a model that is better able to take into account fathers' competencies and specificities that constitute beneficial contributions to the child's development – for example, characteristics related to action, challenging and surprising children, and encouraging them to take risks and stand up for themselves.

From Father Involvement to Parental Involvement

The increased involvement of fathers with their children brought fathers, long neglected by the scientific community, to the attention of researchers (Lamb, 1975). The recognition of the specificity of fathers' contributions made the conceptualization of parental involvement more complex: adding the father component not only doubled the possibilities of influences (cumulative effects); it also made it necessary to adopt a systemic perspective that took the multiple sources of influence of the different family subsystems into account. Researchers sought the best ways of combining the maternal and paternal characteristics within the parental component in their studies.

In some studies, the operationalization of involvement has taken the form of a combined measurement of task sharing by the two parents. The rating scale used is often of the following type: (1) I always do it; (2) I do it more often than my partner; (3) I do it as often as my partner; (4) my partner does it more often; (5) my partner always does it.[3] Sometimes, studies have each parent do the evaluation separately, to obtain a more accurate view of the division of tasks between them, since fathers tend to overrate their participation. It is still difficult, however, to know whether the gap between the two parents' results is due to an overestimation by one or an underestimation by the other. This type of instrument has the advantage of measuring both the maternal and paternal characteristics at once, but it does not allow for a quantification of the frequency of the concrete involvement of each parent in the different activities assessed.

Other studies, albeit few in number, measure each parent's involvement using a scale of high, average, or low, with the range of combinations of these categories figuring in parental scores (for example, high involvement of both father and mother; high involvement of father/low involvement of mother; high involvement of mother/low involvement of father; and so on). This is an interesting strategy, but it often significantly limits statistical treatment possibilities due to an inadequate number of informants in certain categories. A non-parametric statistical treatment is therefore recommended, and often brings significant results. Bourçois (1997), on the effects of the father's presence on the social development of preschool children, illustrates this methodological approach. The study considers three types of father involvement. In the first group, the mother alone is responsible for caregiving and child rearing. The other two groups are characterized by an equal division of child-related responsibilities, but in one group the father and the mother adopt similar roles, while in the other these roles are clearly differentiated. The results support Bourçois's hypothesis that children show greater openness towards their peers when their father is involved and when his involvement is differentiated from that of the mother.

Today the emphasis placed on co-parenting reflects the importance of anchoring studies in a systemic family perspective. This is less a matter of the influence exercised by one parent or the other than of their combined influence, which is operationalized according to a typology or pattern that considers the characteristics of each parent. This involvement typology considers the degree of involvement (frequency), as well as the nature of the involvement (the kinds of involvement activities the parents engage in and the quality of their involvement). At this juncture, the results of studies have begun to underline the importance of the nature, rather than the degree, of involvement (as long as a minimum level of involvement is present). In two studies carried out among preschool children, we contrast maternal and paternal involvement measures in relation to characteristics of the child's social adaptation and the family climate (Dubeau et al., 2013). We found that quantitative measurements (time interacting alone with the child or being accessible to the child, number of meals eaten as a family, and so on) and the measurement of task sharing between the parents were weakly linked to the child's adaptation and the family climate. However, cognitive measures of involvement – that is, those related to the importance each parent gives to the different roles and functions fulfilled within the family (for example, to work, to the child's emotional support, to discipline) – proved to be the best predictors of both family climate and the child's social adaptation.

These results bring out the importance of moving beyond behavioural dimensions to take cognitive dimensions of parental involvement into account, to be able to understand fully the meaning of father involvement. Parents' representations of their own specific roles and contributions to their children's development have been little studied as yet, but they unavoidably guide parents' behaviours. This niche is promising terrain for the qualitative (inductive) research approach, which is frequently used to explore and document new research topics. The consideration of the multiple realities affecting families is also a relatively unexplored aspect of studies in this field. Recognition of a measure of parental involvement that includes the particularities of each parent requires flexible models that reflect the diversity of today's families.

A Qualitative Vision of Father Involvement

As mentioned above, the advancement of knowledge of a newly perceived phenomenon or little-studied social group is generally the fruit of studies that use a qualitative (inductive) approach. In this approach, researchers set out to be receptive to the discourse of the people targeted by the investigation. They use data-gathering methods, such as interviews, that allow them to collect as much information as possible, while taking care, by means of open-ended queries, to avoid leading questions. In contrast to the deductive approach, here the steps of data gathering and analysis are often carried out simultaneously and feed into each other. The conceptual framework (key concepts and the links between them) emerges progressively from the points of view of the informants. Finally, the objective of these studies is not to obtain a generalization of the results that can then be applied to the population under study, but to arrive at a first phenomenological description of the situation as it is experienced and felt by the actors concerned, taking several facets of their situations (such as family history, work history) into account. Anthropology and sociology are the disciplinary fields that turn most frequently to this research paradigm.

The qualitative approach attributes a central importance to the perceptions and meanings given to a phenomenon by the participants in a study (Goertz & Mahoney, 2012). Thus, it complements quantitative research, which, by emphasizing the frequency or duration of a behaviour, aims to establish the importance or the amplitude of a phenomenon. Stated more simply, in quantitative research on father involvement, the questions asked have to do with how much time the father spends with his child and what type of activities they do together. In qualitative research, the aim is to understand how the father experiences these moments and what subjective meaning he gives to them. The different aspects of the father's life that have a potential impact on his involvement with his child are also considered. In this approach, fatherhood is viewed as a social, psychological, and historical phenomenon.

The focus on the meaning and the understanding of phenomena that characterize the qualitative approach makes it possible to move beyond the criticism that has often been directed towards it by the scientific community. This criticism has mainly concerned small sample size and the exploratory nature of this type of study. It is interesting to note that the results of qualitative studies have become more easily accessible through traditional dissemination channels (academic journals, monographs, and so on). In *Conceptualizing and Measuring Father Involvement*, edited by Day and Lamb (2004), several chapters are dedicated to these studies.

Overall, qualitative research on fathering corresponds to two principal niches: studies that aim to better understand and describe the realities of various subpopulations of fathers – see, for example, Devault et al. (2008), on young fathers, and Schacher, Auerbach, and Silverstein (2005), on gay fathers – and studies that aim to better define or refine concepts and conceptual frameworks in this field. The grounded-theory approach of studies by Daly and Dienhart (1998; Dienhart & Daly, 1997) shed new light on parental involvement by analysing the discourse of fathers and mothers on balancing work and family responsibilities. In their work, parental involvement is defined in a broadened social and systemic perspective that includes consideration of the pressures of work and of individual and jointly held values that guide parents' choices in the sharing of tasks.

The Integration of Paternal Cognitions to Add Nuance to Traditional Definitions of Father Involvement

We conclude this chapter by discussing studies by Prospère that adopted a qualitative approach to identifying certain little-known aspects of fatherhood. These studies have contributed to the advancement of knowledge by: (1) integrating cognitions to nuance the traditional definitions of father involvement; (2) making room for interdisciplinarity; and (3) adopting a rich methodological mixture.

One such study that adds nuance to traditional definitions of father involvement in well-designated life contexts is that of François Fournier and Anne Quéniart (1994). The originality of this study lay in its aim to gain a clearer understanding not only of the father's place in the family, but also of the family's and the child's place in the father's life. The qualitative approach allowed the construction of three father profiles. This typology emerged from some twenty interviews with fathers who had above-average education and income. The interview dealt with various aspects of the father's life, such as the decision process leading to the child's conception, the construction of paternal feeling, the parents' everyday routine, the importance of fatherhood in his life, and so on. The father profiles issued not only from a content analysis of each question, but also from a transversal analysis of the aspects of the fathers' lives that were examined. Table 2.1 summarizes these profiles.

Quéniart's later studies, on father involvement following divorce or separation, retain this methodological framework (Quéniart, 2001). Interestingly, her results show that not all fathers disengage for the same reasons after the couple breaks up. Instead, she identifies three typical trajectories in which: (1) the conjugal separation is seen as liberating for fathers whose sense of fatherhood is completely absent; (2) the separation is seen as a catastrophe that causes the cutting off of the father's relationship with the child; and (3) the separation is mainly experienced only as the breakup of a romantic relationship.

Although it is difficult to summarize the rich content of the framework of qualitative studies, these briefly presented results illustrate the complementary contribution of this methodological approach to the concept of father involvement. More specifically, the multidimensional view of father involvement goes beyond observable behaviour to integrate the spheres of cognitions and emotions related to fathering (Schoppe-Sullivan et al., 2004). The relevance of combining the behavioural, affective, and cognitive spheres principally depends on the objectives of the study. With respect to intervention concerns, these qualitative studies are proving particularly useful in gaining a better understanding of fathers' behaviour.

Table 2.1. Fathers' Profiles, as Compiled by Fournier and Quéniart (1994)

---

1. Family-oriented fatherhood
  The family is a central reference for these fathers. To them, the child represents family life more than anything else; their social status as father is paramount, and their paternal identity hinges on the family relationship. On the level of daily parenting behaviour, the paternal and maternal roles are seen as clearly differentiated. These fathers are chiefly concerned with protecting the family and ensuring its continuation, with the mother giving the children the necessary care, attention, and affection.

2. Fatherhood as a responsibility shared with the mother to meet the child's needs and encourage his or her optimal development.
  For these fathers, the relationship with the child is direct, close, and intense. These fathers are often in a two-earner family situation; thus, raising a child is a challenge in the parents' conjugal life. The totality of the household tasks is generally shared by the two parents, eventually leading to an interchangeable view of parental roles. These fathers consider fatherhood a life change that requires adjustments to balance the different spheres of existence: work, fatherhood, the conjugal relationship, and leisure activities.

3. Peripheral, sporadic fatherhood
  Most of these fathers are younger and are either beginning their careers or still studying. Most have become fathers following an accidental or undesired pregnancy. Their fatherhood is experienced as a form of resistance to change, with the child seen as an irritant. On the level of daily parenting behaviour, these fathers take few initiatives and lack enthusiasm. The mother, therefore, takes on most of the family responsibilities.

Source: Adapted from Fournier and Quéniart, 1994.

Room for Interdisciplinarity

Métiers de pères (Profession: Fatherhood)[4] was a participatory action research project implemented in a context of skill training and social intervention (see Chapter 6). The results illustrate the contribution of a qualitative definition of father involvement based on characteristics related to the individual, co-parental, and socio-professional histories of vulnerable young fathers. The research sought not only to establish the meaning of father involvement for fathers in a context of economic and social vulnerability, but also to identify the reasons underlying the fathers' perceptions. One of the strengths of this study is that it went beyond the fathers' discourse on their relationship with their children to reach an understanding of fatherhood as a phenomenon experienced within a historical and multidimensional context and, therefore, as a context influenced by the fathers' individual, socio-professional, and social histories. For this reason, the fathers were questioned not only about their relations with their offspring, but also about their families of origin and their relationship with their parents, their transition to school and to the job market, and their relationship with the mothers of their children. In this approach, fatherhood is perceived as a dynamic process that can be understood in light of what fathers are experiencing, have experienced, and wish to experience.

In this study, seventeen young fathers participating in a socio-professional integration program were interviewed to elicit their life stories. One challenge of the qualitative approach is to be able to grasp fully the content of interviews, to appropriate the information obtained, and, above all, to establish correlations among the variables, all from the discourse of the participants. On the other hand, researchers adopting this approach usually work as a group to ensure the validity of the analysis, and so did those who undertook the Profession: Fatherhood project.

From the analysis of the interviews with the young trainees emerged a *father involvement continuum*. The variables considered in evaluating the relative degree of father involvement on the continuum are: (1) physical accessibility to the child; (2) the father's participation in the various dimensions of father involvement; (3) the father's steps to assume responsibility for himself and his family; and (4) the father's ability to focus on his child's needs and to empathize with the child's mother. The first two variables are related to the behavioural and dimensional aspects of father involvement, while the latter two are more closely related to the meaning given to fatherhood and its representations.

In the study sample, three types of fatherhood situations are defined within the incremental father involvement continuum: *suspended father involvement* in the case of three of the seventeen young fathers; *halfway father involvement* in the case of seven fathers; and *sustained father involvement* for the remaining seven fathers. *Suspended father involvement* refers to the situation of fathers who, due to personal factors or constraints imposed by their former partner or the judicial system, faced obstacles that made access to the child difficult or impossible, which led to the father's withdrawal from his parental role. Interaction with the child was almost non-existent in these cases. Father involvement was reduced to the evocation dimension (thinking about the child) or simply to the payment of child support. These fathers seemed to have entered a process of disengagement with respect to fathering, and the child had gradually moved to the periphery of their concerns.

Half-way father involvement corresponds to the situation of men whose fathering showed in concrete practices and concerns, but was lacking in certain areas of father involvement. These fathers seemed to regret the loss of the freedom of their adolescence, and they emphasized the sacrifices associated with fathering. Their discourse centred more on their own difficulties and challenges than on the needs of the child and the child's mother. Shared custody arrangements were often a matter of constant negotiations. The life situations of *half-way involved* fathers indicated that their fatherhood was located in a zone of fragility.

Sustained father involvement refers to the situations of participants whose fatherhood was anchored strongly enough to predict that they would continue to be regularly involved with their children in all the aspects of fathering. These fathers were fully engaged in a significant, ongoing process of assuming their fathering responsibilities, leading them towards steady employment, increased availability to care for the child, and the abandonment of risky life habits. Fatherhood had become an integral element of their identity. *Sustained involved* fathers seemed to focus more on the child and less on themselves. They showed empathy in the way they talked about the child and an understanding attitude towards the child's mother.

The typology the study established, ranging from disengaged fatherhood (*suspended father involvement*) to well-anchored fatherhood (*sustained father involvement*), differs from existing typologies in that it places fathers' behaviour within a process of relation building with the child, rather than categorizing it according to social norms. The study takes fathers' accessibility to the children into account, along with their concrete and psychological involvement. This typology also considers the social and personal maturation of the young fathers – that is, their capacity to assume social responsibility after the arrival of a child, to focus on the child's needs, and to establish a *modus operandi* with the mother. Through its dimensional aspect, the typology manages to combine a psychological and a sociological perspective of father involvement.

A Rich Methodological Combination

An illustration of the innovative mixed methodology in Prospère's research, combining the quantitative and qualitative approaches, is the doctoral thesis by Dufour (2001) entitled *La santé mentale des enfants de milieux défavorisés: conceptions, pratiques et profils de pères* (The mental health of children in lower-income families: fathers' perceptions, practices, and profiles). Dufour's objective was to describe how fathers in a low-income milieu perceived their child-rearing role with a preschool child, and how they carried out this function.

Dufour uses the quantitative approach in constituting a maximum variation sample. Prospère's FIQ allowed her to divide the sample of thirty fathers into two contrasting groups: fifteen highly involved fathers with a strong sense of parental competency; and fifteen not noticeably involved fathers with a weak sense of parental competence. Within a qualitative perspective, Dufour interviewed the fathers to obtain their perceptions of the psychological well-being of their children, desirable child-rearing objectives and practices, the father's role, and the social environment, including the neighbourhood. At the first stage, the data underwent descriptive analysis by subject category. At the second stage, the principal dimensions extracted for each category allowed Dufour to draw up a father typology. She identifies five profiles of child-rearing fathers based on their parental practices, rating participants as possessing a low, medium, or high variety of child-rearing practices, and their attitudes (proactive versus reactive), as shown in Table 2.2.

The reactive fathers include the family men and the worrying fathers, and are characterized by a low level of involvement and a weak sense of parental competence. These fathers generally have an anxious attitude regarding resources and their social network. The reactive fathers are similar to traditional fathers in many ways. The *proactive fathers* correspond to the profiles of the accommodating fathers, the guiding fathers, and the down-to-earth fathers. Compared to the reactive fathers, the strong majority of the proactive fathers are very involved with their children and have a strong sense of parental competence. These fathers are comfortable in their parental role and possess a wide repertory of child-raising practices.

These results clearly show that there are many ways to be a father. Furthermore, they bring out the pertinence of studying the subjective experience of father involvement, which might differ from the observable, concrete behaviour of fathers with respect to their children.

Conclusion

Recent studies have made many advances towards a better understanding of the nature of father involvement, its diversity, and its influence

Table 2.2. Fathers' Profiles, as Compiled by Dufour (2001)

---

1. *Family men (n = 7)*
   These fathers generally have a low level of direct involvement with their children and a poor opinion of their parenting skills. They see their role as centring on the basic needs and socialization of the child. They have a limited repertory of practices corresponding to their child-rearing goals. The family is of central value to them, and their view of the psychological well-being of their child mainly concerns adaptation to the milieu and conformity to the norm.
2. *Worrying fathers (n = 7)*
   These fathers are particularly worried about support demands in their parental role (resulting in doubt, questioning, and guilt). Their concept of the psychological well-being of their children centres on self-reliance and the expression of individuality.
3. *Accommodating fathers (n = 7)*
   These fathers are characterized by a relatively high level of involvement and sense of parental competency. Their view of their children's psychological well-being combines a focus on individuality and conformity to the norm. They see their paternal role exclusively in terms of availability and affection, although a few mentioned meeting the child's basic needs.
4. *Guiding fathers (n = 4)*
   These fathers are strongly involved with their children and feel competent in their role, which they assumed with ease, in their view. They see the psychological well-being of their children above all in terms of self-reliance and the expression of individuality. These fathers possess a varied repertory of child-rearing practices.
5. *Down-to-earth fathers (n = 5)*
   These fathers have the most diversified repertory of child-rearing practices. They see their parental role principally in terms of availability, affection, and the socialization of the child. Their requests for assistance are motivated mainly by a search for a solution to immediate worries or difficulties.

Source: Adapted from Dufour, 2001.

on children's developmental outcomes. The quantitative approach that guided earlier studies attempted to validate for fathers the principal results obtained for mothers. Thus, *a priori*, they placed little emphasis on the specificity of fathers' roles, since the conceptual and theoretical frameworks they adopted were essentially supported by data on mothers. An important contribution of these studies was the creation of instruments to measure parental involvement, with some adopting a one-dimensional perspective (the unitary concept) and others considering separately each parent's investment in different areas of activity (the multidimensional perspective). In addition, the instruments developed in the framework of these studies took into account the division of family tasks between the parents and, therefore, were appropriate for a systemic approach to the family. The choice of instrument, however, depends on a study's objectives. In some cases, the principal aim is to translate findings into knowledge that is useful at the level of intervention and practice. For example, the study by Lacharité and Lachance (1998), carried out among families characterized by significant social adaptation difficulties (referral or the risk of referral to the youth protection authorities for child neglect), found that those fathers saw themselves as being just as involved with their children as fathers in the general population. This finding is obviously useful in the intervention milieu, since fathers' perceptions might clash with those of practitioners who discern important gaps in the levels of energy invested by the fathers.

Studies guided by a qualitative approach have also contributed to the multidimensional view of father involvement by considering – beyond the behavioural spheres (direct or indirect interaction) – the cognitive and affective dimensions associated with fathering. Access to the fathers' representations and perceptions investigated in greater depth in interviews and focus groups allows us to better understand and report the psychological and social realities of lesser-known subgroups of fathers, and to construct comprehensive conceptual frameworks that integrate both the maternal and the paternal entities within the parental component. Carrying out studies on smaller samples of fathers is justified by the wide range of dimensions investigated – for example, the individual, conjugal, parental, social, cultural, and even political dimensions that influence these fathers' life stories and their parental involvement. The integration of all these dimensions requires familiarity with a range of disciplinary currents within a comprehensive perspective, and mastery of the contents and the terminologies associated with them is essential. We hope this brief survey has conveyed the multifaceted nature of the concept of father involvement, as well as the subtleties and nuances that should be taken into consideration in this field of study.

The current challenge for research is to arrive at an understanding of father involvement that also encompasses the characteristics of subgroups of fathers (Marsiglio, Day, & Lamb, 2000). As with the research on mothers, for many years fathers were treated as a homogeneous group. Quantitative studies have dealt mainly with the situations of fathers in two-parent families with relatively high educational attainment and income levels (Coley, 2001). More recent studies indicate that father involvement is strongly influenced by the father's individual, family, and social characteristics. Diversified experiences of fatherhood imply diversified needs, and, ultimately, the necessary development of more finely tuned interventions to support these fathers in the exercising of their parental roles.

NOTES

1 This particular review of the literature gives a detailed description of the various measurement instruments, their advantages, and their limitations.
2 Several studies have also looked at the impacts of father involvement on other family members (spouse/partner in Dienhart & Daly, 1997), their interrelations (between siblings in Volling & Belsky, 1992), and on the father himself (in Allen et al., 2012; Forget, Dubeau, & Rannou, 2005; Garfield, Clark-Kauffman, & Davis, 2006).
3 See the instruments for evaluating father involvement developed by Lacharité (1997): the *Inventaire de participation à la vie familiale* (Family life participation inventory).
4 A portion of the content in this section is taken from Devault et al. (2008).

REFERENCES

Allen, S., Daly, K., & Ball, J. (2012). Fathers make a difference in their children's lives: A review of the research evidence. In J. Ball & K. Daly (Eds.), *Father involvement in Canada: Diversity, renewal, and transformation* (pp. 50–88). Vancouver, BC: UBC Press.

Bourçois, V. (1997). Modalités de présence du père et développement social de l'enfant d'âge préscolaire. *Enfance, 3*, 389–399.

Coley, R. L. (2001). (In)visible men: Emerging research on low-income, unmarried, and minority fathers. *American Psychologist, 56*(9), 743–753. http://dx.doi.org/10.1037/0003-066X.56.9.743

Cox, M. J., Owen, M., Henderson, V., & Margand, N. A. (1992). Prediction of infant-father and infant-mother attachment. *Developmental Psychology, 28*(3), 474–483. http://dx.doi.org/10.1037/0012-1649.28.3.474

Coyl-Shepherd, D. D., & Newland, L. A. (2012). Mothers and fathers' couple and family contextual influences, parent involvement and school-age child attachment. *Early Child Development and Care, 183*(3-4), 553–569. http://dx.doi.org/10.1080/03004430.2012.711599

Daly, K. J., & Dienhart, A. (1998). Negotiating parental involvement: Finding time for children. In D. Vannoy & P. J. Dubeck (Eds.), *Challenges for work and family in the twenty-first century* (pp. 111–122). New York, NY: Aldine de Gruyter.

Day, R. D., & Lamb, M. E. (2004). *Conceptualizing and measuring father involvement.* Mahwah, NJ: Erlbaum.

Deutsch, F. M., Lussier, J. B., & Servis, L. J. (1993). Husbands at home: Predictors of paternal participation in childcare and housework. *Journal of Personality and Social Psychology, 65*(6), 1154–1166. http://dx.doi.org/10.1037/0022-3514.65.6.1154

Devault, A., Milcent, M. P., Ouellet, F., Laurin, I., Jauron, M., & Lacharité, C. (2008). Life stories of young fathers in contexts of vulnerability. *Fathering, 6*(3), 226–248. http://dx.doi.org/10.3149/fth.0603.226

Dienhart, A. (1998). *Reshaping fatherhood: The social construction of shared parenting.* Thousand Oaks, CA: Sage. http://dx.doi.org/10.4135/9781483345482

Dienhart, A., & Daly, K. (1997). Men and women co-creating father involvement in a nongenerative culture. In A. J. Hawkins & D. C. Dollahite (Eds.), *Generative fathering: Beyond deficits perspectives* (pp. 147–164). Thousand Oaks, CA: Sage.

Dollahite, D. C., Hawkins, A. J., & Brotherson, S. E. (1997). Fatherwork: A conceptual ethic of fathering as generative work. In A. J. Hawkins & D. C. Dollahite (Eds.), *Generative fathering: Beyond deficits perspectives* (pp. 17–35). Thousand Oaks, CA: Sage.

Dubeau, D., Coutu, S., & Lavigueur, S. (2013). Links between different measures of mother/father involvement and child social adjustment. *Early Child Development and Care, 183*(6), 791–809. http://dx.doi.org/10.1080/03004430.2012.723442

Dubeau, D., Devault, A., & Forget, G. (2009). *La paternité au XXIe siècle.* Quebec City, QC: Presses de l'Université Laval.

Dufour, S. (2001). *La santé mentale des enfants de milieux défavorisés: conceptions, pratiques et profils de pères* (unpublished doctoral dissertation). Université du Québec à Montréal, Montreal.

Dulac, G. (1997). *Promotion du rôle des pères: revue de la littérature et analyse d'impacts prévisibles.* Montreal, QC: McGill University, School of Social Work.

Fagan, J., & Cabrera, N. (2012). Longitudinal and reciprocal association between coparenting conflict and father engagement. *Journal of Family Psychology, 26*(6), 1004–1011. http://dx.doi.org/10.1037/a0029998

Feldman, R., & Klein, P. S. (2003). Toddlers' self-regulated compliance to mothers, caregivers, and fathers: Implications for theories of socialization. *Developmental Psychology, 39*(4), 680–692. http://dx.doi.org/10.1037/0012-1649.39.4.680

Forget, G., Dubeau, D., & Rannou, A. (2005). *Images de pères: une mosaïque des pères québécois,* Quebec, City, QC: Institut national de santé publique du Québec, Retrieved from http://www.inspq.qc.ca/pdf/publications/347-ImagesPeresQuebecois.pdf

Fournier, F., & Quéniart, A. (1994). *Les formes contemporaines du rapport à la famille, à la parentalité et à l'enfant chez les pères québécois: un essai de typologie sociologique.* Montreal, QC: Université du Québec à Montréal, Laboratoire de recherché en écologie humaine et sociale.

Garfield, C. F., Clark-Kauffman, E., & Davis, M. M. (2006). Fatherhood as a component of men's health. *Journal of the American Medical Association, 296*(19), 2365–2368. http://dx.doi.org/10.1001/jama.296.19.2365

Goertz, G., & Mahoney, J. (2012). Concepts and measurement: Ontology and epistemology. *Social Sciences Information, 51*(2), 205–216. http://dx.doi.org/10.1177/0539018412437108

Grimm-Thomas, K., & Perry-Jenkins, P. (1994). All in a day's work: Job experiences, self-esteem, and fathering in working-class families. *Family Relations, 43*(2), 174–181. http://dx.doi.org/10.2307/585320

Grossmann, K., Grossmann, K. E., Fremmer-Bombik, E., Kindler, H., Scheuerer- Englisch, H., & Zimmermann, P. (2002). The uniqueness of the child-father attachment relationship: fathers' sensitive and challenging play as a pivotal variable in a 16-year longitudinal study. *Social Development, 11*(3), 301–331. http://dx.doi.org/10.1111/1467-9507.00202

Hoffman, J. (2011). Attachment research and fathers: Just getting acquainted. In J. Hoffman (Ed.), *Father factors: What social science research tells us about fathers and how to work with them* (pp. 25–32). Peterborough, ON: Father Involvement Research Alliance.

Jacobs, J. N., & Kelley, M. L. (2006). Predictors of paternal involvement in childcare in dual-earner families with young children. *Fathering, 4*(1), 23–47. http://dx.doi.org/10.3149/fth.0401.23

Lacharité, C. (1997). *Inventaire de participation familiale: manuel d'utilisation.* Trois-Rivières, QC: Université du Québec à Trois-Rivières.

Lacharité, C., & Lachance, D. (1998). Perception de la participation du père à la vie familiale dans les familles manifestant des difficultés psychosociales: une étude exploratoire. In L. S. Éthier & J. Alary (Eds.), *Comprendre la famille: actes du 4e Symposium québécois de recherche sur la famille* (pp.134–148). Quebec City, QC: Presses de l'Université du Québec.

Lamb, M. E. (1975). Fathers: Forgotten contributors to child development. *Human Development, 18*(4), 254–266.

Lamb, M. E. (Ed.). (2010). *The role of the father in child development* (5th ed.). Hoboken, NJ: John Wiley.

Lamb, M .E., & Lewis, C. (2013). Father-child relationships. In N. J. Cabrera & C. S. Tamis-LeMonda (Eds.), *Handbook of father involvement: Multidisciplinary perspectives* (pp. 135–151). New York, NY: Routledge.

Lamb, M. E., Pleck, J. H., Charnov, E. L., & Levine, J. A. (1987). A biosocial perspective on paternal behaviour and involvement. In J. B. Lancaster, J. Altman, & A. Rossi (Eds.), *Parenting across the lifespan: Biosocial perspectives* (pp. 11–42). New York, NY: Academic Press.

Le Camus, J. (1997). La paternité sous les regards croisés de la psychologie du développement et de la psychanalyse. In C. Zaouche-Gaudron (Ed.), *La problématique paternelle* (pp. 145–151). Ramonville-Saint-Agne, France: Érès.

Marsiglio, W., Day, R. D., & Lamb, M. E. (2000). Exploring fatherhood diversity: Implications for conceptualizing father involvement. *Marriage & Family Review, 29*(4), 269–293. http://dx.doi.org/10.1300/J002v29n04_03

McBride, B. A., et al. (2005). Paternal identity, maternal gatekeeping, and father involvement. *Family Relations, 54*(3), 360–372. http://dx.doi.org/10.1111/j.1741-3729.2005.00323.x

Newland, L. A., & Coyl, D. D. (2010). Fathers' role as attachment figures: An interview with Sir Richard Bowlby. *Early Child Development and Care, 180*(1-2), 25–32. http://dx.doi.org/10.1080/03004430903414679

Palkovitz, R. (1997). Reconstructing involvement: Expanding conceptualizations of men's caring in contemporary families. In A. J. Hawkins & D. C. Dollahite (Eds.), *Generative fathering: Beyond deficit perspectives* (pp. 200–216). Thousand Oaks, CA: Sage.

Paquette, D. (2004). Theorizing the father-child relationship: Mechanisms and developmental outcomes. *Human Development, 47*(4), 193–219. http://dx.doi.org/10.1159/000078723

Paquette, D., & Dumont, C. (2013). Is father-child rough-and-tumble play associated with attachment or activation relationships? *Early Child Development and Care, 183*(6), 760–773. http://dx.doi.org/10.1080/03004430.2012.723440

Pleck, J. H. (2007). Why could father involvement benefit children? Theoretical perspectives. *Applied Developmental Science, 11*(4), 196–202. http://dx.doi.org/10.1080/10888690701762068

Pleck, J. H., & Masciadrelli, B. P. (2004). Paternal involvement by U.S. residential fathers: Levels, sources, and consequences. In M. E. Lamb (Ed.), *The role of the father in child development* (4th ed., pp. 222–271). Hoboken, NJ: John Wiley.

Quéniart, A. (2001). Le désengagement paternel, un phénomène social aux multiples visages. In H. Dorvil & R. Mayer (Eds.), *Problèmes sociaux* (Vol. 2, pp. 83–102). Quebec City, QC: Presses de l'Université du Québec.

Radin, N. (1981a). Childrearing fathers in intact families: Some antecedents and consequences. *Merrill-Palmer Quarterly, 27,* 489–514.

Radin, N. (1981b). The role of the father in cognitive, academic, and intellectual development. In M. E. Lamb (Ed.), *The role of the father in child development* (3rd ed., pp. 379–428). New York, NY: John Wiley.

Schacher, S., Auerbach, C., & Silverstein, I. (2005). Gay fathers expanding the possibilities for us all. *Journal of GLBT Family Studies, 1*(3), 31–52. http://dx.doi.org/10.1300/J461v01n03_02

Schoppe-Sullivan, S. J., Kotila, L., Jia, R., Lang, S. N., & Bower, D. J. (2012). Comparisons of levels and predictors of mothers' and fathers' engagement with their preschool aged children. *Early Child Development and Care, 183*(3-4), 498–514. http://dx.doi.org/10.1080/03004430.2012.711596

Schoppe-Sullivan, S. J., McBride, B. A., & Ringo Ho, M. H. (2004). Unidimensional versus multidimensional perspectives on father involvement. *Fathering, 2*(2), 1–14.

Volling, B. L., & Belsky, J. (1992). Infant, father and marital antecedents of infant father attachment security in dual-earner and single-earner families. *International Journal of Behavioral Development, 15*(1), 83–100. http://dx.doi.org/10.1177/016502549201500105

Youngblade, L. M., Park, K. A., & Belsky, J. (1993). Measurement of young children's close friendship: A comparison of two independent assessment systems and their associations with attachment security. *International Journal of Behavioral Development, 16*(4), 563–587. http://dx.doi.org/10.1177/016502549301600403

3 Mobilizing Actors in Participatory Action Research: Promoting Father Involvement in Two Vulnerable Communities in Quebec

GENEVIÈVE TURCOTTE AND FRANCINE OUELLET

Prospère initiated its first participatory action research (PAR) project by mobilizing the actors in two vulnerable communities in Quebec. Researchers, practitioners, and the public collaborated for almost a decade, building partnerships and implementing and evaluating a project aiming to instil, reinforce, and maintain father involvement. This chapter and Chapter 4 give an in-depth view of the project, named Prospère after the research team.

In the mid-1990s a group of volunteers in a township west of Montreal and actors in a low-income neighbourhood of that city agreed to participate in the Prospère project when it was proposed to their communities. Through this PAR project, the actors from the two sites came to feel that they were an integral part of a unique social innovation, and were pioneering an area of intervention that was little developed as yet.

This chapter presents the principal parameters of the intervention model elaborated by the Prospère team, and shows how the actors in the two communities translated, reinterpreted, and applied the guiding principles of this PAR project. It describes the main phases of the implementation process, and summarizes the actions carried out between 1995 and 2000, the period during which the researchers evaluated the project's implementation – see Chapter 4. The chapter concludes by looking at the principal conditions for success, as well as the challenges encountered in the mobilizing of a community around a project aiming to promote father involvement.

Context of the Emergence of the Project

At the beginning of the 1990s practitioners and communities were adjusting to the transformation of the father role. Social services had either done little to address fathers' needs or ignored them completely. Instead, they had assumed that fathers were absent from their children's lives and difficult to reach, and – put simply – they had assigned a much greater importance to the mother-child relationship (Dudley & Stone, 2000; Dulac, 1998, 2001a, 2001b; Ménard, 1999). Researchers and practitioners came to realize, however, that the absence of support for the paternal role limited fathers' abilities to live up to social expectations and, wishing to redefine that role, they began to emphasize the importance of including fathers in programs for families (Meyers, 1993; Palmer & Palkovitz, 1988). In 1991 the recommendations of a Quebec advisory group's report on the health and well-being of children and adolescents, entitled *Un Québec fou de ses enfants* (A Quebec crazy about its kids) (Quebec, 1991), gave priority to the establishment of father support programs that would link fathers, institutions, workplaces, and community-based organizations.

Activities, services, programs, and resources aimed at supporting fathers emerged during the following decade in Quebec and the rest of Canada (Arama, 1997; Bolté, Devault, St-Denis, & Gaudet, 2002; Dubeau, Clément, & Chamberland, 2005; Dubeau, Villeneuve, & Thibault, 2011; Dubeau et al., 2013; Forget, Devault, Allen, Bader, & Jarvis, 2005; Hoffman, 2007), as well as in the United States (Levine & Pitt, 1995; Solomon-Fears, 2012). However, as most of these initiatives were individual or single-sector efforts, they did little to bring about fundamental changes in practices, despite their praiseworthy conviction. They generally took the form of focus groups or workshops modelled after those designed for mothers, and tended to target the micro-social level with a view to improving individual awareness and skills. Moreover, few of these programs targeted fathers living in contexts of economic vulnerability or exclusion, and even fewer adopted a global approach that took account of the risk and protective factors linked to father involvement. Yet such an approach is considered an essential condition for the success of programs aiming to improve the well-being of families in general and father involvement in particular (Devault, Gaudet, Bolté, & St-Denis, 2005; Doherty, Kouneski, & Erickson, 1998; Dufour & Chamberland, 2004; Prilleltensky, Nelson, & Peirson, 2001).

Within this context, Prospère's goal was to find the best way to promote and support father involvement among fathers of very young children (ages zero to five) living in contexts of vulnerability, with a view to preventing child victimization. After several months of discussion and reflection, the Prospère team agreed on a PAR project that it planned to implement in two communities with a high proportion of families living below the poverty line.

The Prospère Intervention Model: Principal Parameters

The intervention model presented to the actors in the two communities was open ended: although it provided guidelines, its structure was flexible with respect to the activities that would be developed to attain the various objectives. Its conceptors essentially saw the model as a blank canvas upon which content would be defined and constructed in a process involving all the actors associated with the project, and which would take the characteristics of each site into account. The Prospère team posited that appropriate "ways of doing things" would emerge as the actions were carried out in the field and, more specifically, from the ongoing interchange between the actions and the critical review of those actions.

In Prospère's model, two main parameters would guide the action: the ecological approach, a theoretical framework that takes account of the complexity of fathers' needs and roles; and a local approach inspired by the principles of health promotion and intersectoral action.

The Ecological Approach

The reference framework of the Prospère project implied that solutions to encourage father involvement must reflect the complexity of the roles and needs of fathers and their families. This led to the adoption of the ecological approach, in which the degree of a father's involvement with his children is viewed as the result of a system of complex interrelations between the father's characteristics and the changing properties of both his proximal environment (the characteristics of the mother and the family context) and his distal environment (the characteristics of the workplace and of social services policies) (Bronfenbrenner, 1979, 1996; Bronfenbrenner & Ceci 1994).

On the intervention level, the ecological approach implies acting globally on several fronts at once. Applied to the promotion of father involvement, this entails:

- working with fathers and mothers from the perspective that parental roles are complementary, and at the same time with service providers, to bring them to attribute as much importance to the father-child relationship as to the mother-child relationship;
- intervening in several spheres of fathers' lives (personal, paternal, co-parental, professional, and civic) through action plans that aim to encourage not only self-development and the improvement of the father-child relationship, but also the development of social links (improvement of support networks, learning to accept and benefit from social support and solidarity) and experiences of citizen participation in improving the common good; and
- stimulating collective as well as individual change by targeting: services, so that they will be more father friendly and inclusive with respect to men; the employment sector, so that consideration will be given to the effects of unemployment and job loss on the paternal role; the workplace, to facilitate the work-family life balance; and the general population and social policy-makers, so that a new concept and culture of fatherhood can take root.

A Local Approach

The ecological approach also echoes intensive community-based programs, a local perspective borrowed from the concepts, principles, and strategies of the health promotion domain. Applied in such diverse areas as cardiovascular health (Goodman, Wheeler, & Lee, 1995; Nissinen & Puska, 1991,) juvenile delinquency (Wiebush, McNulty, & Le, 2000) and the street-gang phenomenon (Spergel, Wa, & Sosa, 2006), this particular concept advocates massive community intervention focused on a single social issue by means of a variety of actions: individual follow-up, community accompaniment, support groups, recreational and cultural activities, public communication campaigns, support for citizen participation, and collective action.

Collaboration between actors from different sectors of activity is an essential condition for carrying out intervention based on a global, ecological approach. This strategy also relies on the mobilization of actors through a local steering committee representing different activity sectors in the community that hold complementary mandates (Hamel, Cousineau, & Vézina, 2006; Ouellet, Paiement, & Tremblay, 1995; White, Jobin, McCann, & Morin, 2002).

The Pilot Sites

Five criteria determined which pilot sites would be chosen for this PAR project. The sites had to: (1) have a minimum number of families with at least one child between the ages of zero and five; (2) have at least 25 per cent of families living below the poverty line; (3) have a high rate of referrals for child abuse and neglect; (4) be relatively culturally homogenous (more than 70 per cent of the population with French as their first language); and (5) have not been the subject of a previous experiment or intensive investigative study. The choice fell upon the township of Pointe-Calumet (site A), a small community west of Montreal, and an inner-city neighbourhood in the ward of Rosemont in Montreal (site B).

With almost a third of its families living below the poverty line, site A is one of the poorest communities in its region. Nonetheless the township was in the midst of a profound transformation. As a result of urban sprawl in Montreal, long-established families with deep roots in the area were now the neighbours of recently arrived families who had moved into new housing developments. This had resulted in a certain socio-economic cleavage in the community.

Often described as a "pretty tough place," Pointe-Calumet was trying to rid itself of this negative image. To resolve its problems, it had traditionally relied on mutual support, which constituted its major strength. This was all the more important since social and health services are located outside the municipality's limits. This physical distance, combined with a mistrust of public services, seemed to account for the low level of recourse to formal aid organizations. There was, on the other hand, a thriving informal support system based on volunteerism: many citizens of Pointe-Calumet belonged to associations and clubs that contributed socially and financially to different causes in the community. Although these organizations were quite dynamic, their relations were characterized by a spirit of rivalry, and they generally had little inclination to work together. In addition, representatives of the local elite had blocked any collective mobilization initiatives they perceived as threatening to their interests. The exclusive nature of this power had contributed to the isolation of the community.

This was the context at site A when a social action committee was created, the first step in a larger process of joint action and self-management. This committee was made up of citizens – informal leaders and members of social clubs – who decided to join together to fight poverty, counter the control exercised by the local elite, reinforce social inclusion, and empower their fellow citizens. When the PAR project promoting father involvement began, this committee was in the process of establishing a family services centre with the support of a community worker from the local Centre de santé et de services sociaux (CSSS, health and social services centre). The existence of this project provided a base for mobilizing the community around the promotion of father involvement.

Site B is a densely populated urban neighbourhood where most people rent apartments. When the Prospère project was first taking shape, over a third of the families at site B were living below the poverty line and 46 per cent were single-parent households, the large majority of which were headed by women, an aspect which can make the implementation of programs for fathers particularly difficult. The local CSSS was adjacent to the targeted neighbourhood; one daycare centre lay within it. Rosemont, in which site B is located, possessed more than thirty community organizations and had become known for the cooperation that existed between the community, public, and economic sectors. The previous few decades had seen a series of epic struggles for affordable housing and economic and community development. Due to the financial crisis facing the majority of the community organizations, the priority had changed to consolidating existing organizations, rather than creating new ones. When the Prospère project was proposed in spring 1995, there was no locus of joint action bringing together the principal resources for families with young children, despite a long tradition of collaborative action in the youth sector.

Implementing the Project

A field study in each site was carried out to assess needs, existing services, and the relative openness to a social innovation project centred on father involvement. The objectives in the researchers' intervention model were based on the findings of these studies. A promotion committee was formed to introduce the project to the actors in the sites. Once the actors expressed interest in participating, the project was launched in the following stages, each with its specific issues and challenges: (1) the mobilization of relevant actors through the creation of a local steering committee responsible for implementing the project in each pilot site; (2) the search for consensus based on a logic of action; and (3) the creation of yearly action plans (Butterfoss, Goodman, & Wandersman, 1993; Florin, Mitchell, & Stevenson, 1993; Ouellet et al., 1995; Goodman, Wandersman, Chinman, Imm, & Morrissey, 1996). Almost eighteen months went by from the time the Prospère project was proposed to the two sites until the first action plans were drawn up. This latter process took place each year, with certain adjustments made according to evolving circumstances, experience acquired, and the first perceived effects of the project. The Prospère researchers were active in all stages of the project.

Mobilizing Community Partners through Steering Committees

From the beginning, Prospère considered an alliance with the CSSS near each site to be indispensable to the local mobilization process. Several factors facilitated this collaboration. For the two centres, the main interest lay in the opportunities provided by a partnership with university representatives and the Montreal public health department. By collaborating on this PAR project, they would be able to further develop their expertise, increase their visibility, and gain access to certain subsidized programs. For the CSSS adjacent to site A, the alliance was also perceived as a chance to encourage an incipient mobilization in a community that had shown resistance to using formal services. For the CSSS at site B, the project was seen as a springboard to develop community-based action in the early childhood sector.

To prepare a basis for collaboration with the researchers, the affiliated CSSS delegated community workers to promote the project in each site; these individuals were well known to other actors in the milieu and were familiar with local issues. They had the task of convincing, recruiting, and bringing onto a steering committee the people most likely to be interested in the project. In both sites, the innovative aspect of father involvement promotion and the prospect of being part of a PAR project based on a flexible model that left room for creativity were important factors in the actors' decision to join the steering committees. Furthermore, the practitioners at site A saw the benefit of having credible partners to help launch their family services centre. The actors at site B, for their part, saw the proposal as an opportunity to establish services for fathers in their respective organizations and to work jointly with other organizations in this area.

The composition of the steering committees differed somewhat between the two sites. At site A, to facilitate grafting the project onto the social mobilization effort already in progress, the community worker chiefly recruited for the steering committee volunteers involved in the creation of the family services centre. Of the nine local members, five were citizens active in various social organizations in the community, and four were health and social services professionals from the CSSS, le Centre jeunesse des Laurentides, and the public health department. During the years the project was under way, the number of members representing formal services diminished and the role of professionals remained peripheral. Throughout the project, it was difficult to recruit people who occupied upper-management positions in the organizations and whose support would have made it easier to gain access to material and financial resources. On the other hand, a stable core of volunteers actively involved in their community guaranteed a certain dynamism, openness to new ideas, and the ability to work together. At every stage of the project, the actors at site A would have liked to have had more men on the steering committee to ensure that the process was "on the right track." The characteristics of the community dynamics at site B, on the other hand, made it possible to recruit a majority of male service professionals as members of the steering committee. The site B committee comprised thirteen actors who worked at eleven local community and institutional organizations serving families with young children, and who were interested in promoting father involvement through concrete actions.

The participative role of the Prospère team implied active involvement by a researcher on each steering committee. Besides following and documenting the project's unfolding and measuring its impacts, the researcher's role was to encourage the sharing of knowledge, to invite critical reflection on different issues of the implementation process, to provide support for fundraising and the logistical organization of activities, and to assist in the writing of annual reports. All of this was made easier by the friendly relations that prevailed among the steering committee members, which were based on trust and mutual respect.

Searching for a Consensus

The actors took several months to appropriate the Prospère model and to translate it into accessible language. They adapted it to local characteristics, arrived at a common vision of the paternal role, and decided which actions should be given priority. To do this, the committee members first drew on their own experiences as fathers or mothers. Their discussions were nourished by theoretical knowledge shared with them by the researchers associated with the project. Working sessions were organized, based on a review of the literature on father involvement (Turcotte, Bolté, Dubeau, & Paquette, 2001; Turcotte & Gaudet, 2009) and the results from the field study that had been carried out among fathers and mothers in both sites (Forget, 1995, 1996); for details of the field study, see Chapter 4. This stage of the implementation process was particularly fruitful at the level of the development of interpersonal relations and group solidarity. The actors' sense of belonging was reinforced by the creation of branding elements to identify the two participating groups: the corporate names *Initiative Place-O-Pères de Pointe-Calumet* (A Place for Fathers of Pointe-Calumet) and *CooPère Rosemont* (Cooperative Fathers of Rosemont), together with logos, and slogans. In addition, over the years, the partners developed promotional tools such as flyers, posters, T-shirts, and banners.

This stage of the project brought out five areas of consensus to guide the actions of the steering committees. Three of these areas were common to both sites; the other two differed in the community action strategies that were given priority. These differences can be explained in large part by the specific contexts in which the project was implemented.

A Common Vision of the Father's Role: Getting Away from a Single Model

In deciding on a suitable message to disseminate within the community, the actors in the two sites first sought to arrive at a common vision of the father's role. They concluded that the concept of fatherhood cannot be reduced to a single model and that there are several ways of being a good father. Each must "be a father in his own way" – that is, choose how he wants to be a good father, at his own pace. This concept is consistent with the concern to reduce social exclusion and self-blame (for example, rejecting the deficit paradigm of the inadequate father, or "deadbeat Dad") and to help fathers recognize the positive things they do with their children. The actors in the steering committees adopted a perspective that emphasized the different and complementary nature of parental roles, highlighting things fathers can do with their children that are different from things mothers do. Thus the steering committee members made it clear that the father's role should not be defined by reference to the mother's role, that fathers have a style of interaction with children specific to them, and that this specificity correlates positively to child developmental outcomes.

The Starting Point: Raising Awareness of the Importance of the Paternal Role

While keeping in mind that actions would be carried out on several fronts at a time, the actors of the two sites saw the need to establish priorities that took into account the context, the stage of the project, and the circumstances of the moment. Aware that social innovation allowing a broadened concept of the father's role could come about without a change in mentality, the steering committee members decided that the first action plans should prioritize the promotion of fatherhood in the community. In their view, the setting up of activities that would establish the credibility of the project and emphasize the value of father involvement for the community at large was a precondition to the adoption of strategies to bring about behavioural change. Thus it was first necessary to get the message across that fathers are important for children's well-being.

An Approach Centring on the Family and Co-Parenting

The PAR project's partners favoured a global approach that would include a concern for father involvement within intervention directed towards the family. The aim of the intervention was first and foremost the child's well-being, based on the complementarity of the mother's and father's roles within this common goal. This approach implied mobilizing fathers and bringing them to interact with their children in non-threatening activities that highlighted family enjoyment.

At Site A, a Desire to Inscribe the Project within a Community Development Perspective

At site A, the local context (the absence of joint action, the low level of democratic participation, and the isolation of citizens) moved the members of the steering committee to add a community development objective to the promotion of father involvement. The actors at site A considered that, for the message concerning father involvement to reach its target audience effectively, it was necessary to create conditions that would empower the community. Therefore the steering committee decided that the following objectives should guide its actions: (1) to consolidate the family services centre as the vehicle for the father involvement project; (2) to obtain the support of municipal politicians and other local leaders to ensure that they would not hinder the implementation of the project; and (3) to enhance the community's image among local and regional decision-makers. In advocating an approach of empowerment and self-management, the committee members also agreed that it was up to the fathers – they being most aware of their own needs – to design the activities that suited them, with the aim of eventually managing the project on their own, thus becoming agents of change themselves.

At Site B, an Intersectoral Action Practice

The strategy adopted at site B determined that each organization represented on the steering committee would contribute to the action plan by introducing father-related activities in its annual programming or by adapting the content of existing activities to fathers' needs within the framework of its mandate. In this way the project would benefit from the spheres of action of all the organizations, ultimately "immersing the whole community." The organizations also agreed to develop collaborative links to be able to carry out joint action in the future.

At this stage the development of the project benefited from three major assets: (1) the presence of experienced community workers to mobilize the steering committee members, translate concepts into accessible terms, and foster feelings of solidarity among the members; (2) close links with the research team as a whole, which constantly nourished reflection; and (3) the time necessary for the actors to appropriate the project's principles by examining and situating them within the context of the social debate on gender relations and changes to social roles and responsibilities, including the sharing of domestic chores. A visit by internationally known fatherhood specialist Michael Lamb[1] gave crucial impetus to the remainder of the mobilization process. His observations validated the intuitions of the members of both steering committees, giving them the confidence needed to forge ahead to the stage of drawing up and implementing the action plans.

The Action Plans from Year to Year

After months of reflection and discussion, the steering committee members at the two sites were eager to move forward to the implementation stage. A first action plan was produced, and four others followed during the time the researchers were involved in the implementation of the project. Over the years, a wide range of activities – between twelve and twenty each year – was carried out in the two communities despite the low level of financial resources available to the steering committees – an average of $25,000 per year. The search for funding to carry out the activities was a challenge that occupied much of the project coordinators' time from year to year. In compensation the steering committees were able to rely on the strong participation of all the actors, often on a volunteer basis; the collaboration of the researchers and some of the actors in the conception, funding, and organization of certain activities; and, in the case of site A, many hours of community work by volunteer citizens who were not on the steering committee.

The Principles behind the Development of the Action Plans

The contents of the yearly plans had to be coherent with the logic of action adopted by the actors. From year to year the steering committees at both sites ensured that the plans comprised varied and complementary activities that could be carried out simultaneously on several fronts in different kinds of venues (such as community halls, arenas, parks, malls) and that reflected a varied choice of strategies.

During the activities planning, the actors at site A felt it was important to maintain a certain amount of flexibility. With the view that the action plan should not be a straitjacket, they allowed for the possibility of adding new activities during the year, depending on opportunities that might arise and the needs expressed by the fathers. Their action plans issued from the desire to empower citizens, particularly by involving them in the choice and organization of the activities from the perspective of eventual self-management of the project. Thus, in the project's second year, the members of the steering committee were already dedicating much of their energy to establishing a fathers' group that would gradually assume the planning of most of the family activities.

At site B the actors showed originality in the way they drew up and disseminated their action plan, presenting it in a calendar that was distributed to all the resources of the neighbourhood. Each organization was asked to adapt its annual programming to include activities related to fatherhood. In addition the steering committee oversaw activities that the organizations carried out together, including Family Day, a neighbourhood party that over the years proved an excellent occasion for mobilizing both families and practitioners. The activities were planned with a view to reaching out to vulnerable fathers and supporting them through a continuum of services offered by resources with a common approach towards fatherhood issues.

Finally, the actors and researchers felt it was important to integrate research and knowledge-transfer activities into the action plans. Organizing discussion groups within the community and presenting the results of the field studies, in which mothers and fathers were questioned in one-on-one interviews, were seen as additional ways to stimulate reflection on father involvement and to make the project better known.

The Strategies and Activities Supporting the Principles

In accordance with the ecological approach, the actors at the two sites ensured that the action plans comprised activities that touched upon a range of diversified targets, and stemmed from strategies inspired by the health-promotion approach. Four main strategies determined the development of the activities: public awareness raising, direct support for fathers, support for families, and the development of father-friendly resources. Table 3.1 presents the content of an annual action plan at the two sites, with the activities grouped according to the appropriate strategies.

RAISING PUBLIC AWARENESS

The first strategy, raising public awareness, aimed to emphasize the value of the father's role and to make the father involvement project known in the two communities by organizing public events (press conferences, launches, information sessions), by using the media (articles or columns in the local press, and radio and television interviews), and through promotional tools (the distribution of T-shirts, brochures, and posters, the setting up of information booths). Two activities promoting the father's role were particularly effective. *Dessine-moi un papa* (Draw Me a Daddy), a travelling exhibition of children's drawings of their fathers, aimed to raise awareness of the importance of father involvement through children's conceptions of fathers' roles. The drawings in the exhibition were done by local school children ages four to six. The exhibit also featured short, evocative texts dealing with different dimensions of the father's role and underlining the benefits of father involvement for all members of the family. In addition, the exhibition included an interactive component in which visitors could rate the frequency of their activities with their children through a comparison with the results of the family survey. The second successful activity,

Table 3.1. Activities Carried Out within the Four Principal Action Strategies at Both Sites

Site A	Site B
Public awareness activities	
Information booth in shopping mall	Promotion of father involvement at the *Magasin-Partage* (shared food outlet)[a]
Dessine-moi un papa (Draw Me a Daddy) travelling exhibition	Screening of films on fatherhood during Family Week
Participation in television programs on fatherhood	
Les cent pères (100 Fathers), a fundraising campaign addressed to business people and community leaders	
Publication of columns and articles in local newspapers and community organization newsletters	
Presentations at conferences, symposiums	
Distribution of promotional tools at public events (T-shirts, posters, brochures, educational kits accompanying the *Dessine-moi un papa* exhibit)	
Distribution of 8 issues of *Accroche-père* (Attract Fathers) doorknob-hanger cards	
Direct support for fathers	
Individual follow-up	*Père-à-père* (Father to Father): individual follow-up
Fathers' group oriented towards action, mutual support and the development of father-child activities	*À deux vitesses* (In Two Gears): father-child group activities followed by discussion periods for fathers
	Papa-cuisine (Father Cooks): initiation to basic cooking techniques for fathers of young children
Support for families	
Meetings between men and women on the conjugal relationship	Storytelling on fatherhood presented at the local library
Dinner/discussion meetings on expectations regarding parental roles	
Fun in the Snow Day (emphasis on father-child activities)	
Family Day during Family Week (emphasis on father-child activities)	Family Day, part of Family Week (emphasis on father-child activities)
Father-child ice-fishing expedition	
Developing father-friendly resources	
Activities to raise awareness among decision-makers	Prenatal meetings with fathers and fathers-to-be
	Group meetings (postnatal sessions)
	Fatherhood workshops
	Seminar-exchanges and training for practitioners
Distribution of posters and brochures in service resources	

[a] A food market where low-income residents can obtain groceries with a suggested contribution equivalent to 10 per cent of the cost.

Accroche-père (Attract Fathers), based on an original knowledge-transfer strategy, was a play on words that evoked the idea of catching fathers' attention and getting them involved; it also alluded to the format (a doorknob hanger). Inspired by commercial advertising, it consisted of the door-to-door distribution of a doorknob-hanger card that presented selected results of the family survey in plain language. The activity had a dual purpose: to present the father's role as actually experienced in the two pilot sites, and to publicize the activities promoting father involvement. The doorknob-hanger cards were distributed to all households in both sites eight times over a thirteen-month period, with different content each time (for details, see Chapter 7).

DIRECT SUPPORT FOR FATHERS

Direct support for father aimed to increase fathers' sense of parental competency, and help them take steps to assume a more active role with their children and build social links with others through support networks. These goals were realized through a number of activities, including individual follow-up of fathers facing particular difficulties, parenting education workshops in which fathers and children interacted, father-child recreational activities, and discussion and support groups for fathers. At site A, a fathers' group was formed at the initiative of two members of the steering committee. Defining themselves as a group oriented towards action and mutual support, rather than a focus or a therapy group, the participants set three objectives: to take their place as fathers in the community; to organize activities that would bring them into a close relationship with their children in order to provide a visible father model for them; and to highlight the enjoyable aspects of fatherhood. A similar father-managed activity at site B called *À deux vitesses* (In Two Gears) combined structured games with the children and a discussion group on fatherhood and co-parenting.

SUPPORT FOR FAMILIES

Support for families involved a set of activities that aimed to place fathers in the foreground and create occasions for them to interact with their children at various neighbourhood get-togethers. At both sites, the steering committees collaborated in organizing events whose prototypes were Family Day and Fun in the Snow Day. In addition to the father-child activities organized for these two events, we should mention the Daddies' Quiz, which tested fathers on their knowledge of their children's tastes and preferences, as well as a stroller rally, a father-child snow sculpture competition, and a father-child Olympics. These events gave committee members a good opportunity to put up banners and posters, which contributed to the project's visibility and the promotion of the father's role in the community. The adoption of a family-oriented approach led to the inclusion of additional activities to foster co-parenting and children's well-being.

DEVELOPING FATHER-FRIENDLY RESOURCES
The action plans at the two sites also included activities that aimed to foster a more father-friendly approach in practices and programs. Lectures and training seminars were organized among practitioners in the two communities to raise awareness of the importance of father involvement for children's well-being. Posters and brochures were distributed to organizations at both sites. At site A, a major effort was directed towards raising awareness among local elected representatives. This undertaking proved important for fostering decision-makers' acceptance of the project, which facilitated access to local resources (including better premises, advertising space in the town newsletter, and so on). At site B, coherent with the steering committee's logic of action, each partner organization adapted its services to meet fathers' needs. They held workshops led by male staff on the father's role, and adjusted their schedules to make services more father friendly. For example, the CSSS added a discussion group among fathers, facilitated by a male practitioner, to its program of prenatal meetings.

The Target Population

The message conveying the importance of the father's role reached a large number of citizens, practitioners, and local elected representatives. During the reference period, most families in the two sites received information several times by means of the various promotional tools generated by the project: the distribution of the eight messages attached to residents' doorknobs; the regular appearance of columns and articles in local newspapers and newsletters; electronic media features; and the distribution among public service and community resources of brochures and posters highlighting fatherhood. In addition, at each site, approximately two hundred families were contacted yearly in the context of the family activities underlining the importance of fathers, and almost four hundred fathers and mothers with a child under age six were brought to reflect on father involvement by participating in the family surveys carried out during the field study and the impact evaluation stages of the project. At site A, at least two hundred and fifty people attended the Draw Me a Daddy exhibition, which was also widely disseminated in Quebec, other parts of Canada, and abroad, and was an important motive for pride, not only among the members of the steering committee, but all of the municipality's residents. It is also estimated that about fifty men participated in the father-child activities organized by the fathers' group. At site B, more than two hundred fathers and mothers in the community attended the prenatal meeting for fathers each year. Furthermore, some thirty fathers participated in a mutual support or discussion group established by the project partners.

Conclusion

The experience at the two sites allowed us to identify aspects that should be taken into account when planning future actions in community-based research in general, and in PAR projects promoting fatherhood involvement in particular.

The analysis of the project's implementation, detailed in Chapter 4, confirmed first and foremost that local mobilization efforts must be adapted to the characteristics of the milieu in which they are carried out (Ouellet, Forget, & Durand, 1993). At site A, for example, the community's isolation, the absence of collaborative action among groups, and the low level of civic participation led the project's actors to add a community development objective to the promotion of father involvement in their area. They organized activities to get citizens involved and to obtain decision-makers' recognition of the project. Furthermore, the desire to graft the father involvement initiative onto the citizen mobilization effort that had already begun when the project was proposed to the municipality, combined with the residents' physical distance from public services and their mistrust of institutions, explains why, contrary to what was observed at site B, the steering committee was built upon a base of volunteer citizens, rather than of representatives of organizations. At site B, on the other hand, a tradition of collaboration and solidarity among the actors of the community, public, and economic sectors, the will to develop community action in the early childhood sector, and the physical proximity of resources led the actors to set up an intersectoral procedure that was largely taken in hand by practitioners who desired to provide accessible services to fathers and to encourage collaboration among practitioners.

The partners at the two sites realized that ample time was needed to deal with the challenge of appropriating the promoters' model, translating it, and adapting it to local conditions, while advancing towards a shared concept of the paternal role. Given the newness of the concept and its inclusion in the social debate on gender relations, sufficient time should be allotted for the discussion of social roles and for bringing individuals to reassess their values. Since the question of father involvement affects people in their personal lives, they should re-examine their personal values before they can develop mutual familiarity and group solidarity.

It was observed that the theme of father involvement and the perspective of joining a PAR project were strong mobilizing factors for the actors. Despite a global economic context that discouraged innovation, the two steering committees did not encounter major financial difficulties that would have hindered their functioning or productivity. The community workers emerged as key actors in the process of mobilizing their respective communities around father involvement. The presence of researchers and highly respected institutional partners helped to overcome implementation challenges by conferring visibility and credibility to the project among local decision-makers and the community as a whole.

As the years passed, the actors at the two sites acquired convictions regarding the best means to reach fathers and to work with them. They considered it necessary to seek fathers out through accompaniment/ support activities in their life situations and by creating occasions for them to meet one another and exchange ideas – for example, by enlisting their help and collaboration in a concrete activity. This required the availability of a male practitioner willing to establish a stable, known presence in the community and thus ensure continuity in the interventions.

The actors at both sites came to adhere firmly to certain intervention principles. They opted for a flexible approach that relied on the fathers' strengths, stressed the positive things they did with their children, and considered family enjoyment an important function. Based on the assumption that competence and confidence are mainly acquired through fathers' successful experiences with their children, they saw the importance of giving fathers opportunities to interact with their children and to observe other men in their fathering role at community celebrations, local recreational activities, and outings.

With regard to planning, the actors at the two sites became aware that, although continuing to diversify targets and action strategies, in the first years the emphasis should be on activities designed to: (1) confer legitimacy to the project – that is, to obtain its recognition in the community and to win the support of decision-makers; and (2) to heighten public awareness of the value of father involvement. Such activities are necessary conditions for the adoption of strategies that aim to bring about behavioural change. In this, they agreed with the observations of other researchers (Goodman et al., 1995, 1996).

Experience at each site showed that, by pooling strengths and having the support of actively involved researchers, it was possible to put in place a plan that targeted several areas at a time, using diversified strategies. At both sites, the plans reached the entire community through a number of activities that emphasized the value of fatherhood. They targeted fathers directly through discussion groups, individual follow-up, and father-child activities within the framework of family-oriented events. Couples were also targeted through activities that encouraged parental alliance. Finally, the plans targeted service resources and local elected representatives through awareness and training activities.

During the reference period, it became clear that the intervention was not having a noticeable effect on the workplace, employment organizations, or institutions responsible for developing social policy. This gap motivated a further PAR initiative by Prospère: *Métiers de pères* (Profession: Fatherhood), a project described in Chapter 6.

NOTE

1 Michael Lamb is a senior research scientist and chief of the section on Social and Emotional Development at the National Institute of Child Health and Human Development in Bethesda, MD. Since 1975 he has published multiple books, reviews, and articles on fathering. His book *The Role of the Father in Child Development* (Lamb, 2010) is in its fifth edition.

REFERENCES

Arama, D. (1997). *Promotion du rôle des pères: inventaire des ressources et projets d'interventions spécifiques à la paternité au Québec*. Quebec City, QC: Ministère de la Santé et des Services sociaux.

Bolté, C., Devault, A., St-Denis, M., & Gaudet, J. (2002). *On father's ground: A portrait of projects to support and promote fathering*. Montreal, QC: Université du Québec à Montréal, Groupe de recherche et d'action sur la victimisation des enfants – Alliance de recherche pour le développement des enfants dans leur communauté.

Bronfenbrenner, U. (1979). *The ecology of human development*. Cambridge, MA: Harvard University Press.

Bronfenbrenner, U. (1996). Le modèle "processus personne contexte temps" dans la recherche en psychologie du développement: principes, applications et implications. In R. Tessier & G. M. Tarabulsy (Eds.), *Le modèle écologique dans l'étude du développement de l'enfant* (pp. 9–59). Sainte-Foy, QC: Presses de l'Université du Québec.

Bronfenbrenner, U., & Ceci, S. J. (1994). Nature-nurture reconceptualized in developmental perspective: A bioecological model. *Psychological Review*, 101(4), 568–586. http://dx.doi.org/10.1037/0033-295X.101.4.568

Butterfoss, F. D., Goodman, R. M., & Wandersman, A. (1993). Community coalitions for prevention and health promotion. *Health Education Research*, 8(3), 315–330. http://dx.doi.org/10.1093/her/8.3.315

Devault, A., Gaudet, J., Bolté, C., & St-Denis, M. (2005). A survey and description of projects that support and promote fathering in Canada: Still work to do to reach fathers in their real-life settings. *Canadian Journal of Community Mental Health*, 24(1), 5–17. http://dx.doi.org/10.7870/cjcmh-2005-0001

Doherty, W. J., Kouneski, E. F., & Erickson, M. F. (1998). Responsible fathering: An overview and conceptual framework. *Journal of Marriage and the Family*, 60(2), 277–292. http://dx.doi.org/10.2307/353848

Dubeau, D., Clément, M. E., & Chamberland, C. (2005). Le père, une roue du carrosse familial à ne pas oublier! État des recherches québécoises et canadiennes sur la paternité. *Enfances, familles, générations*, 3(Autumn). Retrieved from http://www.erudit.org/revue/efg/2005/v/n3/012534ar.html

Dubeau, D., et al. (2013). *Soutenir les pères en contexte de vulnérabilités et leurs enfants: des services au rendez-vous, adéquats et efficaces*. Quebec City, QC: Ministère de la Santé et des Services sociaux et Fonds de recherche société et la culture.

Dubeau, D., Villeneuve, R., & Thibault, S. (2011). *Être présent sur la route des pères engagés. Recension québécoise 2009–2010 des modalités de soutien pour les pères*. Montreal, QC: Regroupement pour la valorisation de la paternité.

Dudley, J. R., & Stone, G. (2000). *Fathering at risk: Helping nonresidential fathers*. New York, NY: Springer.

Dufour, S., & Chamberland, C. (2004). The effectiveness of selected interventions for previous maltreatment: enhancing the well-being of children who live at home. *Child & Family Social Work*, 9(1), 39–56. http://dx.doi.org/10.1111/j.1365-2206.2004.00302.x

Dulac, G. (1998). L'intervention auprès des pères: des défis pour les intervenants, des gains pour les hommes. *PRISME*, 8(2), 190–206.

Dulac, G. (2001a). *Aider les hommes... aussi*. Montreal, QC: Éditions VLB.
Dulac, G. (2001b). Les stéréotypes sociaux sur les rôles et l'implication des pères dans les services à la famille. *Défi jeunesse, 7*(2), 26–32.
Florin, P., Mitchell, R., & Stevenson, J. (1993). Identifying training and technical assistance needs in community coalitions: A developmental approach. *Health Education Research, 8*(3), 417–432. http://dx.doi.org/10.1093/her/8.3.417
Forget, G. (1995). *Un modèle communautaire de soutien à l'engagement paternel: analyse du milieu à Pointe-Calumet*. Montreal, QC: Direction de la santé publique de Montréal-Centre.
Forget, G. (1996). *Défis et opportunités pour la promotion de l'engagement paternel dans le quartier Rosemont*. Montreal, QC: Direction de la santé publique de Montréal-Centre.
Forget, G., Devault, A., Allen, S., Bader, E., & Jarvis, D. (2005). Les services destinés aux pères: une description et un regard sur l'évolution des pratiques canadiennes. *Enfances, familles, générations, 3*(Autumn). Retrieved from http://www.erudit.org/revue/efg/2005/v/n3/012538ar.html
Goodman, R. M., Wandersman, A., Chinman, M., Imm, P., & Morrissey, E. (1996). An ecological assessment of community-based interventions for prevention and health promotion: Approaches to measuring community coalitions. *American Journal of Community Psychology, 24*(1), 33–61. http://dx.doi.org/10.1007/BF02511882
Goodman, R.M., Wheeler, F.C., & Lee, P.R. (1995). Evaluation of the heart to heart project: Lessons from a community-based chronic desease prevention project. *American Journal of Health Promotion, 9*(6), 443–455. http://dx.doi.org/10.4278/0890-1171-9.6.443
Hamel, S., Cousineau, M.-M., & Vézina, M. (2006). *Guide d'action intersectorielle pour la prévention du phénomène des gangs*. Retrieved from http://www.santecom.qc.ca/Bibliothequevirtuelle/Irds/2922588343.pdf
Hoffman, J. (2007). *Supporting Father Involvement in Canadian Families: An Overview*. Peterborough, ON: Father Involvement Initiative – Ontario Network.
Lamb, Michael E. (Ed.). (2010). *The role of the father in child development* (5th ed.). Hoboken, NJ: John Wiley.
Levine, J., & Pitt, E. W. (1995). *New expectations: Community strategies for responsible fatherhood*. New York, NY: Families and Work Institute.
Ménard, A. M. (1999). *La vision du rôle paternel et les pratiques auprès des pères de milieux défavorisés et d'infirmières oeuvrant dans les services de périnatalité en CLSC* (unpublished master's thesis). Université du Québec à Montréal, Montreal.
Meyers, S. A. (1993). Adapting parent education programs to meet the needs of fathers. *Family Relations, 42*(4), 447–452. http://dx.doi.org/10.2307/585347

Nissinen, A., & Puska, P. (1991). Community control of chronic diseases: A review of cardiovascular programmes. In B. Bandura & I. Kickbush (Eds.), *Health Promotion Research*, European Series, 37 (pp. 393–421). Copenhagen, Denmark: World Health Organization Regional Publications.

Ouellet, F., Forget, G., & Durand, D. (1993). *Une ville et deux quartiers en santé: étude de cas des trois premières initiatives dans l'île de Montréal*. Montreal, QC: Direction de la santé publique de Montréal-Centre.

Ouellet, F., Paiement, M., & Tremblay, P. H. (1995). *L'action intersectorielle: un jeu d'équipe*. Montreal, QC: Direction de la santé publique de Montréal-Centre & CECOM de l'Hôpital Rivière-des-Prairies.

Palmer, G. F., & Palkovitz, R. (1988). The challenge of working with new fathers: Implications for support providers. *Marriage & Family Review*, 12(3-4), 357–376. http://dx.doi.org/10.1300/J002v12n03_17

Prilleltensky, I., Nelson, G., & Peirson, L. (2001). *Promoting family wellness and preventing child maltreatment: Fundamentals for thinking and action*. Toronto, ON: University of Toronto Press.

Quebec (1991). *Un Québec fou de ses enfants: rapport du groupe de travail sur la santé des jeunes*. Quebec City, QC: Ministère de la Santé et des Services sociaux, Direction des communications.

Solomon-Fears, C. (2012), *Fatherhood initiatives: Connecting fathers to their children*. Washington, DC: Congressional Research Service. Retrieved from http://www.fas.org/sgp/crs/misc/RL31025.pdf

Spergel, I. A., Wa, K. M., & Sosa, R. V. (2006). The comprehensive, community-wide gang program model: success and failure. In J. F. Short & L. A. Hughes (Eds.), *Studying youth gangs* (pp. 203–224). Lanham, MD: Altamira Press.

Turcotte, G., Dubeau, D., Bolté, C., & Paquette, D. (2001). Pourquoi certains pères sont-ils plus engagés que d'autres auprès de leurs enfants? Une revue des déterminants de l'engagement paternel. *Revue canadienne de psychoéducation*, 30(1), 65–93.

Turcotte, G., & Gaudet, J. (2009). Conditions favorables et obstacles à l'engagement paternel: un bilan des connaissances. In D. Dubeau, A. Devault, & G. Forget (Eds.) *La paternité au 21e siècle* (pp. 39–70). Québec (QC): Presses de l'Université Laval.

White, D., Jobin, L., McCann, D., & Morin, P. (2002). *Pour sortir des sentiers battus, l'action intersectorielle en santé mentale*. Quebec City, QC: Les Publications du Québec.

Wiebush, R. G., McNulty, B., & Le, T. (2000). Implementation of the intensive community-based aftercare program. *Juvenile Justice Bulletin* (July). Retrieved from https://www.ncjrs.gov/pdffiles1/ojjdp/181464.pdf

4 The Challenging Evaluation of Complex Interventions

DIANE DUBEAU, GENEVIÈVE TURCOTTE, FRANCINE OUELLET, AND SYLVAIN COUTU

A complex problem requires a complex solution. This truism applies when an evaluation is undertaken to discuss or document the intrinsic value of a project, initiative, or an intervention program. A frequent error is to imagine that an evaluation will answer all our questions. Naturally there are various evaluative approaches, each one with a different perspective on the realities of a study subject (Bledsoe & Graham, 2005; Rossi, Lipsey, & Freeman, 2004). To obtain the fullest and most valid portrait possible of these realities, however, researchers should observe them from different angles and use a variety of evaluation tools and methodologies. This was the approach adopted by Prospère to arrive at a triangulated evaluation of the health-promotion project implemented at two experimental sites (see Chapter 3). Because methodology is often seen as one of the main challenges of research on father involvement, this chapter describes in detail different stages and components of this evaluation. Both practitioners and researchers will find in this chapter a comprehensive and father-focused measure of father involvement and the different methods used to measure the implementation and evaluation of a participatory action research (PAR) project focusing on fatherhood. First, for readers who are not well acquainted with this domain, we present a brief synthesis of program evaluation. Second, we provide an overall view of the evaluative studies done at the two sites. We then look at the results of the implementation evaluation, principally the perceived effects of the project and the process that produced those effects at the participating sites. The presentation of the implementation data is particularly relevant for introducing the fourth section, which deals with the evaluation of the effects. We also include a synthesis of an evaluation by an outside researcher, as well as an interview with two of our partners at the respective sites, who give their assessments of this collaborative experience.

Program Evaluation: A Field to Be Discovered

The evaluation of intervention programs is a relatively new area of research, with the first writings on the subject emerging in the 1970s. The domain rapidly expanded and made important strides forward (Labin, 2011; Madaus & Stufflebeam, 2000). Readers less familiar with this area of knowledge should know that there are several types of evaluation, which are usually categorized according to the stage of the program's development (Chen, 2005). In sequential terms, *needs assessment* is the first type of evaluation, carried out before a program is drawn up. The purpose of this assessment is to identify needs as they are seen by the principal actors involved (targeted clientele, practitioners, and others). A *field study* then assesses the existing resources available, the collaboration possibilities, and the degree of openness to the research topic. *Implementation evaluation* is usually undertaken during the first years a program is in place. The information gathered through this evaluation process serves to document what has been achieved and to obtain a more complete description of the ways local decision-makers have appropriated the program. Ideally, the objective of this evaluation is to allow the progressive adaptation of the program as the data are gathered, in order to be able to better respond to the needs identified. The *effects, efficiency, and impacts evaluations*, done at the end of the program's development, aim to measure its effectiveness in terms of the changes that can be attributed to the intervention. The notion of causality is important here, and this requires methodologies that allow maximum control of the variables. One can foresee the difficulties associated with these types of evaluations when they take account of realities prevailing in the field that might not comply with the scientific rigour of standard research principles. Here, a distinction must be made between the context of the research and that of the program evaluation. The researcher's methodological freedom of choice is limited in program evaluation, as the methodology must be adapted to the characteristics of the milieu. To give an example, although a high number of participants might be desirable for a study, the researcher is often obliged to work with small sample sizes in a particular setting, which restricts the types of statistical analysis that can be done. Creativity then becomes an important asset for the evaluator, who must develop innovative methods adapted to the particular setting while maintaining the required scientific rigour in the research.

Although we have placed evaluations of effects, efficacy, and impacts in a single category, certain nuances should be pointed out. The *effects evaluation* focuses more specifically on the short-term changes observed (for example, at the end of the program); the expected effects of participation in a program are often identified according to the program's objectives. The *efficiency evaluation* adds consideration of the cost effectiveness of the program. We might ask, for example, if the same effects could be obtained at a lower cost by holding ten workshops instead of fifteen. Finally, the *impacts evaluation* requires the adoption of a broader perspective that takes into account the short-, medium-, and long-term effects; effects that are not identified according to the program objectives; and effects on individuals or groups not directly targeted by the program.

Overview of Prospère's Evaluative Perspectives

The PAR presented in Chapter 3 relied on joint action by the researchers and the practitioners in the steering committees at the two experimental sites. These entities worked together, combining their complementary expertise to promote father involvement. Evaluation activities were undertaken throughout the implementation of the project. In this chapter, after presenting an overview of the evaluative parameters, we briefly discuss the main aspects of the project. We then take a look at the issues, results, and outcomes specifically associated with the implementation and community impacts evaluations.

The first evaluative stage of Prospère's PAR was a field study carried out at the sites participating in the project. This evaluation aimed to measure the degree of openness on the part of local agencies offering services to families with young children, and to document the perceptions of practitioners and the population in general regarding father involvement. This descriptive study was conducted by means of one-on-one interviews, a review of existing documents, observation, and focus groups held at the two sites with practitioners, with fathers, and with mothers. The conclusions that emerged from this analysis informed the yearly action plans drawn up by the steering committees of each site.

The second part of the evaluation process was an implementation analysis covering a five-year period (the reference period). This analysis charted all the factors associated with the implementation of the project, relying on a multiple-case-study method (Yin, 1998) that combined (1) semi-structured interviews with the principal actors; (2) a documentary analysis; (3) participative observation of the steering committees; and (4) direct observation of the activities. The results obtained made it possible to consolidate or reorganize certain aspects of the project, to contextualize the results measured by the impacts evaluation, and to identify success factors to retain for the eventual dissemination of the project to other communities. Two implementation reports were published following this evaluation stage (Ouellet, Turcotte, & Desjardins, 2001; Turcotte, Desjardins, & Ouellet, 2001).

The third evaluative exercise concerned the analysis of the community impacts of the project. Data collection was carried out during two periods: at the beginning of the reference period for the pre-test measurements, and at the end of the reference period for the post-test measurements. The impacts were categorized according to: (1) the clientele targeted (the population in general, service agencies, practitioners and managers, families, and fathers); (2) the intermediary results obtained during the implementation period (creation or reorganization of services, number and quality of joint action initiatives among practitioners or service agencies, and changes in the attitudes and practices of service providers); and (3) the expected outcomes (fathers' parental competency, increased father involvement, improved attitudes towards child rearing, and better-quality family relations). One element in this type of evaluation that illustrates the complexity alluded to in this chapter's title is undoubtedly its duration. There was a long interval between the two data-collection times, necessary to ensure that all the planned activities had been put in place, as, according to Goodman, Wheeler, and Lee (1995), five to ten years are needed for a joint action initiative to produce the expected outcomes in the targeted phenomenon. This interval posed challenges for the evaluators regarding the choice of samples and measurement instruments. We discuss this aspect later in the chapter.

With hindsight it is easy to perceive the richness and abundance of results that can be generated by applying these three evaluative perspectives to a single study object. This type of approach is recommended by Richard, Gauvin, and Raine (2011) for complex programs (community-based interventions) adopting an ecological approach. To our knowledge, very few intervention projects or programs have benefited from such a wide range of data gathered at different stages of their development. For Prospère's project, the data, collected over a period of years, and the conclusions drawn from analysing them made it possible to establish a solid basis for a community-based intervention aiming to promote father involvement, by fostering, guiding, questioning, and validating the concrete actions put in place at each site. On the research level it is interesting to note that, despite the differences between the objectives of the respective evaluation exercises, the methodologies first adopted were subsequently co-constructed with the principal actors in the project, thus creating a broader range of possible interpretations of the results. Prospère's implementation and community impacts evaluations are good illustrations of this synergy.

The Implementation Evaluation

A research team followed the unfolding and evolution of the project at the two sites by regularly gathering data during the five-year reference period. This evaluation had three objectives:

1) To help the steering committees find solutions and make decisions by providing them feedback on strengths and areas needing improvement during the evaluation process. The adoption of a participatory action approach (Jason, Keyes, Suarez-Balcazar, Taylor, & Davis, 2002; Green, Daniel, & Novick, 2001) centring on utilization (Patton, 1997) led the researchers to become actively involved in the steering committees of the two sites and to take part in promotional activities. The research team members offered to take the minutes of meetings, which facilitated their integration in the steering committees and allowed the keeping of a detailed, validated record of the matters discussed and the decisions made by the actors. While the evaluation was being carried out, activity reports and summaries of certain implementation issues were produced to encourage critical reflection on the developing project.
2) To produce knowledge regarding the intervention model being constructed, with a view to its eventual generalization in other environments. The researchers aimed to keep a clear record of how the project was built up and how it evolved through the years. During the first years, the goal of identifying the elements that best lent themselves to generalization was added to the action theory guiding the intervention.
3) To identify the processes involved in the production of the ultimate effects of the project. As explained in the previous chapter, the

proposed intervention model was relatively open ended and loosely structured. The model was viewed as a blank canvas upon which content would be defined and constructed in a process involving the participation of all the actors associated with the project, and which would take the local context into account. The implementation analysis focused on this concrete appropriation process. The question asked by the researchers was the following: How did the actors redefine, reorganize, and reinvent (translate) the guiding principles of the project?

The Chosen Approach

The traditional approach to an implementation evaluation (relying on the logic of dissemination) emphasizes the gaps between the planned and the implemented model and attempts to explain them (Dusenbury, Brannigan, Falco, & Hansen, 2003). This model is based on the premise that the program to be implemented is a finished product, stable in time and space. In this perspective, any modification to the original product is seen as detrimental to its effectiveness. The model we chose (the logic of translation) aimed to track the project throughout its transformations, bringing into evidence the process of mutual adaptation between the program and the context. By context we mean the characteristics of the respective communities, the global environment, the actors (for example, their interests, assets, roles, negotiation strategies), and the meaning given to the action by the actors (Bilodeau, Chamberland, & White, 2002).

This alternative approach to the classical evaluation model is based on the principle that transformation of the program is inherent in any implementation process. This principle is justified, first, by the fact that a program absorbs the elements of the context in which it is introduced, and therefore is influenced by changes likely to occur in both the proximal and distal environments (for example, in the resources available, the clientele, social policy priorities, or organizational dynamics). Second, it is justified because a program generally brings into play a set of heterogeneous actors who might have different, even conflicting, interests and objectives. Consequently the implementation can lead to resistance and result in negotiations between the actors, inevitably producing alignments and adjustments of greater or lesser import to the program as initially planned. Thus the program is seen as an evolving product subject to a plurality of visions within an environment in a state of perpetual change.

The Methodological Strategy

To follow the evolution of the project, the researchers adopted a case-study methodology, a recognized qualitative research strategy that combines scientific rigour, flexibility, and depth of data collection and analysis (Yin, 1998). This methodology is particularly indicated when analysing the unfolding of a project that is indissociable from the context in which it is carried out. More specifically a multiple-case-study design was used, with the intervention at each site constituting a case study.

The explanatory potential of the case study is based on a conceptual framework that guides data collection and analysis, and multiple sources of data that are analysed in convergence through a mode of triangulation. As shown in Figure 4.1, the conceptual framework comprised six major variables: (1) the promoters' model; (2) the local environment (characteristics of the test sites); (3) the characteristics of the actors (interests, resources, assets, and roles in the implementation of the project); (4) the actors' theoretical model (representations of the issues linked to father involvement and the solutions chosen to promote it in their community); (5) the action plans; and (6) the perceived effects in the community.

Four data sources were used: (1) over forty semi-structured interviews with the principal actors in the project (members of the promotion and steering committees and other partners in the communities); (2) written documents (minutes of committee meetings, proposals written by the initiators of the project, activity reports, and promotional materials); (3) participant-observation notes on the procedures and content of the committee meetings at which the researchers were present as actors in the process; and (4) activity sheets compiling factual data on the nature and unfolding of the activities (the resources invested, the tools used, the degree to which the objectives were achieved, and the perceived impacts in the community).

Results: A Chain of Effects on Father Involvement

In the multiple-case-study method, the researcher carries out a descriptive task that allows him to understand what has occurred in specific contexts. Simultaneously a theoretical and explicative investigation will bring out the processes that led to the production of the results. Thus, beyond the perceived outcomes at the end of the implementation of a

Figure 4.1. A Conceptual Framework for the Implementation Evaluation

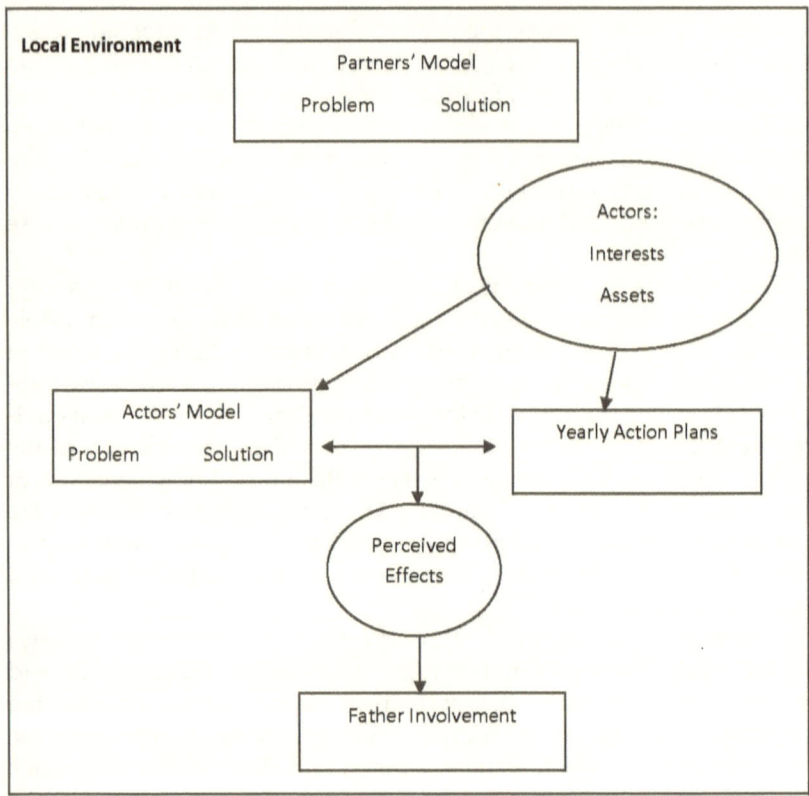

project, hypotheses can be formulated regarding the processes underlying the outcomes. The analysis of the data collected throughout the reference period of the Prospère PAR contributed to, among other things, a conceptualization of the process of results production that allowed us to formulate hypotheses regarding the effects of the project. This conceptualization is illustrated in Figure 4.2.

In undertaking the Prospère PAR, decision-makers, practitioners, and researchers were called on to demonstrate that it was possible, through a massive community-based intervention effort, to increase fathers' levels of involvement with their children. Since the goal of the project implied a veritable shift in culture, it would have been illusory

Figure 4.2. The Process of the Production of Effects in the Prospère Project

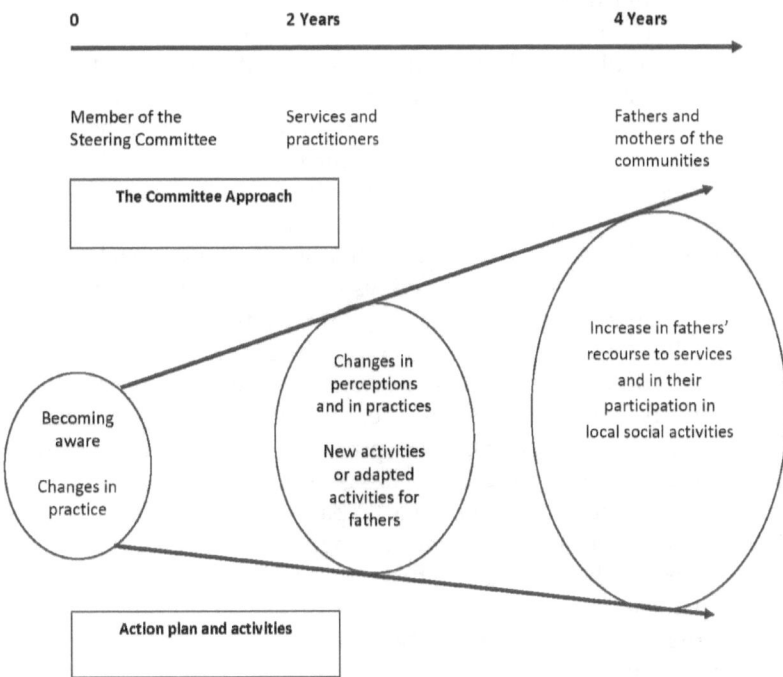

to expect significant results regarding father involvement levels in the community before several years had passed – that is, until a major community mobilization and awareness-raising campaign had been carried out (Goodman et al., 1995). Although joint action initiatives might not solve a problem directly, they can strengthen the links among organizations and enhance the activities and services offered, as well as raise awareness of the issue in the community. These first steps were seen as a springboard on the project's path to achieving the ultimate objective of increased father involvement (Goodman, Wandersman, Chinman, Imm, & Morrissey, 1996).

These considerations led the evaluation team to gather information on the effects and the mechanisms that had produced them in their periodic collection of data. Data analysis confirmed other findings on the effectiveness of community-based interventions. The data obtained from the actors, as well as from several external observers, indicated that changes had occurred on different levels according to the developmental stage of the project.

As shown in Figure 4.2, the first changes were observed among the steering committee members, with improvements noted in the quality of their discussions and in the sharing of expertise with the researchers associated with the project; the actors reported a better knowledge of the issue, a positive evolution in their perceptions of the father's role, and changes in their personal and professional behaviour. Then, in a chain reaction, beginning in the second year and intensifying each subsequent year, the effects were felt in the organizations at each site, following the awareness-raising activities in the action plans. At site A, a greater openness to fatherhood among local leaders and in the population as a whole was reported. At site B, the practitioners of four community organizations and the Centre de santé et de services sociaux (CSSS, Health and Social Services Centre) early intervention team said that their perceptions and some of their practices had changed. Starting in the fourth year, the actors at both sites observed an increase in fathers' recourse to services and in their participation in local social activities. These changes were viewed as positive signs of a desirable evolution in the attitudes and behaviour of fathers towards their children.

During those five years, our key informants also pointed out the changes they noticed in community dynamics. At site A, the support of important partners, such as the Université du Québec à Montréal, the CSSS, and the Agence de la santé et des services sociaux (Health and Social Services Agency) of Montreal, made it possible to enter into a dialogue with the local authorities, with the result that participants now felt listened to, recognized, and supported by their local elected representatives. In addition, this site acquired credibility in its region by breaking new ground in the area of father involvement promotion. Finally, by the end of the project, the objective of citizen participation in the choice and organization of the activities, from the perspective of future self-management of the project, was in the process of being achieved: a group of fathers had taken charge of organizing most of the activities in the action plan, and had developed strong feelings of belonging with respect to the program. At site B, where no formal joint action structure supporting families with young children had previously existed, the project gave the organizations in this sector the opportunity and motivation to, in their words: "do things together and get to know each other better" and "learn to cooperate." Their collaborative association is now recognized by the other coordinating committees in the district.

Summary: A Useful Approach in Implementation Evaluation

Prospère's proposed model was based on the health-promotion strategies of territory immersion and intersectoral action. It was a complex model requiring the participation of numerous actors from various organizations, often from very different professional realities. The steering committee at each site guided the actions. Among the acknowledged advantages of this model is the pooling of resources and expertise to carry out joint action regarding an issue that cannot be resolved by a single organization. This model also eliminates the duplication of services. Despite the model's convincing quality, empirical evidence of the effectiveness of the steering committees was difficult to demonstrate. According to Berkowitz (2001), this difficulty is largely due to obstacles associated with traditional scientific methods, in which little attention is paid to the realities of the milieu. Indeed, during the implementation of the Prospère project, two premises that stemmed from the model were questioned: (1) the premise that the steering committees' formation and workings would be linear processes; and (2) the premise that the implemented activities would be inspired by best practices.

Traditional research methods presuppose a linear process in the operations of a steering committee in a health-promotion project that, in time, will produce a progressively dynamic membership and a smoother mode of functioning (for example, in the choice of partners, consensus in the vision of the problem and its solutions), and, therefore, increase the effectiveness of the actions. In our case the process was not entirely linear, mainly due to turnover in the personnel of the local agencies and institutions, which included people participating in the steering committees. This inevitably produced changes in the group dynamic. Fortunately a major asset of the Prospère project was the constancy of the actors at both sites and of the members of the research team. This stable nucleus facilitated the integration of newcomers in accordance with the objectives pursued, without compromising the common vision of the model adopted at each site. This observation was supported by the results that emerged from the implementation evaluation carried out over the five-year reference period. Moreover the evaluation model adopted by Prospère (the logic of translation) proved particularly useful in documenting the points of view of the different actors and in analysing, in a dynamic perspective, the changes noted in the yearly action plans and in the perceived effects. Sequentially these effects were first seen in the members of the steering committees as described above, then in practitioners working with young families, through their greater openness towards fathers, and, ultimately, in the fathers themselves, through their more frequent recourse to the agencies' services.

The implementation evaluation model also informed us with respect to the second premise of classical research methods, which concerns the implementation of activities that are inspired by best practices. In reality the choice of activities was often guided by the organizations' practical imperatives, such as existing programs and available resources. Moreover the topic of father involvement itself was a challenge due to the scarcity of documentation on promising programs in this area. The alliance of actors and researchers generated new ways of reaching fathers that were translated in the yearly action plans at each site. The implementation evaluation also contributed to the regular gathering of quantitative data on the action plans (for example, number of activities, objectives pursued, clientele reached) during the reference period. This information was particularly useful when formulating hypotheses regarding the production-of-effects process (in terms of, for example, the links between the activities in the yearly action plans and the effects noted at a given development phase of the project). At the same time the information collected raised relevant questions, such as: What is a good local action plan? How many different interventions should it involve? What place should be given to continuous and intensive individual interventions? How, over the years, should individual or group interventions be combined with interventions targeting the community? In a more global perspective, future reflections should consider prospective ways of meshing local actions with regional and national programs. Indeed, acting locally might be insufficient for achieving the expected outcomes.

To summarize, Prospère's implementation evaluation model overcame certain obstacles stemming from classical research methods, and was able to maintain scientific rigour while taking account of the realities of the intervention settings and the model proposed by the promotion committee (Durlak & DuPre, 2008). The results of this evaluation were relevant at the action level. At the research level, they guided the last step: the assessment of whether the project's main objective, an increase in father involvement, had been achieved. In this respect, the data compiled on the perceived effects of the project during the implementation stage proved an indisputable asset in relation to the subsequent impacts evaluation.

The Impacts Evaluation

As yet, few empirical studies have produced evidence-based results demonstrating the effectiveness of strategies to promote father involvement (Devault, Gaudet, Bolté, & St-Denis, 2005; Holmes, Cowan, Cowan, & Hawkins, 2013). A recent review of published writings on program evaluation indicated that, after a long period of neglect, evaluations related to needs and implementation are now receiving the attention they deserve (Hughes & Traynor, 2000). The field of impacts evaluation remains to be further developed, particularly when dealing with complex health-promotion programs, in order to be able to validate results and outcomes. The methodological problems inherent in this type of evaluation have often been pointed out, including the difficulty of respecting rigorous scientific research norms while taking account of the realities of the milieu. The numerous obstacles that arise in this type of evaluation should not, however, curtail the practice of it, nor should they cast doubt on its relevancy. In direct continuity with the results obtained by the implementation evaluation, and inspired by them, the members of Prospère took on the ultimate challenge of a community impacts evaluation. The next part of the chapter presents the impacts evaluation strategy and its results, as well as recommendations for carrying out this type of evaluation.

Impacts Evaluation Strategy

In accordance with the approach of the Prospère project, the impacts study had to comply with a PAR model (Jason et al., 2002). In this perspective, steps were taken with the local steering committees at the beginning of the PAR so that the chosen evaluation model would be compatible with their expectations as well as those of the researchers (Bea van Beveren & Hetherington, 1997).

The first step was to determine the dimensions that would be evaluated. By analysing the action plans of the two sites for each of the years that the project was carried out, and by consulting the implementation evaluation reports, we drew up an exhaustive list of the implicit and explicit objectives of the activities. These were then classified separately for each site and according to Prospère's four principal objectives, which were: (1) to establish a father-friendly environment; (2) to influence the general population; (3) to influence the family network; and (4) to strengthen the fathers' individual potential. Two meetings with each steering committee were needed to reach agreement on a few modifications and to validate the classification system. A consensus was also reached regarding priorities.

The second step was to carry out a combined analysis of the classifications for the two sites to determine their compatibility (60 per cent of the objectives identified were common to both sites). The results of this analysis were presented to the two steering committees. Meetings were held with all the members of the Prospère team to report the steps taken and the results obtained. The researchers expressed their expectations regarding the impacts evaluation, and their expertise was sought to provide conceptual guidelines for an impacts evaluation model.

Figure 4.3 presents the community impacts evaluation model that resulted from the above-mentioned procedures. The impacts (dependent variables) are divided into four categories of outcomes according to the target clientele (the general population, organizations, families, and fathers). The expected impacts shown in Figure 4.3 were operationalized according to the objectives prioritized by the steering committees.

The presentation of the methodology of evaluative research often seems to weigh down a text. Although we are aware of this inconvenience, we find it pertinent to present a minimum amount of information to ensure that the methodology used is well understood. For the sake of conciseness, a summary of the methodology is provided in Appendix B.

The impacts evaluation was based on two types of methodological strategies involving quasi-experimental and pre-experimental designs: (1) a pre-test/post-test design, with a control group to evaluate the impacts on the level of father involvement (the ultimate result); and (2) a post-test design, with a control group to evaluate a set of impacts closely related to the activities of the local action plans (intermediate results). The impossibility of assigning (non-equivalent) groups randomly and the lack of certain measurements before the implementation of the intervention (missing data for Time 1 of the evaluative study – pre-test measurements) justified the adoption of these two research designs.

Pre-test/post-test design with comparison groups: The impacts on the level of fathers' involvement with their children was the object of a pre/post comparison between the two test sites and the control sites, paired according to a set of criteria (for example, the number of families with a child under the age of five, the number with low or unstable income, a high youth protection referral rate). As the ultimate expected result of

Figure 4.3. Prospère's Community Impacts Evaluation Model

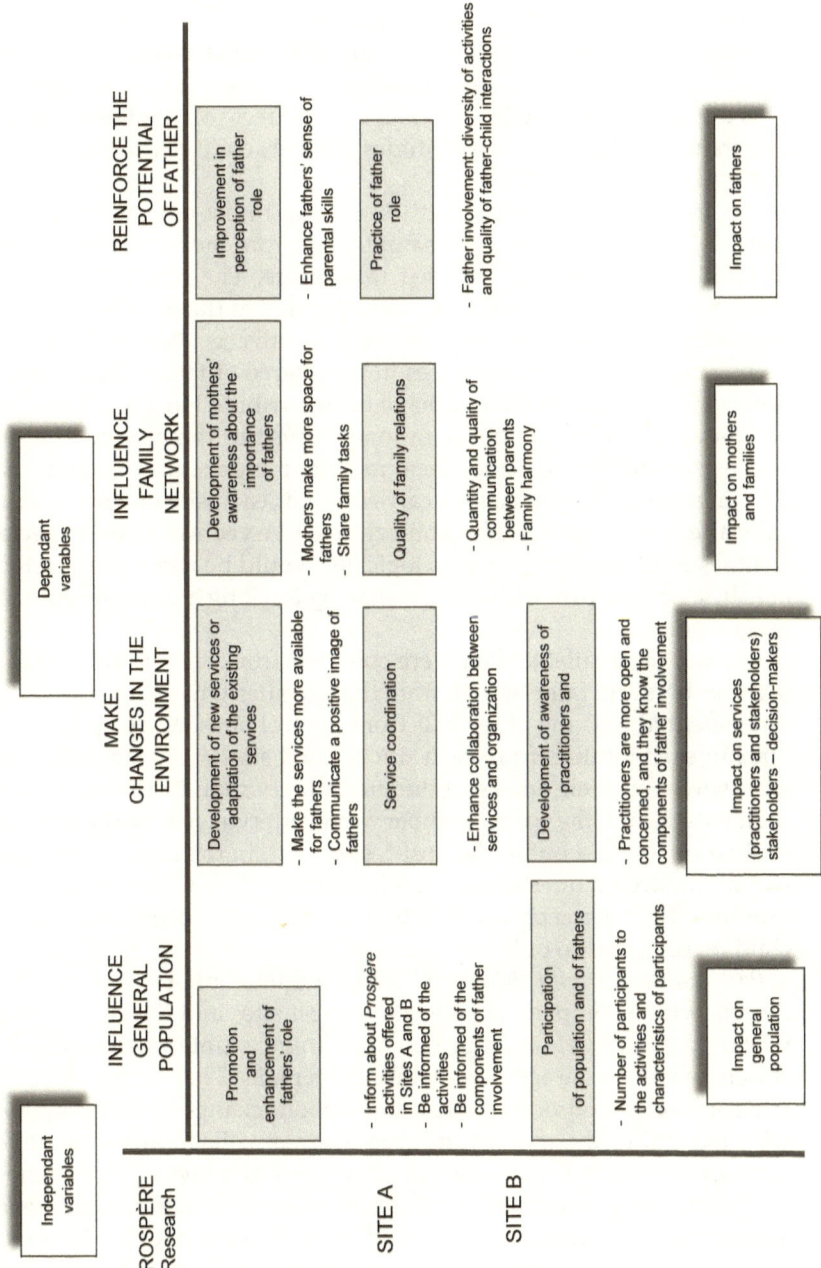

the project was a higher level of father involvement, we felt it important to evaluate that variable by means of an experimental design that would reveal if this effect could actually be attributed to the project. This design also allowed us to analyse the effects on the fathers' sense of parental competence and attitudes towards child rearing associated with father involvement.

It is important to specify that the pre- and post-test measurements were not taken from the same sample, but from independent samples of families. Two reasons justified this choice. The first was the long interval (five years) between the data collected at the pre-test and post-test times. The use of the same sample of subjects, tracked longitudinally, might have shown changes in the degree of father involvement; however, these changes could have been attributed just as well to the child's development, rather than to any effect of the project. The second reason that made us decide to recruit an independent sample was that, in monitoring the actions carried out at each site (actions specifically affecting families with a child zero to five years old), the expected changes in fathering behaviour, logically, would be more easily detectable by a comparison with cohorts than by tracking a single population longitudinally.

In total, the available data were collected from eight hundred families (mothers and fathers); half from the two sites where the project was implemented and the other half from control sites. More specifically, one hundred families from each site (100 × 4 sites = 400 families) were interviewed in their homes in the preliminary inquiry (pre-test measurements),[1] and the same number were interviewed in the impacts evaluation, carried out in the post-test period. In the home interviews, parents answered questionnaires related to the dimensions studied (for example, their perceptions of father involvement, attitudes towards child rearing, and so on).

Post-test design with the control group (without pre-test): A post-test design, with a comparison between the test sites and the control sites, was used to evaluate a set of potential impacts (intermediate results) closely related to the activities in the action plans. These aimed to create father-friendly environments and bring about changes in interventions with fathers, in the quality and frequency of collaborative initiatives among practitioners, and in practitioners' attitudes towards fatherhood. As mentioned above, these measures were the object of a single evaluation time (post-test only), since the impacts were not clearly operationalized until after the evaluation model was drawn up. This process required numerous meetings with the actors to ensure its adequacy and to take the results of the implementation evaluation into account.

Four data sources were used: (1) semi-structured interviews with mothers and fathers (n = 383 families);[2] (2) semi-structured interviews with service providers and managers (approximately twenty-five people in each community); (3) follow-up charts and reports on the activities; and (4) notes based on direct observation in the service agencies (for example, images of fathers, participation of fathers in social services, at the vaccination clinic, at report card day at school, accompanying the child to the daycare centre or picking up the child).

Promising Results

The results presented in this chapter concern only quantitative data obtained from the parents, and therefore deal only with the ultimate impacts of the project.[3] It was expected that, in a sequential perspective of the impacts, changes initially would be noted on the level of the cognitive variables: the fathers' attitudes towards child rearing, their perceptions of parental roles, and their sense of parental competence. Ultimately the changes noted on the cognitive level would also translate to the behavioural level. Table 4.1 presents a synthesis of the fathering dimensions evaluated with their associated sub-scales, as well as the measurement instruments used.

To simplify the presentation of the results, we include only those showing statistically significant differences – that is, where the threshold of significance was lower than 0.05 in the two-tailed t-test. More specifically, we conducted variance analyses, which brought out the principal effects linked to the measurement times (the difference between the pre-test and post-test measurements, irrespective of the groups) and to the groups (the difference between the experimental and control sites, irrespective of the measurement times), as well as to the interaction effect between the measurement times and the groups (the difference between the measurement times, according to group). We particularly expected results from this last effect (the time/group interaction measurement). We hoped that we would observe changes between the two evaluation times, and also that these changes would differ according to whether or not the fathers had received the intervention. We present the results according to the four principal fathering dimensions evaluated: attitudes towards child rearing, perception of parental roles, sense of parental competence, and father involvement.

110 Diane Dubeau et al.

Table 4.1. Measurement Synthesis

Dimensions of fathering	Sub-scales	Measurement instruments
Attitudes towards child rearing	1. Empathetic 2. **Warm** 3. Strict 4. Punitive 5. **Abusive**	Sommer et al. (1993) Easterbrooks & Goldberg (1984): warmth scale – 32 items
Perception of parental roles	1. **Maternal instinct** 2. **Parental specificity** 3. Attention given to fathers 4. Resistance by child's mother	Questionnaire inspired by Beitel (1989) – 16 items
Sense of parental competence	Total score	Parenting Sense of Competence Scale, Gibaud-Wallston (1977) – 16 items
Father involvement	1. Emotional support 2. **Physical care** 3. **Physical play** 4. Openness to outside world 5. Discipline 6. Evocation 7. **Household chores**	Father Involvement Questionnaire (Prospère) – 52 items; see Appendix A

Note: Statistically significant results are identified in bold.

On attitudes towards child rearing, in two of the five attitudes significant differences were revealed between the two measurement times and between groups, according to whether or not they had received the intervention (the combined time/group interaction effect). More specifically, the fathers in the sites where intervention had taken place showed warmer and less abusive child-rearing attitudes at Time 2 than at Time 1. Among the fathers in the control groups, we observed no difference between the two measurement times.

Data on the perception of parental roles were gathered only at Time 2 of the study. We did, however, have assessments completed by the mothers and fathers regarding the four dimensions evaluated. These results indicated that the mothers and fathers at the intervention sites were less inclined to agree with the maternal instinct notion ("Because of the maternal instinct, women look after children aged 0 to 2 years better than men do"), and were more inclined to assign a positive value to the specificity of the roles assumed by each parent ("It's good for a child if each parent has their own way of looking after him/her"). We noted no distinctions regarding the awareness of fathering behaviour ("I have the impression that I notice more what fathers do with their children") or the perception of the mother's resistance towards father involvement ("My partner often thinks I'm not doing things with the children the right way").

The sense of parental competence, as evaluated by the fathers, increased from Time 1 to Time 2. However, we observed this result as much at the control sites as at the sites where intervention had occurred. Several correlational studies have found a link between perceptions of parental involvement and the sense of parental competence; therefore, it is possible that the increase in father involvement observed between the two measurement times for all the sites combined is also reflected in the increase in the sense of parental competence.

The father involvement dimension allowed us to verify whether there was a change in the fathers' behaviour with their children during the reference period. The results showed no significant difference when a global measurement scale of father involvement was used (with a total of forty-seven items).[4] On the other hand, the use of the father involvement sub-scales brought out differences between the groups. Specifically, fathers at the sites where intervention had taken place showed a greater involvement at Time 2 than at Time 1 in three of the seven dimensions evaluated: physical care, physical play, and participation in household chores. In both the intervention and control groups, fathers obtained lower results in the emotional support given to their children at Time 2. This result, which appeared to counter our expectations for fathers at the intervention sites, might be explained by the age difference in the intervention sample between Time 1 and Time 2 (the children being older at Time 2). In the measurement of openness to the outside world, fathers in both the intervention and control groups obtained better results at Time 2 than at Time 1; here, no effect associated with the intervention was revealed. Finally, in the discipline measurement, the significant difference obtained concerned only fathers in the control groups (less involvement by the fathers on the disciplinary level). We observed no significant difference in the evocation sub-scale.

To sum up, three considerations allowed an encouraging evaluation of the results regarding the impacts of the project on the fathering dimensions. First, except in the case of one item, the significant differences we observed in the group/time measurements corresponded to the expected effects (improvements in the groups where intervention had taken place). Second, the use of control sites provided an important advantage in that it allowed us to nuance results, which, in certain cases, had pointed to an effect of time, rather than of the intervention. Third, the pattern of the results obtained showed effects in both the cognitive sphere (attitudes towards child rearing, perception of parental roles) and the behavioural sphere (father involvement).

The Researcher-Evaluator: A Tireless Questioner

The emergence of the positive outcomes of the intervention was a pleasant surprise, given the relatively weak empirical evidence of the effectiveness of similar programs to date. As previously mentioned, the difficulty of obtaining evidence-based data is often related to methodological obstacles associated with this type of evaluative study (Berkowitz, 2001); therefore, it seemed pertinent to investigate certain methodological aspects in greater depth to make sure they did not invalidate the results obtained.

METHODOLOGICAL CONSIDERATIONS

We asked and analysed three questions within the scope of the data obtained: Are fathers good self-evaluators? Did the social desirability factor skew our results? Was the pairing of the sites done correctly?

Regarding the first question, two elements assured us of the reliability of the fathers' answers. The first was provided in the evaluations by both mothers and fathers regarding father involvement. Despite some differences that agreed with those observed in other studies (Pleck & Masciadrelli, 2004), fathers' evaluations of their fathering behaviour were generally superior to those done by the mothers on the same subject. We noted no distinction between the sites, however, irrespective of whether or not they had undergone intervention. The second assurance of the validity of the fathers' answers was based on the results obtained in the rating scale that aimed to evaluate fathers' willingness to be involved with their children.[5] We applied this scale only to the mothers, and here, the results differed according to the site. On a statistically significant level, more mothers at the intervention sites perceived the fathers' involvement as voluntary, compared with mothers at the control sites. This result was interesting, as it indicated that the increase in father involvement at the experimental sites was not the result of pressure from the mothers.

Since the majority of the evaluative study's measurements were self-reported, consideration of the *social desirability* factor was needed to eliminate response bias; the inclusion of a social desirability questionnaire (Crowne & Marlowe, 1960) allowed us to deal with this question. A principal group effect was obtained, which showed higher social desirability scores for fathers at the sites that did not undergo the intervention. Therefore, the results concerning father involvement behaviour and the cognitive fathering dimensions (attitudes towards child rearing, perception of parental roles, and sense of parental competence) could well have been overestimated at the control sites, producing a smaller gap between them and the intervention sites. This factor made us more confident that the differences obtained were real and not skewed by the fathers' desire to give answers reflecting socially desirable attitudes or behaviours.

Finally, the difficulty of *pairing with control sites* is often mentioned in connection with this type of evaluation. The identification of pairing criteria does not necessarily guarantee the relative equivalency of the groups with respect to other characteristics that might be important to consider. Apart from certain geographical differences in a pairing with one of the intervention sites, principally concerning the organization of services,[6] the analysis of the socio-demographic characteristics of the samples showed few significant differences between the compared populations. These characteristics were more closely associated with the dimensions evaluated, and are presented in this chapter. Thus, we observed no significant difference in site pairings in the educational attainment levels of the parents (mother and father), in the number of years the couple had been together, in the number of children in the family, or in the ratio of girls to boys in the targeted children.[7] The only significant differences we observed, for all the sites combined, concerned the ages of the parents and the children. Thus, we noted that mothers and fathers were significantly younger at Time 2, while the average age of the children was higher. It was this result that led us to hypothesize about the reason we obtained weaker scores for the emotional support dimension of father involvement at Time 2 at all the sites, whether or not they had been subjected to the intervention. It is very likely that the behaviours described in the items associated with this dimension, such as "I comfort my child when he/she is afraid" or "I comfort my child when he/she is crying," were less frequent since many of the children were older.

Contributions of the Intervention

Beyond the methodological issues, it was also pertinent to ask questions about the contribution of the intervention to the results we obtained. Two aspects of the results reassured us regarding the real impacts of the program. First, the data issuing from the implementation evaluation confirmed that the intervention activities were established in accordance with the yearly action plans, and that participation in these activities had steadily increased during the reference period. Second, in the interviews done in the impacts evaluation (post-test measurements), we asked respondents if they had noticed any differences between their own community and a similar community in four specific areas: (1) services offered to families with young children; (2) services specifically offered to fathers; (3) socio-economic level; and (4) overall quality of life. The results fulfilled expectations, as the answers by the fathers at the intervention sites revealed perceptions of superiority with respect to services offered to families with young children, services specifically intended for fathers, and overall quality of life, in contrast to the perceptions of the fathers at the control sites. In addition, we questioned the fathers on: a) their perception of the degree of openness to fathers in local services intended for families with young children; b) the attention given to them and to their partners by the personnel in these services; and c) the presence of images of fathers in the service agencies. The only (marginally) statistically significant difference obtained concerned images of fathers, which were perceived as being more numerous at the sites where the intervention was implemented.

The global picture of the results we obtained supported the perception that the project generated the effects expected by the actors and the researchers – that this community-wide intervention based on a public health model and an ecological approach (Porche, 2004) was producing positive results in the cognitive and behavioural dimensions of father involvement.

As this chapter was written, some of the data were being subjected to more advanced analyses to establish, among other purposes, the importance of the intermediate variables in the process leading to the increase of father involvement in a community. The results that have been disseminated to date can be compared to pieces of a jigsaw puzzle: we now possess a number of these pieces, but we can only know how to put them together to obtain a comprehensive picture when they have been thoroughly analysed. The evaluation team is fully aware that prudence is essential in interpreting and disseminating the results if justice is to be done to the efforts by the many people who believed in this project and in the importance of promoting fatherhood involvement to improve the well-being of our children.

Conclusion

After a five-year exercise of sharing the complementary expertise of actors and researchers, we were able to affirm that Prospère rose to the challenge of a complex evaluation. Taking a critical look at the project from various evaluative angles allowed us to pinpoint strengths and assets, as well as the difficulties that arose in this community-based social innovation initiative. We discuss these under the following headings: the topic of the project, the methodological choices, and the often conflicting imperatives of practice and research.

THE TOPIC OF THE PROJECT

Father involvement is an issue that concerns both mothers and fathers, since talking about what makes a good father inevitably refers back to our concept of what makes a good mother. That no parent is indifferent to this issue was an important factor in launching the project, as it motivated people to participate and also held their interest on a sustained basis. During the five-year reference period, the constancy shown by the members of the steering committees at both sites could be attributed to their interest in the subject of father involvement and the many issues it raised on the theoretical/conceptual, methodological, and practical levels. The analysis of the outcomes-producing process, an aspect of the implementation evaluation, showed that the outcomes were first manifested in the members of the steering committees. Furthermore, with regard to the encouraging results obtained by the community impacts evaluation, the researchers hypothesized that the media campaign highlighting the father's role might have accelerated the effects of the intervention. Several media channels (newspapers, radio, and television, advertising) brought the population to focus on, address, and discuss the new realities of fatherhood in the wake of several decades of social change that have affected family organization, leading to, among other things, a more active role for fathers. This increase in public awareness was clearly an asset in the implementation of the project.

THE METHODOLOGICAL CHOICES

Several methodologies, all scientifically rigorous, were used in the different types of evaluations carried out. Moreover, the approach that guided the evaluation design (participatory action research and an evaluation centred on utilization) assigned active roles to the actors in the project, and encouraged their participation in carrying out the evaluations. The richness of the information obtained by means of these multiple methods convinced us of their validity. However, three areas of questioning remained when the evaluation ended. First, the results of the implementation and impacts evaluations brought out the need for an implementation period long enough to make appropriate adjustments to the activities scheduled in the yearly action plans, to be able to produce the expected outcomes and to respond to the needs of the targeted clientele. On the other hand, the length of this period implies certain methodological constraints with regard to the impacts evaluation – for example, father involvement measurement becomes complicated when the longitudinal follow-up of a cohort of individuals is influenced by children's developmental changes.

Second, the implementation of a project at different types of sites (urban and semi-urban) is an advantage when considering the generalization of an intervention model. However, this choice also gives rise to important methodological and ethical challenges that must be taken into account. For example, should we continue with comparative analyses of an intervention site and its paired control site at the risk of encouraging one to the detriment of the other? Also, are the research designs used still valid when the sample size is reduced to facilitate the explanation of the specificity of each site? To address this, in the framework of the impacts evaluation, we chose to combine the two intervention sites in the analysis in order to validate the proposed model.

The third interrogation regarding the methodology concerns the use of control sites in the impacts evaluation. The results of this evaluation showed that these sites constituted an essential point of reference, since an increase in father involvement was observed from one measurement time to the next whether or not intervention had taken place. At the same time, there was a statistically significant increase in certain dimensions of father involvement at the sites where intervention had taken place as opposed to the control sites. Thus, one of the difficulties observed remains in determining how far we should go in the pairing of samples. The absence of significant results in evaluative studies of community-based programs is often explained precisely by the difficulty of pairing sites (Bouchard, 1999). Random assignment and the control of socio-demographic characteristics are possible avenues, each of which has its limits and constraints.

THE OFTEN CONFLICTING IMPERATIVES OF PRACTICE AND RESEARCH
This experience brought out some of the inherent challenges associated with the conflicting imperatives that exist in partnerships between practitioners and researchers. Their respective schedules (for example, deadlines for grant requests) might not coincide, thus creating tensions. In this PAR project, the implementation evaluation revealed the pressure felt by the steering committee of site A regarding the establishment of the first yearly action plan. Tensions also arose due to the manner in which the evaluation results were transmitted: to meet expectations regarding their use, the results were transmitted quickly in various forms to the different actors. On the other hand, to avoid compromising the efforts made in the impacts evaluation, numerous controls of the different variables were necessary, leading to delays in the analyses. The scientific and professional communities might have conflicting agendas and priorities that are difficult to reconcile. This situation gives rise to the sensitive question of how the transmission of information should be controlled so that the work of several years will not be cancelled out by the premature or partial release of the evaluation results. Although time is a rare commodity, it seems to be key to resolving some of the difficulties frequently encountered in this type of research. If enough time is allocated for a project, quality relations (respect and the sharing of expertise) are more likely to develop among the partners, and they will have a better knowledge of the realities specific to the communities and of other actors' expectations concerning the different phases of a project (from its implementation to the dissemination of the results of its evaluation, if there is one). Finally, among the motives for potential tensions between practitioners and researchers is the often unequal funding of research activities and intervention activities. In this project, more than $300,000 was allocated to carry out the evaluations, compared with the $25,000 per year obtained by each of the sites to carry out yearly action plans with over twelve different activities each. That funding gap inevitably generated tensions in the partnership. Access to funding sources for intervention, recurrent over a period of at least three years, seems to be an essential condition for ensuring the maintenance of a project of this sort.

Despite these major challenges, the constraints inherent in the project, and the particularities of the experimental sites, we hope we have provided, through the multiple perspectives through which we evaluated the Prospère project, some answers that will help guide intervention aiming to promote fathers' involvement with their children.

NOTES

1 Data gathered in the framework of the Quebec Social Research Council grant for the implementation evaluation.
2 These were the same parents who underwent the post-test of the first research schema mentioned above.
3 A large volume of both quantitative and qualitative data was collated for this evaluation by means of the semi-structured interviews with service providers and parents. The qualitative data treatment will be the subject of an upcoming publication.
4 For the global measurement of father involvement, we excluded the five items that rated participation in household chores. However, these items were taken into account in the father involvement sub-scales.
5 This scale contained four items, including: "My partner only looks after the children when he feels like it, and not as a regular responsibility" and "I have to ask my partner to look after the children."
6 Pointe-Calumet (intervention site A) is close enough to Montreal (50 km) for families to use the health and social services located in this city if they choose, whereas the control territory paired with site A is far from any large metropolitan area (150 km from Montreal) and, therefore, families living there use local services almost exclusively.
7 To answer questions about father involvement in some of the measurement instruments, parents with two children or more were asked to refer to one child in particular, chosen at random by the research assistant administering the questionnaire to avoid bias.

REFERENCES

Bea van Beveren, A. J., & Hetherington, R. W. (1997). The front-end challenge: Five steps to effective evaluation of community-based programs. *Canadian Journal of Program Evaluation*, *12*(1), 117–132.

Beitel, A. H. (1989). *Toward reconceptualization of paternal involvement in infancy: The role of maternal gatekeeping* (unpublished doctoral dissertation). University of Illinois, Urbana–Champaign.

Berkowitz, B. (2001). Studying the outcomes of community-based coalitions. *American Journal of Community Psychology, 29*(2), 213–227. http://dx.doi.org/10.1023/A:1010374512674

Bilodeau, A., Chamberland, C., & White, D. (2002). L'innovation sociale, une condition pour accroître la qualité de l'action en partenariat dans le champ de la santé publique. *Canadian Journal of Program Evaluation, 17*(2), 59–88.

Bledsoe, K. L., & Graham, J. A. (2005). The use of multiple evaluation approaches in program evaluation. *American Journal of Evaluation, 26*(3), 302–319. http://dx.doi.org/10.1177/1098214005278749

Bouchard, C. (1999). The community as a participative learning environment: The case of Centraide of Greater Montreal 1, 2, 3 GO! Project. In D. Keating & D. Hertzman (Eds.), *Developmental health and the wealth of nations: Social, biological and educational dynamics* (pp. 311–321). New York, NY: Guilford Publications.

Chen, H. T. (2005). *Practical program evaluation*. Thousand Oaks, CA: Sage.

Crowne, D. P., & Marlowe, D. (1960). A new scale of social desirability independent of psychopathology. *Journal of Consulting Psychology, 24*(4), 349–354. http://dx.doi.org/10.1037/h0047358

Devault, A., Gaudet, J., Bolté, C., & St-Denis, M. (2005). A survey and description of projects that support and promote fathering in Canada: Still work to do to reach fathers in their real life setting. *Canadian Journal of Community Mental Health, 24*(1), 5–17. http://dx.doi.org/10.7870/cjcmh-2005-0001

Durlak, J., & DuPre, E. (2008). Implementation matters: A review of research on the influence of implementation on program outcomes and the factors affecting implementation. *American Journal of Community Psychology, 41*(3-4), 327–350. http://dx.doi.org/10.1007/s10464-008-9165-0

Dusenbury, L., Brannigan, R., Falco, M., & Hansen, W. B. (2003). A review of research on fidelity of implementation: Implications for drug abuse prevention in school settings. *Health Education Research, 18*(2), 237–256. http://dx.doi.org/10.1093/her/18.2.237

Easterbrooks, M. A., & Goldberg, W. A. (1984). Toddler development in the family: Impact of father involvement and parenting characteristics. *Child Development, 55*(3), 740–752. http://dx.doi.org/10.2307/1130126

Gibaud-Wallston, J. (1977). *Self-esteem and situational stress: Factors related to sense of competence in new parents* (unpublished doctoral dissertation). University of Rhode Island, Kingston.

Goodman, R. M., Wandersman, A., Chinman, M., Imm, P., & Morrissey, E. (1996). An ecological assessment of community-based interventions for prevention and health promotion: Approaches to measuring community coalitions. *American Journal of Community Psychology, 24*(1), 33–61. http://dx.doi.org/10.1007/BF02511882

Goodman, R. M., Wheeler, F. C., & Lee, P. R. (1995). Evaluation of the heart to heart project: Lessons from a community-based chronic desease prevention project. *American Journal of Health Promotion, 9*(6), 443–455. http://dx.doi.org/10.4278/0890-1171-9.6.443

Green, L., Daniel, M., & Novick, L. (2001). Partnerships and coalitions for community-based research. *Public Health Reports, 116*(Suppl. 1), 20–31. http://dx.doi.org/10.1093/phr/116.S1.20

Holmes, E. K., Cowan, P. A., Cowan, C., & Hawkins, A. J. (2013). Marriage, fatherhood, and parenting programming. In N. J. Cabrera & C. S. Tamis-LeMonda (Eds.), *Handbook of father involvement: Multidisciplinary perspective* (pp. 438–454). New York, NY: Routledge.

Hughes, M., & Traynor, T. (2000). Reconciling process and outcome in evaluating community initiaves. *Evaluation, 6*(1), 37–49. http://dx.doi.org/10.1177/13563890022209109

Jason, L. A., Keyes, C. B., Suarez-Balcazar, Y., Taylor, R. R., & Davis, M. I. (Eds.). (2002). *Participatory community research. Theories and methods in action.* Washington: American Psychological Association.

Labin, S.N. (2011). Shaping the future: An integrative methodological agenda. *American Journal of Evaluation, 32*(4), 572–578.

Madaus, G. F., & Stufflebeam, D. L. (2000). Program evaluation: A historical overview. In D. L. Stufflebeam, G. F. Madaus, & T. Kellaghan (Eds.), *Evaluation models* (pp. 4–18). Boston, MA: Kluwer Academic.

Ouellet, F., Turcotte, G., & Desjardins, N. (2001). *À Rosemont, ça CooPère: analyse d'implantation d'un projet d'action intersectorielle sur la paternité.* Montreal: Régie régionale de la santé et des services sociaux de Montréal-Centre et Direction de la santé publique de Montréal-Centre.

Patton, M. (1997). *Utilization-focused evaluation: The new century text* (3rd ed.). Thousand Oaks, CA: Sage.

Pleck, J. H., & Masciadrelli, B. P. (2004). Paternal involvement by U.S. residential fathers: Levels, sources, and consequences. In M. E. Lamb (Ed.), *The role of the father in child development* (4th ed., pp. 222–271). Hoboken, NJ: John Wiley.

Porche, D. J. (2004). Population-based public health practice. In D. J. Porche (Ed.), *Public and community health nursing practice: A population-based approach* (pp. 1–15). Thousand Oaks, CA: Sage.

Richard, L., Gauvin, L., & Raine, K. (2011). Ecological models revisited: Their uses and evolution in health promotion over two decades. *Annual Review of Public Health, 32*(1), 307–326. http://dx.doi.org/10.1146/annurev-publhealth-031210-101141

Rossi, P. H., Lipsey, M. W., & Freeman, H. E. (2004). *Evaluation: A systematic approach* (7th ed.). Newbury Park, CA: Sage.

Sommer, K., et al. (1993). Cognitive readiness and adolescent parenting. *Developmental Psychology, 29*(2), 389–398. http://dx.doi.org/10.1037/0012-1649.29.2.389

Turcotte, G., Desjardins, N., & Ouellet, F. (2001). *À Pointe-Calumet, on fait place aux pères: analyse d'implantation d'Initiative Place-O-Pères, un projet d'action communautaire sur l'engagement paternel.* Montreal: Régie régionale de la santé et des services sociaux de Montréal-Centre et Direction de la santé publique de Montréal-Centre.

Yin, R. K. (1998). The abridged version of case study research: Design and method. In L. Bickman & D. J. Rog (Eds.), *Handbook of applied social research methods* (pp. 229–260). Thousand Oaks, CA: Sage.

5 A Retrospective Look at the Partnership between Researchers and Actors

GILLES FORGET AND DOMINIC BIZOT

How does the researchers' perspective mix with that of practitioners? Five years after the presentation of the preliminary results of the Prospère project to its two steering committees, which also corresponded with the end of the sustained relationship among the partners, we believed it appropriate to review the issues and challenges the researchers and practitioners encountered during the project. To do this, we used two sources of information: a political analysis of the project from an external source and an interview with two practitioners who were involved in the project from the beginning and who comment on participatory action research (PAR) from their own perspective. How was the partnership between researchers and practitioners formed? Who was involved? How did the relationships evolve between partners? What were the more challenging issues for each partner? These are among the questions we address in this chapter, with a focus on the distribution of power in the inherent complexity of PAR. This analytical process leads us to identify certain success factors that can provide directions for future PAR.

Collaboration between Researchers and Actors in the Field

Many publications exist concerning the issues and challenges facing researchers and actors in the field when they collaborate (see, for example, Giese-Davis, 2008; Kesby, Kindon, & Pain, 2009; Minkler & Wallerstein, 2008). As some authors emphasize, "partnership is not a fashion, but a necessity" (Bilodeau, Lapierre, & Marchand, 2003). This is all the more pertinent in a social innovation initiative that acts on several systemic levels and among several people, and that also explicitly promotes an intersectorial approach (Goldenberg, 2010). Bilodeau and his colleagues (2003) state in their conclusion that the conditions fostering high-quality action in a partnership and high-quality collaboration between researchers and actors in the field are: a sufficiently participative dynamic, the equalization of power relations, and the sharing of knowledge. These conditions open up new roles for project researchers and actors, including those of facilitator, mediator, and eclectic innovator. In short, both researchers and practitioners become receptive to the broadening of knowledge.

Besides undergoing an implementation and an impact evaluation, the Prospère PAR project was also the subject of a political analysis carried out by Martine Cinq-Mars (2005), a doctoral candidate associated with the *Groupe de recherche et d'action sur la victimisation des enfants* (GRAVE), with which Prospère was associated. This critical look at the implementation of the project and the relationship between researchers and actors is based on the theoretical perspective of the logic of translation (Callon & Latour, 1986). Contrary to dissemination models, which analyse the degree of compliance between a project as initially planned and its empirical manifestation, the logic of translation advocates that the transformation of the initial product is inherent in the implementation process. This logic leads the promoters of social innovation to have a different perspective on the "planned" product (Cinq-Mars's term) to be put in place. They see it as the result of a joint construction process influenced by their respective characteristics, their interests, and the context in which the innovation is implemented. Within this theoretical framework, Cinq-Mars carried out an implementation analysis of the father involvement promotion project at site A. She identifies this case as "a set of actors with differing horizons, interests and cultures brought together in a joint action to attain a common goal, the construction of a social innovation" (Cinq-Mars, 2005, p. 49). Through a combination of interviews with the principal actors, notes taken in the field, and an analysis of the documents, she principally focuses on how an agreement was reached among the actors who were collaborating on a volunteer basis, without a line of authority determining the nature of the partnership or that of the innovation.

Cinq-Mars first presents site A, where the social innovation was being carried out, and outlines the context that existed when the partnership began. The researchers' stated intention was to involve all the actors in the development, planning, and implementation phases of the project. The actors established a Social Action Committee led by a community organizer who was preparing to launch a family services centre. At first, the actors were wary of the researchers' request for collaboration, as they had previously participated in a research project that failed to meet their expectations. In this case, however, the university-affiliated project was in line with some of their interests, and the members of the Social Action Committee decided to lead the definition and implementation phases of the project. Examining the collaboration between the two groups, Cinq-Mars wanted to validate that the researchers' avowed intention actually translated into the democratization of powers: "Doubt remains as to whether the intentions of democratization legitimizing the appeal for participation constitute rhetoric serving certain interests or whether they support a realistic and feasible undertaking in which diversified interests succeed in interfacing and decisions regarding outcomes are taken equitably" (2005, p. 82).

Cinq-Mars shows that the actors benefited considerably from their association with the researchers on a political capital level, since the local elite recognized their legitimacy. They took advantage of this experience to increase their resources by accessing funding sources for the family services centre and for activities promoting father involvement. The actors also acquired new expertise and increased their knowledge by gaining a better understanding of their own communities and of father involvement.

Cinq-Mars also addresses the controversies and obstructions that are usually part of a partnership situation, which, when they are encountered, bring to light the different meanings and interests of researchers and actors. To resolve the controversies, the literature recommends seeking the help of a recognized mediator to reach a mutual satisfactory solution. In evaluating the Prospère experience, Cinq-Mars points out three main areas of controversy in the implementation of the project at site A. The first concerned the "who": agreeing on which actors to bring into the project. In Cinq-Mars's view, although the partnership brought together actors from various sectors, this conclusion was reached only after much discussion about the actors themselves and their contribution and responsibilities, which, in Cinq-Mars's evaluation, led to some unilateral decisions. The second area of controversy concerned the "how": agreeing on what participation would be required on the part of the actors. Throughout the project, the particular mechanisms put in place to facilitate interactions among the partners might have increased the feeling of power of a few over some others. The third area of controversy concerned the "what": agreeing on the required theoretical models and action. On this point, the flexibility of the models the researchers drew up was questioned, together with the ability of the actors to really contribute to the project. According to Cinq-Mars, these controversial areas were not resolved, as the researchers were more concerned with aligning the elements of the research process with the initial model of dissemination.

Overall, this additional evaluation from a political perspective sheds light on the power relations that exist between researchers and actors in the field. Actors benefit in several ways, but the democratization of the knowledge does not take place.

Two practitioners who were present at the start of the project and who continue to work to support, strengthen, and maintain father involvement in their communities, shared their perspectives concerning the dynamics of the partnership between researchers and actors. They provided us with an update on the projects at the two sites, discussing how the projects developed after the collaboration with the research team ended; they also answered questions about the partnership, and they evaluated their experience in this PAR project.

The Follow-up to the Partnership

The partnership within the Prospère project came to an end in April 2002, following the presentation of the results evaluation to the two steering committees. Since that time, the family services centre at site A has continued to carry out intervention among fathers and is well-anchored in the community. This organization had difficulty obtaining funding for its activities with fathers, however, and was unable to retain the male service providers who had been hired on a temporary basis during the project's implementation phase. Nonetheless the centre remains the reference point for father interventions in the region. In 2005 it received funding from United Way (Laurentian region), allowing it to hire a full-time male practitioner who carries out father support work at both the local and regional levels.

After a period of reflection, site B has continued with monthly meetings, but the local partners have transformed their joint action structure into a non-profit organization. They consolidated this process by holding a founders' meeting in 2005. The non-profit organization, which kept the original name of *CooPère Rosemont* (Cooperative Fathers of Rosemont), receives funding from the United Way of Greater Montreal for the cost of a coordinator and activities for fathers in the neighbourhood. *CooPère Rosemont* continues to draw up a yearly action plan, together with other local organizations and resources. Its actions are now directed more specifically towards vulnerable fathers. It has maintained its collaboration with Prospère, and is now a partner in a new PAR project called *Relais-Pères* (Relaying Fathers); see Chapter 8.

Both researchers and decision-makers often express concern about the sustainability of partnership projects. In the case of Prospère's partners, the current situation indicates that continuity has been achieved, as the two organizations have diversified their funding sources, maintained their support activities for fathers in their communities, and set up activities, resources, and new programs and services for fathers. The organizations are renowned well beyond their respective communities. This was the situation outlined by the two practitioners from these two organizations, whose answers to our questions are detailed below.

An Interview[1]

We met with Diane Grenier, coordinator of the family services centre at site A, who participated in all the steering committee meetings there, and with Jean-François Leblanc, who was an active member on the steering committee at site B for several years.

> Q: What was your interest in associating with a research team?
> DIANE: We were in the process of setting up an organization in our community. Associating with a university research team gave substance to this process, and with respect to regional actors it gave credibility to the actions we wanted to undertake.
> JEAN-FRANÇOIS: The arrival of the research team and their proposal to join a participatory action research project was an opportunity to bring some fifteen organizations working with families and children in our community to the same table. We had wanted a joint action structure in the past, but the right conditions had not come together. The researchers' proposal provided the right conditions for us to join in.
> Q: You spoke of a common vision of father involvement. How did you perceive the discussions between the researchers and the actors in the steering committee regarding the best way to approach the problem and to solve it?
> DIANE: I wouldn't call it a common vision of the problem; that bothers me a bit. Instead, we refer to people's potential. The discussions we had in the steering committee concerning father involvement were enriching because the committee was made up of men and women of different ages

and backgrounds, several of whom contributed their own experiences as parents. I think when we plan a new intervention, we often omit the stage of talking about the ways we view the phenomenon that we want to act upon, a practice I've tried to use. As for the ecological approach, we wanted to start our new intervention from that perspective because we weren't satisfied with the public health approach, which was more a biomedical intervention. In those days, the ecological approach was not promoted very often. When I spoke with the people at the Centre de santé et de services sociaux [health and social services centre] in my region, I felt like an alien. They didn't listen to us as much back then; it was much more difficult.

JEAN-FRANÇOIS: The fact that we represented several organizations proposing the ecological model for the intervention allowed us to see "who" was doing "what." Nobody can do everything alone. But the members of the steering committee needed to make the model their own and understand it properly to really be able to see where we were heading. That took some time. Month after month, we went back to it until people adopted it. The association also allowed us to discuss our respective views on the problem. Until then we were fifteen organizations with about fifteen definitions of father involvement. The presence of the researchers, acting as a kind of foreman, had a unifying effect.

Q: During that period, how did each of you experience the relations between the researchers and the steering committees, which included citizens in both sites?

DIANE: It was a lengthy process. At the beginning, for some of the citizens, it was like two worlds apart, one at the top and the other below. In time I believe we succeeded in reaching each other, because our objectives were pretty much the same. There were some adjustments to make in the way of looking at the objectives and how to achieve them; that is to be expected. We're dealing with two completely different cultures. There were some periods when relations were strained, but by talking and getting to know each other, we succeeded in coming together on the same wavelength, and I believe this was good for all of us.

Q: Was there a pedagogical effort to explain the approach?

DIANE: Yes: first, to bring an understanding of the realities of the research team and those of the milieu. It is difficult to change people's habits quickly. It takes time to work closely together and say things to each. Gradually, there was an exchange of expertise that was to everyone's advantage, the researchers as much as the citizens and the practitioners. We should also remember that we had opportunities to exchange ideas, for example, at the regular meetings of the steering committee, where everyone's point of view was discussed.

Q: Let's talk about the action plan. After having brought the partners together and arriving at a common vision of father involvement, you drew up yearly plans. With respect to those activities, what struck you about the relationship with the researchers?

DIANE: Some of the actions would have been impossible without the researchers – the doorknob-hanger notices targeting fathers, for example. The family services centre did not have the staff or the competency to carry out an inquiry, analyse its results, and produce a tool like the doorknob hanger. I still use that data in my interventions with families when I draw parallels between fathers and mothers. Also, holding discussion groups is a habit I've kept, a technique I use from time to time when dealing with certain issues. Discovering new tools is enriching.

Q: The intention to evaluate the project was present from the beginning, and the evaluation was done. What have you retained from it?

DIANE: Analysis and evaluations are things we cannot afford to do. However, now, if there is any discussion on this subject, it's been written up. In the field we don't have time to sit and write things down so we can refer to it later. But our actions gain credibility when we can say "We're not the only ones saying it. See, researchers looked at what we were doing, and they say it too." Now, when we approach organizations, these writings back up what we are proposing. The evaluation process has greatly helped us in our arguments.

Q: If we tried to pinpoint the major difficulties in this collaborative undertaking between researchers and practitioners, what would they be?

DIANE: A relationship between two worlds, two cultures, can't go on too long without some problems arising. In the first place, there is each person's way of understanding things. Words don't necessarily mean the same thing to everyone. Then there are each person's obligations and deadlines that don't necessarily fit together. There were some quite heated discussions. Those of us in the community expected a bit more feedback from the research than there was in fact.

JEAN-FRANÇOIS: We would have appreciated being able to meet with the principal researcher more frequently. There was also the way the information was transmitted. For example, we were informed of our project's strengths and weaknesses by fax. That was pretty off-hand. We would have preferred a presentation at a steering committee meeting. We would also have liked to have had more information on certain aspects of the project, such as the evaluation of the impacts.

DIANE: The researchers' presence was also inconsistent. The only stable presence was that of people from the community, most of whom were volunteers. They committed themselves for five years and they stayed the course for the five years. On the other hand, the members of the institutions changed. The citizens were a little disappointed, and their feeling of belonging to the project diminished accordingly as these changeovers took place.

Q: What do you retain from this experience?

DIANE: The association with research was stimulating. I'm thinking of the Dessine-moi un papa [Draw Me a Daddy] exhibition. We hadn't planned to do this with the children's drawings, but it ended up becoming an exhibition. There was a whole dynamic that might not have existed if we had just stayed among ourselves, saying "let's go and get the fathers." The exchanges and the sharing happened in a larger group; I think that's what facilitates the exchange of expertise. The association had a mobilizing effect, and in the eyes of the community it gave credibility to our interventions. Throughout the process the association with the researchers gave us an outside view of our actions. In the field we're immersed in the situation; the meetings were an opportunity to put things in perspective, to hear people who put into words what we do by instinct. I think that's the first benefit: having a space for reflection. Being associated with a research team; during the first year, the discussions were interesting. Having the time to reflect on the reasons we find it important to support fathers: writing things down, transferring knowledge, mobilizing people. It opened doors that had previously been closed to us. Knocking on the door by yourself you think you're strong, but associated with the university it looks more serious. An even more important fact was that it made the citizens proud to be an active part of a university research project and to be considered partners. I would say that the project increased the self-esteem of the whole community.

JEAN-FRANÇOIS: I found that the research also nourished practice. When you hold focus groups and you get some feedback, it can confirm that you're on the right track. It also gives us a better knowledge of the people we want to reach, and gives us some feedback regarding results. For example, when we found out that people were collecting the doorknob hangers and that a high proportion of the target audience was being reached, it was stimulating for us.

Q: Talking about fathers, do you think it is easier now to promote father involvement? Have things changed over the last ten years?

DIANE: Ten years ago I was about the only one talking about fathers. Today it's easier for me to talk about the place of fathers in our services with members of our regional association of family services centres. There is less resistance than there was ten years ago.

JEAN-FRANÇOIS: I agree. I have been giving the Pères en mouvement, Pratiques en changement [Changing Fathers, Evolving Practices] training workshops for the last few years. I offered the training again just recently. At the end of the training session, I said to myself "We've come a long way." Younger practitioners are arriving and saying "I've always thought that fathers were important." It's different from the first training sessions I conducted in 2002. There are fewer objections and complaints about men.

DIANE: It's true: ten years ago often this concern didn't even exist. Today there is less negative prejudice, less of the feeling that the father is to blame a priori. Even on the judiciary level, we can see a change: for example, judges do not automatically accept the mother's version. The first years I accompanied fathers to court, the judges always asked for expert testimony to back up the father's point of view.

JEAN-FRANÇOIS: There is still work to be done with parents. When we meet a mother and ask her where the child's father is, we have to go a little deeper to find out if the mother and the children are in contact with the father. We can usually find this out when we ask the father where the child's mother is and he is able to answer. Practice must adopt more of a family perspective instead of a perspective that only focuses on the mother and the child.

DIANE: Indeed, there is still a lot to do to raise awareness among both mothers and fathers. It's not a contest between men and women. We have to stop comparing to see which one of the two is the better parent, and focus on the child's needs. The child needs parents – father and mother. And the more a family is vulnerable, the more difficult it is, because too often the only paternal or maternal model is absence, abandonment by the parents. We must promote a co-parenting solution centred on the child's needs and facilitated by negotiation between parents.

Q: In conclusion, do you believe it's easier to reach fathers today?

JEAN-FRANÇOIS: I also find that the situation of fathers has evolved. Men want to be less committed to their jobs. Work is important, but not at any price, and the family is also a place to have fun and renew our energies. Since I've been working with fathers, middle-class fathers have remained just as involved, and are using services related to pregnancy and birth, as was found in the first inquiry (Forget, 1995). But it was and still is difficult to reach fathers in precarious situations. They are isolated, and we have to establish a relationship of trust with them. It has to be a long-term effort.

DIANE: I've been in contact with some fathers for almost eight years now. I think what Jean-François says may be truer of men, but it applies to women too. In fact I don't see much difference between fathers and mothers who are suffering, are marginalized and excluded. We have to adopt alternative strategies to reach them. We have to focus on their strengths. The father's role as breadwinner has been put aside for too long; it's an important social role, after all.

Conclusion

Collaboration between researchers and actors in the field is at the heart of participatory action research and of the Prospère father involvement promotion initiative. The project has been examined and reviewed from several angles: in a field study, in implementation and impact evaluations, and in a political analysis. Although these analyses might not reach the same conclusions, they all underline the efforts and the constant challenges of innovative health-promotion practices aimed at influencing the cultures of the actors associated with these programs. The following conditions align with recommendations to strengthen collaborative partnerships to assure health for all: (1) establish a monitoring system to detect progress; (2) develop and use an action plan; (3) facilitate natural reinforcement for people working across sectors; (4) assure adequate base funding; (5) provide training and technical support; (6) establish a participatory evaluation system for documenting and reviewing progress; and (7) arrange group contingencies to ensure accountability (Fawcett, Schultz, Watson-Thompson, Fox, & Bremby, 2010). The practitioners' assessments brought out other aspects of these challenges. Most important, they confirmed the sustainability of the action brought about by this PAR and that the knowledge and skills acquired during this period are still being put into practice in the activities for fathers.

NOTE

1 This taped interview took place at the Montreal public health department; the transcript has been slightly adjusted for publication.

REFERENCES

Bilodeau, A., Lapierre, S., & Marchand, Y. (2003). *Le partenariat: comment ça marche? Mieux s'outiller pour réussir*. Montreal, QC: Direction de la santé publique de Montréal-Centre.

Callon, M., & Latour, B. (1986). Les paradoxes de la modernité: comment concevoir les innovations? *Prospective et santé, 36*, 13–29.

Cinq-Mars, M. (2005). *Considérations épistémologiques et étude de cas concernant l'évaluation d'implantation d'un projet communautaire réalisé par la participation des partenaires issus du secteur public et d'une communauté* (unpublished doctoral dissertation). Université du Québec à Montréal, Montreal.

Fawcett, S., Schultz, J., Watson-Thompson, J., Fox, M., & Bremby, R. (2010). Building multisectoral partnerships for population health and health equity. *Preventing Chronic Disease, 7*(6), 1–7. Retrieved from http://www.cdc.gov.pcd/issues/2010/nov/pdf/10_0079.pdf

Forget, G. (1995). *Un modèle communautaire de soutien à l'engagement paternel: analyse du milieu à Pointe-Calumet*. Montreal, QC: Direction de la santé publique de Montréal-Centre.

Giese-Davis, J. (2008). Community/research collaborations: Ethics and funding. *Clinical Psychology: Science and Practice, 15*(2), 149–152. http://dx.doi.org/10.1111/j.1468-2850.2008.00124.x

Goldenberg, M. (2010). Reflections on social innovation. *Philantrophist, 23*(3), 207–220.

Kesby, M., Kindon, S., & Pain, R. (2009). *Participatory action research approaches and methods: Connecting people, participation and place*. New York, NY: Routledge.

Minkler, M., & Wallerstein, N. (2008). Introduction to CBPR: New issues and emphases. In M. Minkler & N. Wallerstein (Eds.), *Community-based participatory research for health: From process to outcomes* (pp. 5–19). San Francisco, CA: Jossey-Bass.

6 Support for Father Involvement in a Socio-professional Integration Context

ANNIE DEVAULT, GILLES FORGET, FRANCINE OUELLET, AND MARIE-PIERRE MILCENT, WITH JEANNE DORÉ

Introduction

The studies of a research team evolve over time according to the results obtained and the members' reflections on the study subject. The results of the program promoting father involvement in two communities (described in Chapters 3 and 4) and those of other Prospère studies led the research team to direct its attention to a subgroup of fathers who have rarely been the focus of studies and who are seldom targeted in intervention efforts: young fathers in a context of social and economic vulnerability. In this chapter we describe *Métiers de pères* (Profession: Fatherhood), a participatory action research (PAR) project undertaken in collaboration with three socio-professional integration organizations in Montreal. The objective of the project was to gain more knowledge of fathers living in a context of vulnerability in order to be able to provide customized support for them. We begin with a brief summary of current knowledge regarding vulnerable young fathers. We then explain the procedures followed to establish a partnership with the three socio-professional integration organizations and to implement a PAR project. Subsequently we present the procedures and results of a field study whose purpose was to document the services offered by the organizations and to assess the fatherhood support needs of the young fathers in the training programs. We then describe an in-depth research study of a sample of seventeen young fathers who were undergoing or who had undergone training in the organizations, and present the results of an analysis of their life stories and a portrait of their characteristics. In the final section we look at the interventions implemented within the organizations and their effects on father involvement as perceived by the fathers.

Fathers in Contexts of Vulnerability

In the scientific literature, a context of vulnerability with respect to fatherhood is generally associated with three risk factors: being an adolescent or a young adult at the time of the birth of the first child; having an unreliable income and low employment status; and having a low educational attainment level. As shown below, these three factors can be obstacles to father involvement. Compared to fathers in the general population, however, fathers in a context of vulnerability have seldom been studied. Thus, we have less knowledge of the factors that influence their involvement with their children (Cabrera, Tamis-LeMonda, Bradley, Hofferth, & Lamb, 2000; Mosley & Thomson, 1995) and their perceptions of the father's role (Lacharité, 2001) than we do for fathers in more stable situations.

On a personal level, becoming a father at a very young age brings a number of challenges that might disrupt normal human development. In Erik Erikson's (1963) stages of psychosocial development, in the transition from childhood to adulthood, one passes through the search for a sense of self and the formation of intimate relationships, before generativity, or the ability to nurture the next generation, can occur. Adolescents normally are situated in an egocentric position – a privileged time of life in which they reflect on who they are and the role they wish to play in society. With the arrival of a child during this period, however, the young father undergoes an accelerated transformation of his identity from that of a young person searching for himself to that of an adult responsible for another human being. He must turn away abruptly from his personal concerns and assume a more empathetic position. Furthermore, in the case of very young fathers, the child often arrives at the beginning of the couple's relationship. Thus, two young people who have not yet adjusted to an intimate relationship must find room in it for an infant needing constant attention. These young fathers must try to achieve a merging of their ongoing search for identity, adaptation to an intimate relationship, and the development of a caregiving (generative) capacity in a much shorter period than young people in the general population (Pratt, Lawford, & Allen, 2012; Quéniart, 2002; Rhoden & Robinson, 1997). In addition, the literature indicates that, compared to other young men, a higher proportion of young fathers grow up without their two biological parents, experience difficulties with their families of origin, and are victims or witnesses of family violence (Anda et al., 2001; Eggebeen, Knoester, & McDaniel, 2013; Furstenberg & Weiss, 2000).

Low educational status and job instability, with accompanying economic hardship, bring their share of problems. Having a job, although it might not be the primordial factor in "good fathering," is still important (Doucet, 2013), particularly for fathers in a context of economic vulnerability (Allen, Daly, & Ball, 2012; Lamb, 1997; Levine & Pitt, 1995; Roy, 2004; Townsend, 2002). Studies confirm that being employed correlates positively with the degree of fathers' involvement in their children's lives (Carlson & McLanahan, 2002; Fagan, Barnett, Bernd, & Whiteman, 2003; Hofferth, Pleck, Goldscheider, Curtin, & Hrapczynski, 2013), although overinvestment in work might be counterproductive in this respect. The low educational and skill levels that characterize the population of vulnerable young fathers constitute a major obstacle in the job market, where specialized qualifications increasingly are required. Therefore, these fathers are more likely to occupy temporary, part-time, low-paying jobs that perpetuate a context of poverty. Studies show that poverty, job instability, and underemployment negatively affect a father's self-esteem, as he is not able to play the role of family breadwinner (Allen et al., 2012; Devault & Gratton, 2003; Walters, 2011). In a context of poverty, fathers find it difficult to meet the food, clothing, and housing needs of their families. Financial problems and the stress associated with them can increase fathers' levels of psychological distress and affect their concepts of the parental role (Simons, Whitbeck, Conger, & Melby, 1990; Tamis-LeMonda & Cabrera, 1999), as well as the degree of their involvement with their children (Allen et al., 2012; Bryan, 2013; Harris & Marmer, 1996; Hijjawi, 2005). However, one variable that reduces the negative impact of poverty on father involvement is the father's good relationship with the child's mother (Cummings, Goeke-Morey, & Raymond, 2004; Hijjawi, 2005; Nelson, 2004). Allen et al. (2012) report, more specifically, that when a father feels trusted by his partner, he tends to be more confident in his own ability to take care of his child. The importance of a good co-parental relationship is underlined for divorced or separated fathers (Palkovitz, Fagan, & Hull, 2013).

Although this review of risk factors conveys a pessimistic image of father involvement among young fathers in contexts of vulnerability, qualitative studies on this population have arrived at more nuanced conclusions. These studies show that these young fathers are strongly motivated to care for their children and their families despite the deleterious context of poverty, and that, through their efforts and resourcefulness, some succeed in this regard (Allard & Binet, 2002; Anderson, Kohler, & Letiecq, 2002; Ouellet & Goulet, 1998; Pratt et al., 2012). It appears that, for some of these vulnerable young men, becoming a father is an incentive to take concrete steps towards social integration and a productive life.

A principal aim of the Profession: Fatherhood PAR was to document the situation of vulnerable young fathers in greater depth, as we discuss below.

Building a Partnership with Socio-professional Integration Organizations

In 2001, to reach young fathers living in contexts of vulnerability, Prospère established partnerships with three social integration enterprises – *Boulot Vers* (Towards Work), *Formétal* (Forsteel), and *Pro-Prêt* (Ready Clean) – located in different neighbourhoods of Montreal. These not-for-profit organizations work to prevent social exclusion among underqualified young people. Their mandate is to train young people in a certified skill (carpentry, metal folding, and cleaning and maintenance, respectively), and to support them in their search for steady employment. Such social integration enterprises possess a strong potential for intervention among young fathers in contexts of vulnerability for several reasons. They target a young (ages fifteen to twenty-five), economically fragile, mostly male clientele who make little or no use of public health and social services, their programs reach both individuals with young children and those about to become parents, and they provide a veritable life milieu for young adults. During the paid training programs, which typically last six months, trainees must attend five days a week, eight hours a day. The follow-up given by in-house practitioners during this period supports helps these young people to acquire a marketable skill; in addition, intervention on a personal level is provided within the organizations. Ongoing individualized support from qualified counsellors addresses issues such as difficulty accepting authority, substance abuse, and psychological problems. Although many of the young men who benefit from these programs have children, the three enterprises had not paid much attention to the fatherhood factor until the beginning of the Profession: Fatherhood PAR.

Towards a Shared Vision of the Issue and Its Solution

The research team aimed to build a bridge between two sectors, economic and social, that traditionally are unconnected with each other by implementing and documenting a fatherhood awareness project within the job-training programs of the three organizations.

First, the PAR project was presented to the organizations' administrators in a series of meetings at which the basis of the partnership between the researchers and the organizations was established by defining the project's purpose and procedures, as well as the roles and responsibilities of all the actors involved. The administrators immediately saw the value of developing a framework for father involvement and of adding this issue to their psycho-social follow-up, as they were aware that their clientele had difficulty balancing the demands of the training program with fatherhood.

These first contacts with the partners were formalized by the creation of a steering committee to guide the implementation of the project and the adoption of its official name, *Métiers de pères*. Besides the researchers, the steering committee was made up of the organizations' administrators and services providers. The actors reflected collectively on the best way to integrate support for father involvement into the organizations' psycho-social mandates. The steering committee members met throughout the implementation of the project. The stages of Profession: Fatherhood generally corresponded to those of the PAR project presented in Chapter 3.

One research goal was to study the life stories of young fathers enrolled in the three socio-professional organizations. The young men in the sample were first interviewed during their programs and then again eight months later. In-depth analysis of the collected data on the histories of these young fathers and their experiences of fatherhood has already been published elsewhere (Devault et al., 2005, 2008), but we include the results here, as well as the fathers' own evaluations of the impacts of the project. Parallel to the research process, the partner organizations obtained funding to carry out the action component of the project: the promotion of father involvement in the three organizations. For three years, each organization drew up an annual action plan outlining activities to raise awareness of the importance of the father's role and to support father involvement; these activities varied according to the objectives and interests of the administrators and practitioners of each enterprise and the characteristics of its clientele. Throughout the process, findings from the research informed the intervention strategies, while the implementation of the intervention gave rise to further reflection at the research level. This reciprocal process allowed the researchers and partners to acquire a deeper knowledge of the fatherhood experience of young men in contexts of vulnerability and of the implementation of father involvement intervention in the job-training milieu.

The Field Study

After the partnership was formalized, a field study was carried out in the milieu where the intervention would take place. The purposes of the field study were to inventory and describe the services already available in the three organizations, and to assess the needs of fathers in the training programs regarding fatherhood and support for father involvement.

The inventory and description of the services provided in the socio-professional integration programs were undertaken by analysing the enterprises' documents and by meeting with the practitioners. The work of practitioners at these organizations is multidimensional, as they help trainees search for employment and support them on a personal level. Trainees are given information on job search techniques and have access to tools related to the search (such as computers, Internet access, photocopy machines, telephones, and fax machines). They receive assistance in drawing up a budget and in finding an apartment, and are referred to resources corresponding to their needs, including legal services. Practitioners also acquaint the trainees with the realities of the workplace and its requirements, such as punctuality and regularity, as well as expectations regarding management-employee relations. A clearer understanding of the intervention dynamic already existing in the organizations showed the feasibility of promoting father involvement within their programs.

The perceptions of the trainee fathers regarding their needs were elicited by organizing focus groups. The researchers coded the content of these groups according to cultural, family, and personal dimensions, social capital, and means of action (Marsiglio, 2000). The information obtained allowed the researchers to identify six principal needs.

On the personal level, the trainee fathers said they needed:

(1) *to acquire more knowledge of parenting skills.* They repeated that desire particularly in the area of discipline. Some fathers said they were not much interested in caring for infants, yet, despite recognizing their lack of parenting skills, they tended to rely on themselves or, in certain cases, asked their close relatives for help.

(2) *to have a time and place to reflect on their identity as fathers.* These young men had neither opportunities nor settings to talk about

fatherhood, their lives with their partners, or their children, or about how the latter were developing. They said their fatherhood status was given little recognition socially, and they felt they were considered simply as providers, to the detriment of their role as fathers and child rearers. Yet, it emerged in the discussions that they had dreams for their children and felt the need for feedback regarding several aspects of their child-rearing practices.

Regarding the larger environment, the young fathers underlined the need for:

(3) the removal of ideological obstacles attached to the paternal role. The young men spoke at length about gender relations, co-parenting, and the prevailing attitudes that disqualified them as fathers – within the area of child care, among other aspects – and all the obstacles these imply. In their view, society wrongly attributes child-rearing capacities preponderantly to women and overestimates the mother-child relationship.

(4) the removal of institutional obstacles to the father's role. This aspect of the young fathers' discourse centred on the judiciary and social services domains. They mentioned that mothers, much more often than fathers, are still granted sole custody of children in divorce and separation judgments. They also complained that most family and child services are addressed mainly to mothers instead of to both parents.

(5) greater attention to the challenge of balancing the demands of work and family. Holding a job is an important element of social interaction, self-esteem, and social inclusion. In the workplace, however, the young men said they had never been identified, nor had they identified themselves, as fathers. Trying to reconcile work and family life was difficult when neither employers nor the fathers themselves drew attention to their fatherhood status and the needs associated with it.

(6) greater awareness of the father's role among practitioners. In referring to their desire to be recognized as fathers, the young men said that training practitioners on issues related to fatherhood was necessary.

This analysis informed the drawing up of the intervention plan and the research questions underlying our life trajectory study of young fathers.

The Young Fathers' Life Stories

The qualitative research was carried out among seventeen young fathers. In two one-on-one interviews, each participant was asked to give information on his personal history, his relationship with the mother of his child or children, and his employment history. The eight-month interval between the two interviews allowed researchers to analyse the results of the first interview and validate them with the participant in the second interview.

Participants were recruited with the help of the practitioners at the three organizations, who identified fathers among the young trainees, as well as others who had completed a training program over the previous six-month period. The data collection relied principally on the theme-based life-story method, which examines the lives of participants from a particular perspective (Mayer & Deslauriers, 2000). Our conceptual framework, illustrated in Figure 6.1, was based on the systemic intervention philosophy of socio-professional integration organizations. Their mandate is to provide personalized accompaniment centred on the individual's needs, using a global approach that combines the personal, social, and employment realms. We felt it was essential to adopt this same approach in our research by documenting the personal sphere (individual history), the socio-professional sphere (schooling and employment history, relation to the resources of the environment), and the parenting sphere (parental history), taking account of the interrelations among these domains and analysing them as elements that might or might not facilitate socio-professional integration and father involvement.

Figure 6.1. Conceptual Model of the Life-Story Study

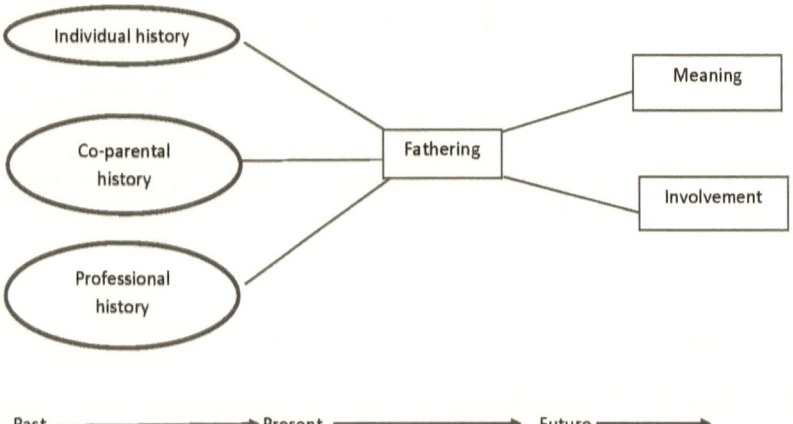

The first interview eliciting the young fathers' life stories focused on the theme of *fathering*. The young men were asked to tell us, in chronological order, how the child had arrived in their lives and to describe their feelings and reactions towards this event. Questions were designed to draw out their perceptions of the paternal role, the meaning of fatherhood in their lives, and the impact of the child's arrival. The fathers provided information on the frequency of their contact with their children, as well as the good and bad moments they had experienced with them. Their *socio-professional* histories were drawn from their experiences at school, the training they had received, and the jobs they had occupied. The second of the two interviews centred on the subjects' *individual* histories in their families of origin. Each participant was asked to describe his relationship with his mother and father, detailing the evolution of these relationships and the part they played in supporting his own fatherhood. The interview also dealt with any traumatic events that might have occurred during his childhood or adolescence, such as bereavements, separations, or placements in foster care. Finally, the *co-parental* history was elicited, including the meeting of the father and the mother of his child, the quality and duration of their relationship, the circumstances of the child's conception, the mother's pregnancy and the birth of the child, as well as the current status of the relationship.

The body of data collected in the interviews was systematically treated using a qualitative data analysis method (Miles & Huberman, 1994). The audiotapes were transcribed, and the researchers identified the salient passages to retain the essential information from the interviews. Each summary was independently validated by another member of the research team. The content of the summaries was coded in an index tree according to the pre-established themes (individual history, socio-professional history, co-parental history, and fathering) to allow a transversal reading of the data.

Characteristics of the Young Fathers

At the time of the second interview, the mean age of the seventeen fathers was twenty-five, with the youngest being twenty and the oldest thirty-two. Ten were born in Quebec and seven outside of Canada. Fifteen (88 per cent) had eleven years of schooling or less; two had attended school for only six years. Thirteen of the seventeen held a job at the time of the second interview; thirteen reported an annual income of less than $20,000, and the rest were earning income of between $20,000 and $25,000 a year.

At the time their first child was conceived, the fathers' mean age was twenty (minimum, fifteen and a half; maximum, twenty-five), and the mean age of their respective partners was twenty-one (minimum, fifteen; maximum, thirty-three). In fourteen cases, the first child had been conceived unintentionally a few months or even a few weeks after the couple's relationship began (minimum, a month and a half; maximum, two years). Except in the case of one father, the children were all biological offspring, although this did not mean that the participants had no contact with non-biological children at the time of the study or before it. Ten subjects had only one child; the others had between two and six children. The mean age of the children at the time of the first interview was slightly over five (minimum, three months; maximum, twenty-one years). Five fathers had daily contact with their children, seven saw their children at least once a week, and two saw their children only occasionally; only three fathers no longer had contact with their children. Three-quarters of the fathers no longer formed a couple with the children's mother at the time of the second interview. The mean length of the romantic relationship with the child's mother was 4.14 years (minimum, a year and a half; maximum, eight years).

To summarize the situation of the vulnerable young fathers in the study sample, most were relatively young with a low level of education, and all had a low income. Each had become a father soon after he met the mother of the child/children. The majority had one child of an average age of five. Although the majority saw their children regularly, most were no longer in a romantic relationship with the child/children's mother.

Individual Histories

The childhood and adolescence of the participants were marked by problems and ruptures (some of the results given here are taken from Ouellet, Milcent, & Devault, 2006). Approximately half of the fathers had experienced the separation of their parents before age twelve. Five had never lived with their biological father, although some had known him. Only one had spent his entire childhood living with his biological parents. Five had experienced the death of a family member due to illness or suicide. Two had been placed in foster care during their childhood. Seven had spent time at a youth detention facility, but, at the time of the interviews none reported involvement in crime or drug abuse.

RELATIONSHIP WITH THE BIOLOGICAL MOTHER

Ten of the seventeen participants reported having had a warm, secure, and positive relationship with their biological mother. They said they still felt that she understood and listened to them, and they retained many clear memories of happy times spent with her. To them, their mother was one of the most important people in their adult life: "I need her often. I need her advice; sometimes, I need to talk to her, so I go to her place and have a cup of coffee with her." Only one father described his relationship with his mother as always having been difficult. The remaining five participants seem to have had a more complex, ambivalent relationship with their mother. Their accounts were often contradictory and incoherent, mixing positive descriptions of their mother with recollections of episodes in which the mother was either absent or an unreliable source of security and affection. Nevertheless these young fathers remained loyal to their mother in their accounts, hardly ever criticizing or questioning her physical or psychological absence. In any case, their mother was particularly important to many of the young fathers: "She's my mother, she's the only one I have, and she's one of the most important people in the world to me. I'd do anything to protect her."

RELATIONSHIP WITH THE BIOLOGICAL FATHER

The accounts of seven of the young fathers indicated a satisfying relationship with their biological father, even if he was authoritarian and emotionally distant. They viewed their father as a person they could rely on: "We were pals and we're still pals...I respect my father." They evoked warm memories of father-son activities, nuancing the positive and negative aspects of the relationship. Their accounts revealed that they felt loved and respected by their father. Several participants reported conflicts with their father during their adolescence, although these quarrels did not prevent them from maintaining positive ongoing contact with him. None of the participants, however, described their father as a model in all the dimensions of parenthood. Rather, he represented a model in certain respects, such as in his role as worker/provider, but not in others, such as that of a giver of affection: "The things I do with [my son] now are the same things my father used to do with me [but] I would have liked it if he had talked to me more." The ten other participants said their fathers had been either absent or dead when they were growing up, or their relationship had been violent or abusive: "My father used to forget about me and leave me on the street corner.

When I'm with my daughter, she's my priority. I wasn't my father's priority ... he was absent, irresponsible, impulsive, aggressive." These participants spoke of the lack of a fathering model: "I didn't really have a father... you want to have a role model, but the models I had weren't so great. The [only] model Dads [were] on TV." Thus, compared to their evaluations of their relationships with their mother, a higher proportion of the participants characterized their relationship with their father as difficult.

Socio-professional histories

All the fathers interviewed had left school at a young age, usually after a series of failures or misadventures. Their adolescence was characterized by rebellion and conflict, particularly with their fathers. Several had experienced stressful family events, such as immigration, suicide, mental health problems, and substance abuse. A significant number had been members of a street gang and had used drugs. All had entered the workforce between the ages of twelve and sixteen, and their first jobs had been unstable ones involving manual labour or factory work. However, having a job had given them a measure of self-esteem they had lacked at school and, consequently, they showed considerable resourcefulness in their job searches. In addition to the impermanent nature of their jobs, the participants had faced various difficulties in their first employment experiences. The unskilled tasks to which they had been assigned quickly became repetitive and boring. Several had attempted to go back to school, but had rarely succeeded due to a lack of money or low levels of motivation. Overall, the young fathers had occupied a series of menial jobs that they would abruptly quit if they found more promising employment or experienced conflict with a superior.

Co-parental histories

Most of the young fathers interviewed had met their partner during their adolescence. A high proportion of the young mothers came from disturbed backgrounds of significant emotional neglect and absent or abusive parents, while others were struggling with drug abuse, alcoholism, or mental health problems. For several of the fathers, the relationship had been their first love: "My first serious relationship was with her. Yeah, I was sixteen, she was fifteen. After I met her, I was always taking care of her." Some of the fathers said that, once they had gotten over the shock of learning about the pregnancy, they were happy about it, while others said they had remained disturbed by the situation. In all cases, the decision of whether or not to keep the child was left to the mother.

The majority of the participants described the pregnancy and the child's first year of life as an extremely tumultuous period in the couple's relationship. The reasons for conflict were many: lack of money, jealousy on the part of the partner, disagreements over the sharing of household chores, and problems related to substance abuse by one or the other partner. Almost half of the young fathers stated that, in hindsight, they had not been ready for so much change in such a short time: "I had skipped too many stages ... I felt like I'd reached adulthood a little bit too fast. [I had] too many responsibilities."

Conflicts in the relationship were mainly related to the couple's precarious financial situation when the baby was born. Although almost all the fathers had looked for a job when they learned of the pregnancy, and most had succeeded, the employment they found was unskilled and unstable.

The separation of the father from the child's mother, which had occurred in the majority of cases, was described as a period of intense emotional distress: "I thought about her all the time ... Every time I looked at a girl, I saw my ex-girlfriend. She was my first love, and it doesn't end just like that." Some fathers added that their sorrow was compounded by the hardship of losing daily contact with their children and the shattering of their dream of a united family. Some felt their ex-partner had used them financially. Following the couple's separation, some of the fathers had lost contact with their children for a time because they had fled the situation, relapsed into drug abuse, or been treated for depression. Other fathers had reorganized their lives following the separation so that they could remain close to their children. Despite the various problems during and after the relationship, ten of the seventeen fathers said they saw the mother of their children as a good mother and as a responsible and trustworthy person, adding that they maintained a good relationship with her.

Fathering

Despite their lack of parental models, the couple's separation, and their poverty, fourteen of the seventeen young fathers maintained regular contact with their children, seeing them every day, every weekend, or every other weekend. Their statements revealed their desire to change the course of their lives. Many wanted to avoid reproducing their own childhood experiences with their children, implying that they wanted to be present, available, and affectionate, rather than strict or violent. All of the fathers said they had to "invent" their own fatherhood roles. The children were an important part of these fathers' lives, and they spoke of them with feeling: "He's my own flesh and blood ... my son belongs to me. I won't let anyone hurt my child ... he's mine, mine and [his mother's]." The fathers were proud of their children and admired them. All reported varying degrees of concrete commitment to their children: walking them in the stroller, taking them to the daycare centre, talking and playing with them, and organizing outings with them. They thought about their children when they were not with them, and worried about their health and future.

Almost all the fathers qualified the arrival of the child as a significant event that had motivated them to take control of their lives and assume their responsibilities towards their families and themselves. Having a baby had made them much more aware of the importance of being financially responsible. Their role as breadwinner was uppermost in their minds; the arrival of the child had motivated them to try to break out of the cycle of perpetual underemployment and job instability. They wanted to be able to buy clothing, shoes, and gifts for the child.

The young fathers also saw having a child as an incentive to realize themselves as individuals. They said it had made them decide to put a definite end to their "wild youth," by which they meant going out to bars, engaging in sexual promiscuity, wasting money, incurring debts, and taking drugs. "It takes a lot to look at yourself and want to change things, to improve yourself, because you know that the effects will be seen in your children. You'll benefit from improving your life, and you won't be the only one. Your children will benefit from it, too."

Naturally, not all of the seventeen fathers engaged in fatherhood with the same intensity (see Chapter 2 for a presentation of the father involvement continuum created in the framework of this study). Approximately half of those who were still in contact with their children showed their involvement in ways that affected not only the children, but also themselves. They were involved in child care, in an affectionate relationship with their children, and in child support payments, but beyond these dimensions, they had a deep personal commitment to fathering. It also appeared that they were more centred on the children and less on themselves; they were re-examining their ways of interacting with their children, and they showed empathy when they spoke about the children and the children's mother. In contrast, the other half of fathers who were in contact with their children did not show an equally intense investment in all the dimensions of fatherhood. They regretted the loss of the freedom of their adolescence, and tended to emphasize the sacrifices and self-denial associated with fatherhood.

Subsequent analysis of specific characteristics of the most involved fathers revealed that they were more likely than the other fathers in the study still to be in a romantic relationship with the mother of their children, to have had the child later in the relationship, and, when they were no longer in a relationship with the mother, to be on good terms with her (for details, see Ouellet et al., 2006).

On the whole, the seventeen fathers revealed complex and unstable life histories, with characteristics corresponding to those found in the literature on fathers in contexts of vulnerability. The overwhelming majority had not spent their childhood in an intact two-parent family, and their adolescence had been marked by conflict, membership in street gangs, and substance abuse. Their meeting of the mother of their children had taken place within this same context of instability, and the baby had arrived early in the relationship. Our study also revealed, however, that, even in these troubling circumstances, certain stable sources of support for the fathers emerged, quite often from their biological mother, occasionally from their biological father, and in some cases from the mother of the children. The presence of these people appeared to confer a certain stability and continuity to the father-child relationship. Support from the practitioners at the three socio-professional organizations and the framework these organizations provided also played a part in stabilizing the relationship, according to the fathers in the study sample.

Actions to Support Father Involvement in the Socio-professional Integration Organizations

To launch the activities to promote father involvement by the participating socio-professional integration organizations during the research study, the researchers and the partners at the organizations drew up yearly action plans based on the ecological approach and the health-promotion model. In each organization, intervention targeting the trainee fathers, their families, the psycho-social services, and the global environment was carried out in accordance with three principal strategies of the health-promotion domain that aim to strengthen individual potential, influence attitudes, and reorganize life environments. These health-promotion strategies were adapted to the project's more specific aims in the ways described below.

The *strategy to strengthen individual potential* comprised a set of activities that aimed to increase the skills of the young fathers and the significant people around them (partners, friends, relatives, services providers) so that they would acquire a greater sense of competence as individuals and as fathers, leading them to play a more active role with their children. The *strategy of influence* took the form of awareness-raising activities. These ranged from information dissemination to more structured persuasion techniques that aimed to develop new attitudes and increase knowledge among individuals, groups, decision-makers, and communities regarding the father's role and support for father involvement. Finally, the *strategy to reorganize the environment* aimed to bring about modifications in the life environments of the young fathers and their families (for example, public services, community organizations, daycare centres, schools, organized recreational activities, the workplace) so that these facilities could provide resources and activities better suited to their needs. This last strategy also aimed to bring young fathers together within their communities to define their own objectives and choose their own means of action.

The three annual action plans drawn up by the socio-professional integration organizations were supported by a two-member intervention team hired specifically for the program's implementation. The team consisted of a coordinator, whose principal tasks were to strengthen the links between the partners in the project, oversee its implementation, and develop specific tools such as information brochures on fatherhood, and a facilitator who conducted workshops upon the request of the organizations and provided individual follow-up for fathers who desired it. The action plans were articulated upon the health-promotion strategies mentioned above, and took account of the needs identified in the focus groups and interviews.

To strengthen their *individual potential*, the fathers were offered personal follow-up, either by the organization's practitioners or by the project facilitator. Intervention activities included non-directed discussion groups, theme-based discussion groups, and support groups. In the non-directed discussion groups, the fathers among new cohorts of trainees met to talk freely with one another about parenting and their relationships with their children. This allowed the practitioners to identify the fathers' needs, to be able to offer them customized support. In the theme-based discussion groups, specific topics for discussion were introduced, such as the conjugal relationship, the relationship with the biological father, and the impact of a parent's absence on a child. The support groups were aimed at fathers who were experiencing particular difficulties, and these provided a framework for targeted action and personalized follow-up. Approximately two hundred trainees benefited from one or another of these activities during the three years that the project was implemented.

Each of the three organizations held awareness-raising activities, supported by the intervention team, as a means of putting the *strategy of influence* into effect. For example, an administrator invited to give a lecture about his organization would add comments on his own fathering experience. The organizations also suggested that the fathers in the programs view a documentary film on father involvement made by young fathers who had trained in another socio-professional integration organization, and talk with the filmmakers about their experience.[1] Finally, four information leaflets addressed to young fathers living in contexts of vulnerability were produced and distributed. The content of the leaflets encompassed the mission of and the services offered in the Profession: Fatherhood project; father involvement; co-parenting; and family mediation.

Regarding the strategy to *reorganize the environment*, all three organizations modified their premises by mounting posters promoting father involvement. One organization took the initiative of asking all the trainees who were fathers to pin up photographs of their children. This increased the fathers' self-esteem and made them aware of the presence of other fathers in the program. Finally, the intervention team established various links with community resources in the surrounding neighbourhoods to facilitate referrals and support for young fathers where they lived.

Fathers' Perceptions of Their Experience with the Fatherhood Training Program and the Support Provided

Within the context of the qualitative research study, the researchers compiled data related to the young fathers' experience with the fatherhood training program and their views on the support received during the Profession: Fatherhood project.

The fathers mentioned various motives for participating in the training program. Some said they wanted to acquire a skill to obtain stable employment, to be paid a salary to enable them to return to school, to receive a training certificate, or to "accomplish something" in their lives. For others, the motive was more closely related to parenting: they felt the training would allow them to assume more control over their lives, to re-establish the relationship with the children's mother, or to obtain custody of their children. A few mentioned the advantage of receiving a salary to provide for their family, together with the opportunity to offer their children the image of a father who "gets up every morning to go to work."

The majority of the young fathers emphasized that their time at the socio-professional organization had been a positive experience from which they had emerged stronger and better equipped. They reported that it had made them feel valued, appreciated, and understood. They described practitioners, who were available to them throughout the training program – even through personal crises – as significant persons who played an important role in their lives or in whom they could feel trust, in some cases for the first time in their lives. For several young fathers, the organization had become a place towards which they felt a real sense of belonging.

Most of the participants felt that the counsellors had been sensitive to their concerns, advised them, and showed interest in their lives and their progress. They had been intent on providing the young fathers with individual follow-up centring on the fathers' life projects and abilities. Being the object of attention was an unfamiliar experience for some of the fathers, who said it was a surprise to realize that someone was concerned about them and believed in their potential, sometimes more than they did themselves: "They opened my eyes and made me see that I could achieve what I wanted." The fathers' motivation and self-confidence had increased accordingly. They said they appreciated being given a chance to succeed, as well as being supported by professionals who stressed the importance of going through with their commitments and encouraging them to persevere to the end.

The support provided by the three organizations also had extended to the fathers' co-parental relations. Several fathers reported receiving support in their relationships with their partners or ex-partners. The counsellors helped several fathers re-establish communication with the mothers of their children in non-conflictual ways; in certain cases, mediation sessions for the father and mother were arranged.

The fathers felt that the counsellors had been close to their concerns as fathers, and that they had provided sympathetic and steady support with respect to the fathers' desire to be fully involved with their children. This was undoubtedly one of the ricochet effects of the awareness-raising work done with the managers and practitioners at the organizations regarding the importance of father involvement, and was a direct consequence of their appropriation of the PAR process. Indeed, at the most difficult moments, the counsellors had encouraged the fathers not to give up and to stay in contact with their children, emphasizing the children's need for their fathers. They had also strengthened the fathers' ability to fulfil their role: "They helped me because my self-esteem went back up, so my relationship with my daughter automatically improved because I wasn't so afraid to take care of her." Some of the fathers made a direct association between their training program and an increase in their involvement with their children: "Having a job made me more responsible, so it came together, from the parenting point of view, with becoming responsible towards my daughter." The support for fathering also took practical forms, such as finding a babysitter for the child, encouraging the father's participation at the child's school, and giving information on the child's development. "She [the counsellor] told me: If your child is crying, it's because he needs you."

To summarize, the fathers who had completed their program felt more responsible and confident, and said they had acquired the assurance that they could finish something they started. They also said the support they had received was a significant factor in their decision to maintain contact with their children, despite their difficult circumstances.

A Team Assessment

At the end of the second year, the research team evaluated the progress of the Profession: Fatherhood PAR. The project coordinator interviewed three partners from the socio-professional organizations and two members of the research team. The questions concerned their understanding of the PAR project, their motivation to take part in it, the obstacles to overcome, and the possibilities it opened up. For the partners in the organizations, the project brought out the importance of highlighting the trainees' paternal status: "The discussion groups opened up the way. One trainee hadn't said he was a father and this was an opportunity for him to say it." For the researchers the particular challenge of the project lay in undertaking joint action with organizations in an unfamiliar socio-economic sector and with which they were not accustomed to collaborating. The research process, however, confirmed the project's relevance in the eyes of the organizations' administrators, one of whom said: "These are young fathers who don't have an easy life, so they need support." Partners and researchers acknowledged that staff turnover had been an obstacle to the project's smooth unfolding. During the five years of the project, a number of services providers left the organizations and were replaced with new ones, which made further awareness-raising efforts necessary. The partners agreed on the importance, in this type of project, of having the necessary human resources to sustain the development and implementation of support activities adapted to the milieu. They recognized that the activities carried out within the PAR process were beneficial for the trainees and helped fulfil the organizations' mandates: "The interviews by the research team were also a good thing for the young people; they would tell me about them the day after." Finally, it is the researchers' hope that the steering committee meetings constituted a springboard towards a collective movement of support for young fathers in contexts of vulnerability.

Conclusion

The participants in the study all presented risk factors associated with a context of vulnerability: they had become fathers early in their adult life, they had low educational attainment levels, did not hold stable jobs, and were living in poverty. The stressful situation in which these young fathers were trying to provide for their families, but lacked the means to do so, made the parenting task that much more difficult. With a similar cohort of fathers, Miller (2011) describes this transition as an "emotional rollercoaster." Nonetheless it is clear from the narratives of some of the young fathers that the arrival of a child was a watershed event in their lives that made them aspire to become productive citizens and responsible parents. The research thus confirmed that fatherhood in contexts of vulnerability need not only be a period strewn with obstacles; it can also be a confidence-building, life-improving experience for young fathers who attribute great importance to their children (Bryan, 2013; Miller, 2011; Nelson, 2004). In the same way, Pratt et al. (2012) indicate that fatherhood can help young men find a purpose in life, settle down, and repair hurt by being more present for their children than their own father was for them.

Since young fathers with their difficult histories and living conditions generally make very little or no use of public health and social services, their time at the integration organization was a crucial opportunity for several reasons. The continuity provided by a six-month training program and the support provided by individualized follow-up engendered the development of relations of trust that these young people so often had lacked in the context of their previous jobs and in their personal lives. The active participation of the organizations in the research process and father involvement support activities also led to a greater openness towards the young men in their role as fathers and to ongoing support specifically related to this role.

This first experience of a father involvement initiative in socio-professional organizations showed that personalized, stable support for young fathers as they are trained in a professional skill holds unequivocal benefits for them, and likely for their children and the children's mothers as well. The results convinced us that the strengthening of parenting skills and fathers' confidence in their own capacities not only could prevent them from giving up on maintaining contact with their children, but even encourage them to increase their involvement with them.

The association of researchers and partners in the joint aim of supporting social inclusion and father involvement among vulnerable young fathers was evaluated positively. The partners not only wanted to help achieve the research objectives; they also proposed solutions and developed intervention tools that facilitated anchoring the project in the organizations. At the heart of this approach lay the mechanisms of the focus and discussion groups, the steering committees, ongoing negotiation, and the periodic dissemination of the research results, all of which served as references for raising awareness among the services providers and supported them in their work. However, carrying out this type of PAR project in its full scope, which implies a process lasting between three and five years, might not always be possible in the current context. Nevertheless these kinds of interventions for disadvantaged fathers are important, since there are fewer program initiatives for fathers in more marginal situations (such as Indigenous, immigrant, and gay fathers) (Hodgins, 2011; Walters, 2011).

The Profession: Fatherhood project continues, thanks to an additional research grant that has allowed us to probe deeper into some of the findings that have emerged to date, particularly in the area of co-parental relations (see Deslauriers & Devault, 2012; Devault, 2014;

Devault, Denis, Lacharité & de Montigny, 2012; Devault & Deslauriers, 2010). The project was fully endorsed by the practitioners and administrators of the three socio-professional organizations in steering committee meetings; the quality of their collaboration has shown that they believe in its benefits. It remains to be seen whether our efforts will lead to the generalization of this intervention model in similar community-based programs or services, and will influence public health programs and raise awareness regarding the rocky paths of youths who become fathers soon after beginning a relationship, in adolescence or just after adolescence, and who are at a high risk of becoming "dropout fathers." We hope that other socio-professional organizations will adopt the Profession Fatherhood model and give young fathers living in contexts of vulnerability more widespread access to this form of support. If so, a dent, however small, will have been made in the perpetuation of exclusion. Even more important, the health and well-being of the children and their parents will be improved.

Profession: Fatherhood II

The study of young fathers' life stories undertaken in the Profession: Fatherhood project shows that, despite personal histories marked by instability and rupture, a significant proportion of young men who become fathers experience this event as a rude awakening that jolts them into taking themselves in hand and eventually becoming more stable on the emotional and financial levels – that is, to be motivated to assume their responsibilities towards their families and themselves (Devault et al., 2005, 2008). Our findings show, however, that not all young fathers are involved with their children to the same degree. This has led us to draw up a new typology of father involvement: Profession: Fatherhood II. The more general aims of this continuation of our first study are to describe the characteristics of the experience of fatherhood among young men in a situation of socio-economic exclusion and to determine which dimensions of their life stories have the greatest influence on their fathering behaviour. The study seeks to deepen our understanding of the mechanisms underlying co-parenting, as this is the most important variable influencing young fathers' relations with their children. We also aim to validate the father involvement continuum, the classification developed by Prospère, which is based on the quality and degree of fathers' involvement with their children.

As in the first research study, the participants in the Profession: Fatherhood II project are registered in training programs offered by the same three socio-professional organizations with which we partnered in the first project. As this study aims to understand co-parenting relations better, we will interview thirty fathers and fifteen mothers, whether or not they still form a couple. The fathers will be between fifteen and twenty-five years of age, and have at least one child, with whom they might or might not have regular contact. Data on the fathers will be collected in a single interview focusing on the fatherhood experience. Information from the narratives will be solicited in such a way as to clearly identify the individual, employment, and co-parenting histories of the fathers. The interviews with the mothers will deal essentially with co-parenting relations. The systematic in-depth analysis of these interviews will serve to inform interventions aimed at supporting father involvement through socio-professional organizations that are frequented by young people living in situations of economic and social vulnerability.

NOTE

1 *Mâle aimé* (Male poorly loved) (2005), a documentary film produced by the socio-professional organization La Réplique, looks at the father's role and paternal abandonment.

REFERENCES

Allard, F., & Binet, L. (2002). *Comment des pères en situation de pauvreté s'engagent-ils envers leur jeune enfant? Étude exploratoire qualitative.* Quebec City, QC: Régie régionale de la santé et des services sociaux de Québec.

Allen, S., Daly, K., & Ball, J. (2012). Fathers make a difference in their children's lives: A review of the research evidence. In J. Ball & K. Daly (Eds.), *Father involvement in Canada: Diversity, renewal, and transformation* (pp. 50–88). Vancouver, BC: UBC Press.

Anda, R. F., et al. (2001). Abused boys, battered mothers, and male involvement in teen pregnancy. *Pediatrics, 107*(2), e19–e36. http://dx.doi.org/10.1542/peds.107.2.e19

Anderson, E. A., Kohler, J. K., & Letiecq, B. L. (2002). Low-income fathers and "responsible fatherhood" programs: A qualitative investigation of participants' experiences. *Family Relations, 51*(2), 148–155. http://dx.doi.org/10.1111/j.1741-3729.2002.00148.x

Bryan, D. M. (2013). To parent or provide? The effect of the provider role on low-income men's decisions about fatherhood and paternal engagement. *Fathering, 11*(1), 71–89. http://dx.doi.org/10.3149/fth.1101.71

Cabrera, N. J., Tamis-LeMonda, C. S., Bradley, R. H., Hofferth, S., & Lamb, M. E. (2000). Fatherhood in the twenty-first century. *Child Development, 71*(1), 127–136. http://dx.doi.org/10.1111/1467-8624.00126

Carlson, M. J., & McLanahan, S. S. (2002). Fragile families, father involvement, and public policy. In C. S. Tamis-LeMonda & N. Cabrera (Eds.), *Handbook of father involvement: Multidisciplinary perspectives* (pp. 461–488). Mahwah, NJ: Erlbaum.

Cummings, E. M., Goeke-Morey, M. C., & Raymond, J. (2004). Fathers in family context: Effects of marital quality and marital conflict. In M. E. Lamb (Ed.), *The role of the father in child development* (pp. 196–221). Hoboken, NJ: John Wiley.

Deslauriers J. M., & Devault, A. (2012). Rethinking services for young fathers. *Fathering, 10*(1), 66–90.

Devault, A. (2014). Commentary on the complicated worlds of adolescent fathers: Implications for clinical practice, public policy, and research. *Psychology of Men and Masculinity, 15*(3), 275–277.

Devault, A., Ouellet, F., Milcent, M.P., Laurin, I., Lacharité, C., & Favreau, L. (2005). Les caractéristiques des trajectoires de vie comme facteurs sous-jacents à l'engagement paternel: le cas des jeunes ayant complété le programme d'une entreprise d'insertion. Research report presented to the Fonds québécois de la recherche sur la société et la culture.

Devault, A., Milcent, M.P., Ouellet, F., Laurin, I., Jauron, M., & Lacharité, C. (2008). Life stories of young fathers in contexts of vulnerability. *Fathering, 6*(3), 226–248. http://dx.doi.org/10.3149/fth.0603.226

Devault, A., Denis, L., Lacharité, C. & de Montigny, F. (2012). Le rôle des femmes dans la vie des jeunes pères vivant en contexte de vulnérabilité. *Nouvelles pratiques sociales, 24*(2), 30–47.

Devault, A. & Deslauriers, J. M. (2010). Work and social integration of young men who become fathers. *International Journal of Adolescence and Youth, 16*(1), 21–46.

Devault, A., & Gratton, S. (2003). Les pères en situation de perte d'emploi: l'importance de les soutenir de manière adaptée à leurs besoins. *Pratiques psychologiques, 2*, 79–88.

Doucet, A. (2013). Gender roles and fathering. In N. J. Cabrera & C. S. Tamis-LeMonda (Eds.), *Handbook of father involvement: Multidisciplinary perspectives* (2nd ed., pp. 297–319). New York, NY: Routledge.

Eggebeen, D. J., Knoester, C., & McDaniel, B. (2013). The implications of fatherhood for men. In N. J. Cabrera & C. S. Tamis-LeMonda (Eds.), *Handbook of father involvement: Multidisciplinary perspectives* (2nd ed., pp. 338–358). New York, NY: Routledge.

Erikson, E. H. (1963). *Childhood and society.* New York, NY: Norton.

Fagan, J., Barnett, M., Bernd, E., & Whiteman, V. (2003). Prenatal involvement of adolescent unmarried fathers. *Fathering, 1*(3), 283–301. http://dx.doi.org/10.3149/fth.0103.283

Furstenberg, F. F., & Weiss, C. C. (2000). Intergenerational transmission of fathering roles in at risk families. *Marriage & Family Review, 29*(2–3), 181–201. http://dx.doi.org/10.1300/J002v29n02_11

Harris, K. M., & Marmer, J. K. (1996). Poverty, paternal involvement, and adolescent well-being. *Journal of Family Issues, 17*(5), 614–640. http://dx.doi.org/10.1177/019251396017005003

Hijjawi, G. R. (2005). *Father involvement in diverse families at one-year follow-up* (unpublished doctoral dissertation). University of Virginia, Charlottesville.

Hodgins, B. D. (2011). Father involvement initiatives: Social inclusion or the (re)construction of hegemonic masculinity? In A. Pence & J. White (Eds.), *Critical perspectives in child and youth care* (pp. 95–117). Vancouver. BC: UBC Press.

Hofferth, S. L., Pleck, J. H., Goldscheider, F., Curtin, S., & Hrapczynski, K. (2013). Family structure and men's motivation for parenthood in the United States. In N. J. Cabrera & C. S. Tamis-LeMonda (Eds.), *Handbook of father involvement: Multidisciplinary perspectives* (2nd ed., pp. 57–80). New York, NY: Routledge.

Lacharité, C. (2001). Entrevue sur l'expérience paternelle. (unpublished manuscript).

Lamb, M. E. (1997). Fathers and child development: An introductory overview and guide. In M. E. Lamb (Ed.), *The role of father in child development* (3rd ed., pp. 1–19). New York, NY: John Wiley.

Levine, J., & Pitt, E. W. (1995). *New expectations: Community strategies for responsible fatherhood.* New York, NY: Families and Work Institute.

Marsiglio, W. (2000). *Understanding the context and consequences of father involvement.* Involving Fathers: Proceedings of the First National Symposium on the Place and the Role of Fathers, Montreal, 11–16 November.

Mayer, R., & Deslauriers, J. P. (2000). Quelques éléments d'analyse qualitative: l'analyse de contenu, l'analyse ancrée, l'induction analytique et le récit de vie. In R. Mayer, F. Ouellet, M. C. Saint-Jacques, & D. Turcotte (Eds.),

Méthodes de recherche en intervention sociale (pp. 159–188). Montreal, QC: Gaëtan Morin.

Miles, B. M., & Huberman, A. M. (1994). *An expanded sourcebook: Qualitative data analysis*. Thousand Oaks, CA: Sage.

Miller, T. (2011). *Making sense of fatherhood: Gender, caring and work*. Cambridge, UK: Cambridge University Press. http://dx.doi.org/10.1017/CBO9780511778186

Mosley, J., & Thomson, E. (1995). Fathering behavior and child outcomes: The role of race and poverty. In W. Marsiglio (Ed.), *Fatherhood: Contemporary theory, research, and social policy* (pp. 148–165). Thousand Oaks, CA: Sage. http://dx.doi.org/10.4135/9781483327242.n8

Nelson, T. J. (2004). Low-income fathers. *Annual Review of Sociology*, 30(1), 427–451. http://dx.doi.org/10.1146/annurev.soc.29.010202.095947

Ouellet, F., & Goulet, C. (1998). *Pôpa: analyse d'entrevues de pères vivant dans des situations d'extrême pauvreté* (original document). Direction de la santé publique de Montréal-Centre, Montreal (unpublished manuscript).

Ouellet, F., Milcent, M.-P., and Devault, A. (2006). Jeunes pères vulnérables: trajectoires de vie et paternité. *Nouvelles pratiques sociales*, 18(2), 156–171.

Palkovitz, R., Fagan, J., & Hull, J. (2013). Coparenting and children's well-being. In N. J. Cabrera & C. S. Tamis-LeMonda (Eds.), *Handbook of father involvement: Multidisciplinary perspectives* (2nd ed., pp. 202–220). New York, NY: Routledge.

Pratt, M. W., Lawford, H. L., & Allen, J. W. (2012). Young fatherhood, generativity, and men's development: Travelling a two-way street to maturity. In J. Ball & K. Daly (Eds.), *Father involvement in Canada: Diversity, renewal, and transformation* (pp. 107–125). Vancouver, BC: UBC Press.

Quéniart, A. (2002). La paternité sous observation: des changements, des résistances mais aussi des incertitudes. In F. Descarries & C. Corbeil (Eds.), *Espaces et temps de la maternité* (pp. 133–143). Montreal, QC: Éditions du remue-ménage.

Rhoden, J. L., & Robinson, B. E. (1997). Teen dads, a generative fathering perspective versus the deficit myth. In A. J. Hawkins & D. C. Dollahite (Eds.), *Generative fathering: Beyond deficit perspectives* (pp. 105–117). Thousand Oaks, CA: Sage.

Roy, K. M. (2004). You can't eat love: Constructing provider role expectations for low-income and working-class fathers. *Fathering*, 2(3), 253–276. http://dx.doi.org/10.3149/fth.0203.253

Simons, R .L., Whitbeck, L. B., Conger, R. D., & Melby, J. N. (1990). Husband and wife differences in determinants of parenting: A social learning and exchange model of parental behavior. *Journal of Marriage and the Family, 52*(2), 375–392. http://dx.doi.org/10.2307/353033

Tamis-LeMonda, C. S., & Cabrera, N. (1999). Perspectives on father involvement: Research and policy. *Society for Research in Child Development, 13*(2), 1–32.

Townsend, N. (2002). *The package deal: Marriage, work and fatherhood in men's lives*. Philadelphia, PA: Temple University Press.

Walters, J. (2011). *Working with fathers: From knowledge to therapeutic practice*. London, UK: Palgrave Macmillan.

7 Fathers behind Bars: A Participatory Action Research Project to Support Father Involvement following Incarceration

DIANE DUBEAU, MARTINE BARRETTE,
AND DENIS LAFORTUNE

Introduction

Over the past three decades, important advances have been made in our understanding of fathers' involvement with their children, its positive effects on child development, and effective strategies for encouraging and maintaining this involvement. Our knowledge is challenged, however, when it come to marginalized fathers who act in ways incompatible with good parenting, such as engaging in substance abuse and antisocial behaviour, including violence (Stover & Morgos, 2013). With this in mind, how can practitioners encourage parental involvement by fathers who are viewed as psycho-socially maladjusted?

This chapter examines a particular context of marginality: fathers who have been incarcerated. Many practitioners working with youth find it difficult to acknowledge the benefits of father involvement when the fathers have been convicted of a crime and are serving, or have recently served, a prison sentence. Some services professionals even adopt the uncompromising position that it is better for the children not to have any contact at all with their father under these circumstances. However, even though an imprisoned father is not be accessible to his children on a daily basis, he continues to exercise an influence on them in various ways and to varying degrees (Walters, 2011). Considering this, and the fact that incarceration is a shocking event that unavoidably affects everyone in the family, it is surprising how so few services in Quebec, and in Canada overall, have a mandate to support families whose father has been sent to prison. To take better account of this reality and to propose appropriate intervention avenues, a participatory action research (PAR) project called *Grandir sainement avec un père détenu* (Fathers behind Bars) was created in 2001.[1]

Without claiming to address all the issues that arise for all family members in the context of a father's incarceration, this chapter aims to shed light on the subject by looking at relevant studies and presenting the results of Fathers behind Bars. First, we discuss the findings extracted from a review of the literature, which justify investing in support structures for families facing the stressful situation of a father's incarceration. More specifically, we discuss aspects related to the extent and complexity of this phenomenon, its effects on family members, and the relevant services or programs available to these fathers and their families. In the second part of the chapter, we adopt a practical perspective, and describe the intervention and prevention components of the Fathers behind Bars project, which are now implemented in several halfway houses in Quebec.[2]

Why Promote Father Involvement among Incarcerated Fathers?

The question of father involvement when fathers are in prison or newly released from prison is a sensitive one. In either case, there are obvious gaps in father involvement on both the quantitative and qualitative levels due to the father's prolonged inaccessibility and his inappropriate behaviour. But we do know that fathers influence their children regardless of the degree of involvement. When it comes to this particular context, we therefore need to ask: why should we support and promote father involvement, and what is the most effective way to do it?

First, what does the scientific literature say about the consequences of a father's physical absence for his children? A number of studies have found that, in general, the perceptions of the father's role and competence with respect to his children are rarely compromised by his absence due to employment reasons or even death (Murray & Farrington, 2008). Similar results have been obtained in studies that look at children who experience divorce or parental separation: for the majority of such children, there is little effect, although some family members might have trouble adjusting to these transitions. According to Cyr and Caroben (2004), although most children whose parents separate or divorce do not experience any serious difficulties, a minority (20 to 30 per cent) is likely to present social, educational, or psychological problems.

What is the case, then, when the father is in prison? Those who doubt the benefits of the father's presence in the child's life under these circumstances not only cite the father's prolonged absence, but also underline the reasons for his absence and the ensuing repercussions on all the family members, questioning the incarcerated father's ability to assume his parental role and function adequately (Lafortune et al., 2004). The concerns most often raised by practitioners working with the families of incarcerated men concern the risk that children will identify with their father's antisocial behaviour, together with the risk of maladjustment problems in the children due to both the separation of the family and the circumstances of the father's imprisonment (Farrington & Welsh, 2007). However, although it might be true that children in this situation are more vulnerable to psychological, behavioural, and social problems, we should not conclude that the father's criminal behaviour inevitably compromises their security and development. Several variables – upon each of which a rigorous in-depth analysis should be performed – can either aggravate or attenuate the children's difficulties. Chief among these are the characteristics of the father (the extent of his involvement with his children before the incarceration), the characteristics of the children (their number, ages, and capacity for resilience), and the characteristics of the family (the quality of the parents' relationship before the incarceration, their economic situation), together with the nature of the father's criminal behaviour (whether it involved the victimization of a family member), and the length of the sentence (Lafortune et al., 2005; Murray, 2010).

Fathers are not automatically stripped of their parental rights due to their known criminal activities and prison terms. Although some jailed fathers do lose contact with their children and withdraw from their parental responsibilities, others wish to maintain their links with their children and fulfil their paternal role. Children, on the other hand, rarely question the parental link, and many want to maintain the relationship: As a son of an incarcerated father said, "When your father goes to prison, you don't see him as often. Sure, it's tough when you have to say your father's in jail. But he's my Dad! And it won't change anything [in] the way I feel about him [even though] he did that" (Barrette et al., 2002). However, even when the mutual desire to maintain the relationship exists, almost a third of incarcerated fathers have no contact with their children after their prison sentences begin (Hairston, 1989). Since many jailed fathers do not maintain the conjugal relationship with the mother of their children, father-child contacts are difficult to maintain. Arditti, Smock, and Parkman (2005), in interviews with fifty-one imprisoned fathers, demonstrated how these men were entirely dependent on the mothers for contact with their children. According to Hairston (1995), one-fifth of incarcerated fathers do not receive visits from their children due to the mother's opposition and the persistence of conjugal conflict. These studies show that father involvement for these particular fathers does not simply hinge on their own desire for contact with their children, but depends greatly on family dynamics and parental relations.

Father Incarceration in Canada and Quebec

Very few Canadian studies tell us how many fathers are in prison or how many children are affected by their father's incarceration. Yet approximately 31,600 people are jailed every year in federal and provincial detention facilities (Beattie, 2005). It should be mentioned that prison sentences of two years or more come under federal jurisdiction, while sentences of less than two years fall under provincial jurisdiction. In 2004, 12,034 men and 379 women were serving prison sentences of two years or more in federal institutions (Canada, 2005). We can assume that a good number of these individuals were fathers or mothers.

Hoping to quantify the phenomenon of father incarceration more accurately, we consulted the data bank of Correctional Service Canada (Canada, 2005). This source, however, provided almost no valid information on the families of most of the fathers incarcerated in federal penitentiaries.[3] Although a few details on families were available through inmate management records, most of these issued from clinical reports and did not allow us to obtain a comprehensive overview. This difficulty reflected the lack of attention paid to the family situations of federal offenders. We therefore recommend that parental status be routinely recorded for all prisoners included in the inmate management records at federal penitentiaries. We hope this addition will make it possible to obtain a more complete picture of the phenomenon in the future.

The data banks of Quebec's Centres jeunesse (Youth Centres) were also consulted to estimate the number of children referred to youth protection who were affected by the imprisonment of a parent. As these data banks do not include information on parental incarceration,[4] again it was difficult to arrive at a representative number. We were able to determine, however, that 13.4 per cent of these children had a father who was involved or suspected of being involved in criminal activity. The study by Pauzé et al. (2000), based on 850 youth protection files in Montreal, Quebec City, the Eastern Townships, and the North Shore region, revealed that between 12.1 and 32.1 per cent of the children had a parent who was known to engage in, or was suspected of engaging in, criminal activities. Therefore it is reasonable to conclude that children of parents involved in the corrections system constitute a sizable proportion of the children referred to youth protection services.

Although these statistics are useful in evaluating the extent of the phenomenon of father incarceration, they do not convey the complexity of the experience of the families of imprisoned men, which would allow us to identify and offer the services they need. The documentation gathered during the first year of the Fathers behind Bars project and from semi-structured interviews with various actors (nineteen fathers, six mothers, two children,[5] and seven practitioners) brought out the diversity of the needs of various family members at different stages of the judicial process (Barrette et al., 2002).

The Complexity of the Experience of the Incarcerated Father's Family

A father's incarceration upsets the equilibrium within the family system and has repercussions on all its members. In general, three principal transition periods in the judicial process affect the lives of the father's family to varying degrees:

1. the arrest, including preventive custody, release on bail, the trial, sentencing, and admission to prison;
2. the incarceration, including contacts with the family and penitentiary visits;
3. the release, including the father's stay in a halfway house.

The *arrest* is usually the first transition period in the incarceration process that causes upheaval within the family. Even though other family members, particularly the children, rarely witness the father's arrest by the police, it is nonetheless a troubling, even traumatic, event for the whole family. Whether the arrest is an unexpected development or the logical outcome of the father's known criminal activities, the procedures surrounding it cause sorrow, anger, disappointment, shame, guilt, and anxiety in family members. The resulting fragility of the family's equilibrium is often exacerbated by other difficulties, such as media exposure, stigmatization, lack of information, lengthy legal procedures, and financial problems. Following the shock of the arrest, the legal process often makes families feel powerless due to their lack of knowledge and access to information. The process also might stretch over a long period, incurring heavy costs and leading to further stress. All of this adds a heavy weight to the situation, which hinders the family reorganization process. Moreover, if the quality of family relations before the incarceration was already poor due to problems between the father and mother, difficulties following the imprisonment might lead to a definite breakup.

The separation resulting from the *incarceration* disrupts family organization and might have serious repercussions on family members at the personal level (fear of a permanent loss of contact, depression and feelings of powerlessness, guilt, loneliness, sadness, and longing for the father), the economic level (a drop in the family income, difficulty in paying for rent, food, and other basics), and the social level (stigma). According to Lanier (1995), incarceration affects the father's parental role in several ways: legally (through difficulty in maintaining his parental rights), economically (through increased economic dependency), socially (through confinement, the unwelcoming atmosphere of the prison milieu), psychologically (through a lowering of self-esteem, sadness, anxiety), and relationally (through separation due to the loss of freedom). Incarcerated fathers whose family relations were already precarious or who were given lengthy prison terms often see these relations deteriorate and eventually break down. Given that many incarcerated fathers do not maintain conjugal or other types of close relationships with the mothers of their children, father-child contact is often put in jeopardy. For fathers who are involved with their children and want to continue assuming their parental responsibilities, the separation caused by the imprisonment is one of the heaviest burdens to bear (Hairston, 1995). Many of these fathers often feel guilty for having disrupted their family's lives and for no longer being available to fulfil their family and parental roles. Some feel uncertainty towards their families, fearing that the bond between them will not withstand the enforced separation.

Beyond the father's interest in maintaining his relationship with his partner and/or children, several studies, including Lanier (1995), show that the deterioration of the father-child relationship can have a negative effect on the offender's rehabilitation process in the correctional setting, and also can reduce the chances of his success in reintegrating into the community. In contrast, good relationships and support from the family can be important positive factors in the prisoner's successful re-entry into society (Withers, 2001b). Indeed, men who maintained a positive family relationship during their prison term and who made efforts to fulfil their parental responsibilities until the end of their sentence had lower recidivism rates than those who did not (Wilczak & Markstrom, 1999).

When the family triad is still intact, the father's imprisonment can be a devastating experience for the children's mother. Many mothers experience psychological and emotional problems, such as feelings of abandonment, since they are frequently subjected to isolation, disapproval, or stigmatization by those around them. They also face a lack of financial resources, housing problems, and the multiple obligations of raising their children alone. These difficulties have a negative effect on the mother-child relationship and on the children's accessibility to the mother precisely at a time when they need increased attention and support. The poverty that often results from the mother's single parenthood following separation or incarceration has been recognized as a significant risk factor for children (Saint-Jacques, Drapeau, & Cloutier, 2001). This factor might increase the psychological distress of the parent left to care for the children, and impair his or her capacity to exercise the parental role, leading to the diminished quality of family functioning, and, consequently, to the worsening of the children's situation.

In terms of more direct effects, the father's incarceration is a stressful event for children, who often experience the separation from their imprisoned father as a situation of insecurity, loss, and even abandonment. In these difficult moments, many children also suffer due to a lack of information regarding the reason for the father's absence. The mother then must take on the sensitive task of explaining the situation to the child, but to lessen the emotional shock to their children and to protect them from the shame associated with their father's jail sentence, mothers might withhold the truth. This well-meaning silence can do more harm than good, as it results in confusion and anxiety in the child (Le Camus, 2002; Withers, 2001a). Moreover, for some children, the father's imprisonment might lead to psychological, behavioural, and social problems, such as anxiety, withdrawal, low self-esteem, difficulty in school, and lack of discipline, perhaps leading to antisocial behaviour, joining gangs, and becoming involved in criminal activities (Murray, Farrington, & Sekol, 2012; Simmons, 2000). According to Adalist-Estrin (1994), children whose parents are or have been incarcerated are five to six times more likely than their peers to adopt criminal behaviour and be incarcerated.

Although it might be true that the incarceration of a parent is an important risk factor (Le Camus, 2002), not all children of fathers serving prison terms develop adaptation problems, despite their vulnerability. What makes some children react better than others to this ordeal? Several factors raise the risk of problems, while others exercise a buffering effect on negative life events and, therefore, play an important role in preventing adaptation problems in the children. Foremost among resiliency factors are the child's individual characteristics. Parke and Clarke-Stewart (2002) show that children with an easy temperament, high self-esteem, self-reliance, and good intellectual abilities cope better with difficult life situations. Also, children's coping abilities are stronger when they receive social support. Positive support, particularly from the mother, can help the child face the family, social, and economic problems that arise when the father is incarcerated. The same authors report that social support from the external environment (peers, the school milieu, and so on) also constitutes a significant resiliency factor in children whose fathers are imprisoned.

On the other hand, a good relationship and regular contact between the father and the child are considered key elements in the child's ability to adjust to the father's prison sentence (Parke & Clarke-Stewart, 2002). Unfortunately, dynamic problems (the prohibition of father-child contact due to the deterioration of the mother's relationship with the father, or the mother's fears regarding the child's reaction to prison visits) and static problems (inconvenient visiting hours at the prison, the cold atmosphere, the uncomfortable, uncongenial physical setting of the visits, the cost of phone calls and transportation) can harm the father-child relationship and diminish contact between them during the prison term.

When family members do manage to maintain contact with the jailed father, and if their relationship survives the incarceration period, they must cope with another important adjustment period: the father's *release* into the community and his reintegration into the family. After a prison term of months or even years, family members face a new situation that often requires a redefinition of each person's position and role within the family. Some mothers adapt to reunification with the father by reorganizing the life habits they established during the prison term, and by re-evaluating the conjugal relationship. They might fear losing the independence and decision-making power they acquired while on their own as sole head of the family, and enter into conflict with the father regarding child-rearing practices. Children, for their part, might experience feelings of insecurity stemming from the fear of a new separation from their father. Some children find it difficult to understand

and accept the many rules associated with their father's residence in a halfway house, such as the restricted schedule, including curfew. For fathers, release from prison brings a number of challenges: the search for employment, the development of a peer network, participation in support programs for newly released detainees, and, above all, the re-establishment of the relationship with their family, including their children. The reunification process does not always run smoothly, and fathers must make certain adjustments. Some fathers we interviewed said they felt like strangers to their own family after their release. They said they had been unaware of the changes in their children during the prison term, and it was only upon their release that they realized how little information they had received about their development (Barrette et al., 2002).

Our review of the literature and the findings that emerged from our interviews with the fathers brought out the significance of the different stages of the judicial process and the cumulative repercussions of the process on family members. This led us to examine the programs and services available to families during the different transitional stages. The following section briefly presents these support services.

Social Services for Inmates and Their Families

The scientific and the intervention communities increasingly recognize the correlation between parent criminality and the high risk of maladjustment in children, which they qualify as the intergenerational transmission of criminality (Gregory, 2004; Smith & Farrington, 2004). Yet Canadian practitioners report a lack of relevant information when they are called upon to intervene between incarcerated fathers and their families, as well as the quasi-absence of services for them. In the United States, by way of contrast, the situation of incarcerated fathers and their families has been given more attention by governmental and other agencies, and a number of programs have been established. Generally speaking, these programs aim to improve incarcerated fathers' understanding of parental roles and child development (*knowledge*), their parenting skills (*know-how*), and their affective relationships with their children (*knowing-how-to-be*). The activities given priority in these programs are parent education classes, support groups, family visit units, transportation and lodging assistance, preparation for active life, support at the time of release, and community extension services.

Several studies of the effectiveness of these programs show that they do benefit inmates and their families. Wilczak and Markstrom (1999) report that fathers who participated in this type of program increased their knowledge of the parental role. Other studies show how these programs ease newly released inmates' reintegration into their family and community, and reduce recidivism rates (see Carlson & Cervera, 1991).

In Quebec, however, there is a lack of services and programs addressing the needs of this specific clientele. Indeed, current correctional policies show a low awareness of the fact that many prisoners have children. The services we surveyed were limited to chaplaincy services within the penitentiaries and those offered by such community-based organizations as the branches of the Canadian Families and Correction Network, *Relais famille* (Family Relay), *Continuité famille auprès des détenues* (Family Continuity with the Prisoner), the Salvation Army, and the Elizabeth Fry Society. Yet many incarcerated fathers say they want to know more about their children's development and about how to be a good parent. They are motivated to take parenting courses, and would like to receive educational material to better understand their children's needs and to fulfil their parental responsibilities more adequately. They also express the need for more frequent contact with their family and increased access to family visiting units, family support groups, and information sessions dealing with inmates and their families (Kazura, 2001; Mendez, 2000). These findings principally focus on the needs expressed by incarcerated fathers, but it is essential to go beyond this perspective and consider the needs of their children and the benefits of such programs for them. Thus, it is important to ask: Do the children wish to maintain the relationship with their father while he is in prison? Will continuing contact have a positive effect on the child's socialization and developmental processes? And, ultimately, will the maintenance of conjugal and family relationships affect all family members positively?

Along with the lack of programs or other services in Quebec and the rest of Canada to help maintain and support family relationships in situations of father incarceration, there is a problem with the distinct mandates of the institutions and organizations working with family members, in that they hinder joint action that would take into account both fathers' and children's interests in a coordinated manner. Services particularly needed during the crucial transitional periods of the judicial process – namely, at the times of the arrest and the release – are practically non-existent. The timeliness of the Fathers behind Bars project lay precisely in its aim to help fill these gaps. Since the project issued from concerns directly related to intervention in halfway houses, a *father component* was developed that focused on the improvement of parenting skills as a lever in the social rehabilitation of fathers released on probation. To this was added a *children's component*, which explored intervention paths to prevent maladjustment problems in children facing the situation of a father's imprisonment.

Fathers behind Bars: A PAR Project

The researchers involved in the Fathers behind Bars project have explored issues related to father incarceration since 2001.[6] Their interest is based on three principal findings that emerged from a review of the literature on the effects of incarceration and from interviews with families: (1) the recognition of the high risk of psycho-social maladjustment among the children of incarcerated parents (the intergenerational transmission of criminality); (2) the lack of necessary information to be able to intervene effectively in families affected by a parent's incarceration; and (3) the quasi-absence in Quebec of programs targeting this clientele. In the context of this project, several concrete actions were put in place to better document the issue so that intervention tools adapted to the specific needs of incarcerated fathers and their children could be developed. These actions were structured around two main areas, intervention and prevention, with the first aiming to improve the parenting skills of incarcerated and recently released fathers, and the second aiming to prevent maladjustment in their children.

The Father-Child Intervention Program

The father-child intervention program of the Fathers behind Bars project is directed at newly released fathers during their stay in a halfway house, and aims to help maintain and strengthen the father-child relationship (see Barrette, Dubeau, Milcent, & Côté, 2005). Theoretical presentations, role playing, practical exercises, and group discussions are carried out to help participants achieve the following three objectives: (1) *knowledge*, by increasing the fathers' understanding of the paternal role, the developmental stages of their children, and the functions fathers fulfil in this respect; (2) *know-how*, by encouraging the fathers' acquisition of parenting skills through discussions with other fathers about their experiences, and by giving them helpful hints on how to improve their interactions with their children and adolescents; and (3) *knowing-how-to-be*, by developing, maintaining, or increasing the quality of the affective relationships between the former inmates and the various members of their family, and making them more aware of their social and family history, how it affects the quality of their family relations, and its link with problems during and after their incarceration.

The father-child program is offered to former inmates living in halfway houses and their children. More specifically, the program targets fathers (biological fathers, stepfathers, or other significant father figures) who have served a federal or provincial prison term and who desire to maintain and strengthen their ties to their children. Although it targets newly released inmates and their children, the program also takes into account other family members, such as the mother of the children and the father's current partner. An approach seeking complementarity with already-existing community resources has been adopted to avoid the doubling of services or interference in the intervention process for certain families.

Through one-on-one meetings, workshops, and father-child activities, the father-child program aims to strengthen the father-child relationship and increase former inmates' knowledge and parenting skills, while encouraging reflection on how to improve the well-being of all the actors concerned (the father, mother, and child).

The *one-on-one meetings* are held to recruit participants in the program. The program's goals and the content of the workshops are explained to potential candidates. In these meetings, practitioners apply the inclusion and exclusion criteria for participation,[7] and assess the needs of the fathers and their children. Some fathers take advantage of the opportunity to meet with counsellors in additional one-on-one meetings during their participation in the program, in order to share personal experiences that they do not want to discuss in front of the group or to obtain further information on specific aspects of family life.

The father-child program's group *workshop*[8] encourages reflection on different aspects of fathering. It is made up of eight mandatory sessions, as well as two optional sessions to which the fathers' partners are also invited (see Table 7.1). The workshop is designed to encourage the sharing of knowledge and parenting experiences. Workshop leaders create a convivial atmosphere in which participants can exchange ideas and express their feelings. The goal is for the fathers to understand content through brief exposés based on the scientific literature and clinical research, as well as through discussion of their own experiences.

Table 7.1. Workshops of the Father-Child Intervention Program

Workshops	Content
Mandatory sessions	
1. Family and social heritage	• Evolution of fathers' roles over time • Differences between mothers' and fathers' roles
2. Fatherhood, a lifelong career	• Roles and functions of fathers • Father involvement and its impacts on children

3. Children: little treasures or little devils?	• Challenges of child development
	   – early childhood
	   – pre-school age
	• Individual differences

4. Children: are they little adults?	• Challenges of child development
	   – school age
	   – adolescence

5. Practical advice on young children	Frequent problems arising during these developmental stages and suggestions to deal with these situations
6. Practical advice on school-age children and adolescents	Encouragement of positive and harmonious interactions between the father and child or adolescent
7. Impacts of separation and incarceration	Discussion of the impacts of the separation and incarceration on various family members
8. Factors related to the children's adaptation problems	Factors associated with maladjustment problems in children and risk of the intergenerational transmission of criminality
Optional sessions (fathers' partners are also invited)	
9. The alliance between the two parents: an asset for the child	Co-parenting: issues and challenges; practical advice for improving communication
10. Communication within the couple	Communication within the couple and conflict-resolving skills

Note: The workshop was adapted from the *Pères en mouvement, pratiques en changement* (Changing Fathers, Evolving Practices) training workshop (see Chapter 9).

The content segments are introduced by exercises, such as role playing or a theme-based discussion led by the workshop leader. Each father receives a *participants' guide* that outlines the structure of the workshop, the different exercises that will be carried out, and a brief summary of the content. The guide is a personalized tool in which the fathers can note down their reflections and questions during the practical exercises. It also includes a supplementary reading list and a directory of relevant support resources and Internet sites.

The final component of the workshop is the father-child activities (such as playing sports and games, doing crafts). According to services professionals questioned for *On Fathers' Ground*, an inquiry into programs supporting fatherhood in Canada, the inclusion of recreational, cultural, sports, or other activities is a winning strategy among fathers and contributes to the maintenance of the father-child relationship (Bolté, Devault, St-Denis, & Gaudet, 2002). Our aim when drawing up the father-child program was that the activities would: (1) allow a relationship of trust to grow between the former inmate and his children; (2) allow the newly released father to progressively re-establish a place in his children's lives; (3) give the father the opportunity to share enjoyable moments with his children and other family members; (4) encourage the exercise of parental responsibilities in a supervised setting; and (5) strengthen the former inmate's confidence in the exercise of his parental responsibilities through group or individual interventions.

The Prevention Program: A Practitioners' Guide

In contrast to the father-child program, the intervention, which focused on the children, met with some resistance from services professionals working with children. In the seminars we held with various groups of practitioners, participants expressed their concern about the lack of information on incarcerated fathers and the prison environment, and voiced lingering doubts about the benefits of strengthening the father-child relationship in this context. They debated aspects of the intervention paths suggested, including the appropriateness of individual or group intervention, from the perspective of avoiding the stigmatization of the children. The points that arose in the seminar discussions brought out the strategic importance of providing information and raising awareness among decision-makers and services professionals working with young people (in, for example, the Youth Centres, schools, and family services centres). The desire for more information practitioners expressed in these meetings also convinced us to develop tools to facilitate knowledge transfer and support practitioners in their intervention work with young people experiencing the incarceration of a parent.

The *Practitioners' Guide* (Lafortune et al., 2005) is a prevention tool that aims to give practitioners the information and guidelines to respond adequately to the specific needs of young people who have a parent involved in the criminal justice system. The guide contains gender-differentiated information in that some sections apply to situations involving incarcerated fathers, and others apply to situations in which the mother is or has been in prison; for this reason, we use the term "parent" when describing the guide. The objectives of the practitioners' guide are: (1) to acquaint practitioners with the realities of the correctional environment; (2) to give them a systemic/ecological perspective of the phenomenon of parental incarceration and its effects on different family members; and (3) to support and, whenever possible, improve their practices, in keeping with children's best interests. The guide suggests interventions to prevent maladjustment problems and the intergenerational reproduction of criminal behaviour.

The ten-point practitioners' guide is divided into three main sections (see Table 7.2). Section A, containing information on the phenomenon of parental incarceration, has four chapters. The first presents statistics and other data essential for understanding the effect of a parent's incarceration on the family. An approximate quantification of the phenomenon of incarceration is given, including the proportions of male and female inmates held in Quebec prisons, as well as the proportion of young people referred to the youth protection system who have a family member involved in or suspected of being involved in crime. The second chapter outlines the difficulties experienced by the incarcerated parent and the family at each stage of the judicial process (arrest, awaiting trial, trial, conviction, imprisonment, awaiting release, release and return to life in society). The third chapter deals with some of the problems that occur in children upon the incarceration of a parent, from psychological reactions (such as regressive symptoms, fear of abandonment, and adaptation and behavioural problems) to subjective experiences (such as loneliness, problems at school, social pressures, shame, and isolation). The first section of the practitioners' guide ends with an outline of the legal implications surrounding the parent's incarceration.

Section B focuses on the parameters underpinning the analysis of each specific case. Reference markers guide practitioners in assessing the child's situation and needs. These reference markers are based on the premise that the consequences associated with parent-child separation should be interpreted from a developmental and systemic perspective, instead of from a linear point of view that implies a direct cause-and-effect relation. The markers are intended to prevent generalizations and to provide a framework to help practitioners better understand the circumstances of the imprisonment, the parent's place in the child's life, and the future prospects of the parent-child relationship (MacLeod, 1986; Richards, 1991). The guide recommends that each child's case be viewed as unique, that the interventions be conceived

Table 7.2. Practitioners' Guide for Working with Young People Facing Parental Incarceration

Points	Description
Section A: Essential information for understanding the phenomenon of incarceration	
1	Extent of the phenomenon
2	Stages of the judicial process
3	Children's psychological reactions and subjective experiences
4	Legal implications
Section B: Reference markers to guide the evaluation	
5	Dimensions to consider in evaluating the needs of the child and his/her family
	5.1 Characteristics of the parent's crime, arrest, and prison sentence
	5.2 Characteristics of the child
	5.3 Characteristics of the family environment
	5.4 Characteristics of the relationship between the incarcerated parent and the child
Section C: Reference markers to guide intervention	
6	Interventions adapted to the stages leading to the incarceration (arrest, preventive custody, release on bail)
7	Interventions adapted to the period of the prison term
8	Interventions adapted to the period of the release/social rehabilitation
9	Whose best interest is being considered, the child's or that of the incarcerated parent?
10	Customized programs

in differential terms,[9] and that the evolution of the situation be monitored at regular intervals. More specifically, this section sets out four parameters that should be taken into account when carrying out a case analysis: (1) the characteristics of the parent's crime, arrest, and prison sentence (such as the type of crime, whether it involved the child, media exposure); (2) the characteristics of the child (such as past experience of loss and separation, gender, personality traits); (3) the characteristics of the family environment (such as ethnic origin, precariousness of living conditions); and (4) the characteristics of the relationship between the incarcerated parent and the child.[10]

Section C of the practitioners' guide describes and provides context for the decisions that must be made when a parent is sentenced to prison. Specifically, it suggests avenues for intervention at each stage of the judicial process, from the arrest to the release. Among other things, it deals with the transmission of information to the children, the reasons that might or might not justify maintaining the parent-child relationship during the prison sentence, the different types of visits allowed, and institutional contingencies restricting visits. The section ends with a list of various intervention strategies to consider and a brief description of the specialized programs available to families affected by parental incarceration.

Knowledge Transfer and Appropriation

The Fathers behind Bars project took a series of actions to encourage knowledge transfer and the appropriation of intervention and prevention tools by practitioners in the field. These actions also led to wide-scale dissemination among relevant Quebec organizations. In both the father and child components of the project, one of the first knowledge-transfer strategies was to write and publish articles in professional and academic journals. Communications were also delivered at conferences to promote the project among professionals working in correctional institutions and youth protection organizations. To disseminate information and raise awareness in the general population regarding the issue of parental incarceration, four promotional tools were developed: (1) a CD-Rom incorporating the principal documents produced in the framework of the Fathers behind Bars project; (2) a section presenting the project on the website of La Maison Radisson (The Radisson House); (3) an information brochure; and (4) a promotional coffee mug featuring the project's logo and the address of the website of The Radisson House (www.mradisson.ca).

Knowledge Transfer and the Appropriation of the Father-Child Program

In the father-child intervention program, seminars and training workshops were the primary dissemination activities. The purpose of these meetings was to facilitate the implementation and appropriation of the program by halfway houses. A first seminar for a wider audience was offered to practitioners working with incarcerated fathers in halfway houses, in order to present the program's content to professionals in the correctional and community milieus and to share with them the results of the pilot implementation of the father-child program. An important part of the seminar was reserved for discussing the terms and conditions under which the program could be integrated into the activities of the respective organizations, in accordance with the needs expressed by practitioners and their clientele.

Following this seminar, in-depth training was given to the personnel of the halfway houses. To facilitate the appropriation of the father-child program, various resources were made available to services professionals. An information brochure and implementation tools were developed. The brochure facilitated the practitioners' introduction of the program to their organizations, while the implementation tools allowed the researchers to determine which information was relevant during the program's implementation, and also gather the elements needed for its evaluation (such as attendance records kept by the organizations, selection and assessment of the participants, action plans of the halfway houses, follow-up notebooks). Training manuals for workshop leaders and participants' guides were also created to facilitate the transmission of the workshops' content. Copies of the training manuals were distributed to practitioners during the seminars to help them prepare to conduct the workshops. For each workshop session, practitioners were given an outline of the structure of the session, suggestions on how to lead the exercises, along with guide notes on the principal subjects to present in each exercise, and a summary of the main points dealt with in the session. Workshop leaders could round out their preparation through readings suggested for each session, which were listed in the manual's bibliography. The training manual also recommended that workshop leaders adapt the content of the sessions to the resources available at their respective organizations, the interests of participants, and their own individual presentation styles. In addition, a research coordinator was specifically assigned to implement and update the father-child program in the organizations. This resource person's principal function was to provide support to practitioners and ensure regular follow-up. The advantage of this strategy was that it allowed practitioners to implement the program according to the human and financial resources at their disposal, giving them greater flexibility. It also provided assistance if they had questions or encountered specific problems. The research coordinator also helped gather the data needed to evaluate the program while it was being implemented.

In total, seven mobile seminars and training sessions were offered to thirty-four practitioners from sixteen organizations (including practitioners from halfway houses, and employees of Correctional Service Canada) working with incarcerated fathers. These meetings led to the implementation of the program in six halfway houses, which included several Community Residential Facilities. In general, the programs offered in the community and on a volunteer basis had higher dropout rates than those offered in the specialized establishments. Forty-four newly released inmates agreed to participate in the father-child program, of whom thirty-seven were fathers, six were men without children, and one was a mother. Of these, eighteen (eleven fathers, six men without children, and the one mother) attended most of the workshop sessions, while twenty-six individuals left before completing the workshops. This low completion rate was mainly due to the departure of several former inmates during the program's ten-week schedule. Of the participants who left before finishing the workshop, 25 per cent returned to prison (either for breaking parole conditions or for reoffending); 16 per cent had attended only a few sessions before the workshop leader was transferred, putting an end to the session; 12 per cent stopped attending due to conflicts with their work schedules or after obtaining full release; and the remaining 7 per cent said that they had lost interest or were unable to tolerate the attitudes of other participants. A high proportion of dropouts from the program had relatively weak links with their families and had hoped to re-establish a relationship with their children through the father-child program. They found this difficult to achieve, however, due to the amount of time that had passed (several years, in some cases) since the relationship had been broken off, legal orders prohibiting some of the fathers from contacting their children, or the fact that some children had been placed in institutions; such factors obviously did not foster adherence to the program. Strategies to reach these "distant fathers" should be developed, including the establishment of closer partnerships with judicial and social organizations.

We found that it is not easy for community-based halfway houses to recruit enough participants for a group intervention or to maintain participant adherence for ten weeks. The evaluation of the project's implementation was carried out by conducting fifteen semi-structured interviews and by gathering data from the practitioners' follow-up notebooks (Barrette, Dubeau, Milcent, & Côté, 2005). The results of the evaluation allowed us to identify the principal positive factors that favoured the program's implementation in halfway houses and the sustained attendance of participants: (1) the availability of human and financial resources at the organization; (2) practitioners' interest in the issue of parental incarceration; (3) practitioners' motivation to provide services to this clientele; (4) the positive perception among practitioners and participants of the father-child program; and (5) participants' motivation to undertake and continue the process. On the other hand, we also identified five factors discouraging participants' adherence to the program: (1) the too-brief period that newly released inmates stayed in some of the halfway houses; (2) the mobility of the clientele; (3) the mobility of practitioners; (4) therapeutic saturation among participants due to the multiple programs and interventions being applied to them; and (5) the time of year that the program was implemented (for example, major holidays are more difficult periods for former detainees, who cannot always visit their families).

Strategies to Encourage the Appropriation of the Practitioners' Guide

Our initial strategy was to approach the Association des centres jeunesse du Québec (ACJQ, Association of Quebec Youth Centres), as we determined that collaboration with the ACJQ would be the best entryway for disseminating the practitioners' guide in Quebec's youth protection system. Our relationship with the ACJQ allowed us to reach a large number of managers and practitioners in the Youth Centres, and to promote the use of the practitioners' guide in several administrative regions of Quebec. A presentation of the guide at a ninety-minute ACJQ directors' meeting was the first step in establishing direct links with the Centres.

The presentations and meetings with practitioners working with young people were among the principal activities promoting the use of the practitioners' guide. These meetings were composed of two parts: first, the objectives and activities carried out in the project were briefly explained; second, the various sections of the practitioners' guide were presented and discussed. Services professionals at the meetings were invited to share their clinical expertise and to take a critical look at the guide. Through these meetings, we reached more than one hundred managers and practitioners in almost a dozen youth organizations in Quebec.

To increase knowledge of the situation of families with a parent in prison and to continue the evaluation and validation of the practitioners' guide, we approached the research directors of the Youth Centres in the Montérégie region, south and east of Montreal, asking that the project be included in the scientific programming of these organizations.[11] In this process, a meeting with eight representatives of the research sector of the Youth Centre network was held to present the guide and to select interested practitioners for the evaluation interviews.

In our meetings with practitioners of the Youth Centres of the Montérégie region, we reiterated the difficulty of quantifying the number of children supported by youth organizations who are affected by the incarceration of one of their parents, as so few data are available regarding parental criminal activity. Not all practitioners dealing with young people encounter situations of parental incarceration. Since we targeted practitioners according to their experience with this particular clientele, we noted that professionals in certain sectors are called upon more frequently to intervene in this type of situation (for example, to carry out needs assessments, to decide between open or closed custody arrangements). Naturally the experiences of each of these professionals are different – some intervene more directly with parents by organizing parent-child prison visits, while others have only sporadic contact, if any, with incarcerated or recently released parents.

Without denying the importance of providing services to these children, we note that parent-child intervention is not appropriate in all cases. According to practitioners, it is not always beneficial to the children to maintain the relationship when the parent has been convicted of family violence or a sexual crime. Other points of resistance that emerged in our meetings with practitioners mainly concerned the lack of available information regarding the incarcerated parent and the prison environment, and the advisability of encouraging the reinforcement of the parent-child relationship in this context. Despite their hesitation, practitioners generally agreed that maintaining contact (through telephone calls, letters, visits, and so on) is essential when the parent-child relationship is deemed significant to the well-being of the child.

The meetings also brought out the fact that several aspects dealt with in the practitioners' guide corresponded to practitioners' concerns, particularly regarding the question of whether or not to encourage the maintenance of the relationship, the information that should or should not be communicated to the child, and the circumstances associated with the incarceration. Practitioners considered the guide a valuable tool in this respect, and as supporting the practices of psycho-social professionals and educators by offering useful markers and guidelines for intervention among young people facing the incarceration of a parent.

Conclusion

An important outcome of the Fathers behind Bars project was that it led to increased knowledge of the effects of a father's incarceration on his family members. Our review of the literature and interviews with the principal actors concerned confirmed the relevance of providing support services to families with an incarcerated parent. As for whether or not we should encourage father involvement among prison inmates and former inmates, the data suggest that an in-depth analysis of this subject should be carried out, taking into account a number of parameters. Above all, the project allowed us to define these parameters and to identify the tools needed to proceed with the analysis.

As to information dissemination and awareness raising, the publication of articles in professional and academic journals and the presentation of the project at conferences proved to be good strategies for reaching a wider audience of practitioners in various regions of Quebec. As the project unfolded, actions taken to mobilize communities and form partnerships – that is, seminars, training sessions, and meetings with practitioners from halfway houses and youth organizations – brought a greater awareness of the problem. The encouragement of direct contact led to the creation of partnerships with more than thirty organizations concerned with issues involving incarcerated fathers and their children. The implementation of the father-child program in several halfway houses with different organizational characteristics (mandatory or voluntary programs, the full or partial administration of the program, individual or group activities, and so on) revealed the project's adaptability and flexibility, both of which are desirable qualities for an intervention program.

As for the practitioners' guide, its dissemination was facilitated by meetings with managers and professionals working with young people, through which more than one hundred practitioners from almost a dozen Quebec youth organizations were reached. The resistance initially expressed by these practitioners brought out practical issues and raised a number of questions regarding the choice of intervention strategies. Most important, the project generated a process of reflection and awareness among the various professionals concerned about the effects of a father's incarceration on his children.

A certain amount of time was needed for the various partner organizations to appropriate the issue and the tools developed in the project. The efforts made during the three years that the project was implemented prepared the ground for intervention among a clientele that has received little attention until now. The results of the evaluation, indicating satisfaction on the part of both participants and practitioners, motivated us to continue and to improve the implemented programs to ensure their sustainability.

At the end of this PAR project, the aim was the ongoing appropriation of the intervention and prevention programs by practitioners in halfway houses and in organizations working with detainees' children. Our hope is that the programs issuing from the project will become permanent and will spread province- and even nationwide. At the same time, we realize that each stage of the incarceration process brings specific problems for the family and requires different forms of intervention. The absence of services for the family during some of the judicial stages (notably, the arrest) and the lack of continuity in services constitute important gaps in support for families. Considering that the intervention component of the project touched upon only one stage of the incarceration process (the parent's release from prison), in the long term we plan to develop and offer services that support families at all stages of this process.

NOTES

1 This project was funded (at separate times) by the Public Health Agency of Canada and the National Crime Prevention Strategy of the Government of Canada, in collaboration with the Quebec Ministère de la Sécurité publique and the Quebec Youth fund.
2 The halfway house is a not-for-profit organization that provides services and programs for prisoners released on probation. It is either a Community Correctional Centre run by Correctional Service Canada (CSC), or a Community Residential Centre run by a company under contract to the CSC.
3 The data obtained from the inmate management records seriously underestimated the number of incarcerated men who were fathers. The information was based on records of prison visits, in which the term "child" was attributed only when the child was unaccompanied and, therefore, these generally applied to much older children. Dependent children who accompanied their mothers were included with the mother under the heading of "spouse /partner," but this notation did not indicate if the inmate was their father.
4 This search was completed on 15 October 2005 on the Centre jeunesse de Montréal–Institut universitaire website. For more information see http://www.centrejeunessedemontreal.qc.ca/.
5 The low number of children interviewed was principally due to the fathers' reticence to give us their children's contact information. This attitude might reflect the father's protective role, as illustrated in the following statement: "They don't have it easy as it is, with me being in jail. I'm willing to answer your questions, but I'd rather not have them questioned about it. It's already hard for them" (statement by an incarcerated father, in Barrette et al., 2002).

6 Several researchers took part in this project. We would like to thank Jacques Baillargeon, Natacha Brunelle, André Plante, and Chantal Plourde of the Université du Québec à Trois-Rivières and Denis Lafortune of the Université de Montréal for their contributions. Diane Dubeau acted as external evaluator. The project was integrated into the programming of GRAVE-ARDEC and Prospère in 2003, on a basis of shared interests and objectives concerning fatherhood.

7 The inclusion criteria are: (1) to be a father, stepfather, or significant father figure having served a federal or provincial prison term and be staying in a halfway house; (2) to desire to maintain and strengthen the child-father relationship and be willing to undertake the appropriate parenting education process. A prison sentence for a crime involving family violence excludes fathers from the program. Fathers legally prohibited from having contact with their children are excluded from the father-child activities of the program.

8 The workshops were initially organized by the researchers associated with the project, who adapted documents and previous training workshops to take the realities of fatherhood and parental incarceration into account.

9 That is, the recommended intervention will depend on the results within each parameter.

10 Twelve dimensions are used to evaluate the parent-child relationship here. The instrument was inspired by the Parent Interview Schedule for Axis V of the Multiaxial Classification Scheme (World Health Organization) by Poustka (1987), translated into French by Lafortune and Laurier (2003). Each dimension is evaluated according to a three-point Likert scale.

11 The scientific programming (the research component) of the Quebec Youth Centre system is an essential complement to clinical interventions among children who have been referred to youth protection services. To be included in this programming is an undeniable asset for a project, as it ensures the wider dissemination of programs and gives access to larger samples and data sources.

REFERENCES

Adalist-Estrin, A. (1994). Family support and criminal justice. In S. L. Kagan & B. Weissbourg (Eds.), *Putting families first: America's family support movement and the challenge of change* (pp. 161–185). San Francisco, CA: Jossey-Bass.

Arditti, J. A., Smock, S. A., & Parkman, T. (2005). "It's been hard to be a father": A qualitative exploration of incarcerated fatherhood. *Fathering, 3*(3), 267–288. http://dx.doi.org/10.3149/fth.0303.267

Barrette, M., et al. (2002). *Rapport de la phase I du projet "Grandir sainement avec un père détenu."* Trois-Rivières, QC: Maison Radisson.

Barrette, M., Dubeau, D., Milcent, M.-P., & Côté, S. (2005). *Guides du formateur et du participant du Programme d'intervention " Père-Enfant."* Trois-Rivières, QC: Maison Radisson.

Beattie, K. (2005). Les services correctionnels pour adultes au Canada. *Juristat, 26*(5), 1–36.

Bolté, C., Devault, A., St-Denis, M., & Gaudet, J. (2002). *On father's ground: A portrait of projects to support and promote fathering.* Montreal, QC: Université du Québec à Montréal, GRAVE-ARDEC.

Canada. (2005). Correctional Service Canada. *Departmental Performance Report.* Ottawa, ON. Retrieved from http://www.collectionscanada.gc.ca/webarchives/20060120070156/http://www.tbs-sct.gc.ca/rma/dpr1/04-05/csc-scc/csc-sccd4501_e.asp#_Toc1_1

Carlson, B. E., & Cervera, N. (1991). Inmates and their families: Conjugal visits, family contact, and family functioning. *Criminal Justice and Behavior, 18*(3), 318–331. http://dx.doi.org/10.1177/0093854891018003005

Cyr, F., & Caroben, G. (2004). L'adaptation des enfants et des adolescents à la séparation des parents. In M.-C. Saint-Jacques, D. Turcotte, S. Drapeau, & R. Cloutier (Eds.), *Séparation, monoparentalité et recomposition familiale: bilan d'une réalité complexe et pistes d'action* (pp. 3–32). Quebec City, QC: Presses de l'Université Laval.

Farrington, D. P., & Welsh, B. C. (2007). *Saving children from a life of crime: Early risk factors and effective interventions.* Oxford, UK: Oxford University Press.

Gregory, N. (2004). Crime and the family: Like grandfather, like father, like son? *British Journal of Forensic Practice, 6*(4), 32–36. http://dx.doi.org/10.1108/14636646200400025

Hairston, C. F. (1989). Men in prison: Family characteristics and parenting views. *Journal of Offender Counseling, Services & Rehabilitation, 14*(1), 23–30. http://dx.doi.org/10.1080/10509674.1989.9963922

Hairston, C. F. (1995). Father in prison. In K. Gabel & D. Johnston (Eds.), *Children of incarcerated parents* (pp. 31–40). New York, NY: Lexington Books.

Kazura, K. (2001). Family programming for incarcerated parents: A needs assessment among inmates. *Journal of Offender Rehabilitation, 32*(4), 67–83. http://dx.doi.org/10.1300/J076v32n04_05

Lafortune, D., et al. (2004). L'expérience des familles aux prises avec l'incarcération du père. In M.-C. Saint-Jacques, D. Turcotte, S. Drapeau, & R. Cloutier (Eds.), *Séparation, monoparentalité et recomposition familiale: bilan d'une réalité complexe et pistes d'action* (pp. 217–243). Quebec, City, QC: Presses de l'Université Laval.

Lafortune, D., et al. (2005). *L'expérience des familles confrontées à l'incarcération d'un parent: un guide de pratique en dix points à l'intention des intervenants jeunesse.* Montreal, QC: Université de Montréal.

Lafortune, D., Laurier, C., & Gagnon, F. (2004). Prévalence et facteurs associés à la prescription de medicaments psychotropes chez les sujets places en Centre Jeunesse. *Revue de Psychoéducation, 33*(2), 157–176.

Lanier, C.-S. (1995). Les pères incarcérés: programme de recherche. *Forum: recherche sur l'actualité correctionnelle, 7*(2), 34–36.

Le Camus, J. (2002). *Rester parents malgré la détention: les relais enfants-parents et le maintien des liens familiaux.* Toulouse, France: Érès.

MacLeod, L. (1986). *Condamnées à la séparation: une étude des besoins et des problèmes des délinquantes et de leur(s) enfant(s).* Report prepared for Public Safety Canada, Department of Programs, Research Division.

Mendez, G. A., Jr., (2000). Incarcerated African American men and their children: A case study. *Annals of the American Academy of Political and Social Science, 569*(1), 86–101. http://dx.doi.org/10.1177/0002716200569001007

Murray, J. (2010). Longitudinal research on the effects of parental incarceration on children. In J. M. Eddy & J. Poehlmann (Eds.), *Children of incarcerated parents: A handbook for researchers and practitioners* (pp. 55–73). Washington, DC: Urban Institute.

Murray, J., & Farrington, D. P. (2008). Parental imprisonment: Long-lasting effects on boys' internalizing problems through the life-course. *Development and Psychopathology, 20*(01), 273–290. http://dx.doi.org/10.1017/S0954579408000138

Murray, J., Farrington, D. P., & Sekol, I. (2012). Children's antisocial behavior, mental health, drug use, and educational performance after parental incarceration: A systematic review and meta-analysis. *Psychological Bulletin, 138*(2), 175–210. http://dx.doi.org/10.1037/a0026407

Parke, R., & Clarke-Stewart, K. A. (2002). *Effects of parental incarceration on young children.* Washington, DC: Department of Health and Human Services.

Pauzé, R., et al. (2000). *Portrait des jeunes inscrits à la prise en charge des Centres jeunesse du Québec et description des services reçus au cours des huit premiers mois.* Sherbrooke, QC: Université de Sherbrooke.

Poustka, F. (1987) Entrevue parentale pour l'axe 5 de la classification multiaxiale des troubles psychiatriques chez l'enfant et l'adolescent: situations psychosociales problématiques associées. J. W. Goethe University Frankfurt-am-Main.

Richards, M. (1991). The separation of children and parents: some issues and problems. In R. Shaw (Ed.), *Prisoners' children: What are the issues?* (pp. 3–12). New York, NY: John Wiley.

Saint-Jacques, M.-C., Drapeau, S., & Cloutier, R. (2001). La prévention des problèmes d'adaptation chez les jeunes de familles séparées ou recomposées. In F. Vitaro & C. Gagnon (Eds.), *Prévention des problèmes d'adaptation chez les enfants et les adolescents. Tome I: Les problèmes internalisés* (pp. 353–381). Quebec City, QC: Presses de l'Université du Québec.

Simmons, C. W. (2000). Children of incarcerated parents, *California Research Bureau, 7*(2), 1–11. Retrieved from https://www.library.ca.gov/crb/00/notes/v7n2.pdf.

Smith, C. A., & Farrington, D. P. (2004). Continuities in antisocial behavior and parenting across three generations. *Journal of Child Psychology and Psychiatry, 45*(2), 230–247.

Stover, C. S., & Morgos, D. (2013). Fatherhood and intimate partner violence: Bringing the parenting role into intervention strategies. *Professional Psychology, Research and Practice, 44*(4), 247–256. http://dx.doi.org/10.1037/a0031837

Walters, J. (2011). Domestic violence and fathers in prison. In J. Walters (Ed.), *Working with fathers: From knowledge to therapeutic practice* (pp. 141–157). London, UK: Palgrave Macmillan.

Wilczak, G. L., & Markstrom, C. A. (1999). The effects of parent education on parental locus of control and satisfaction of incarcerated fathers. *International Journal of Offender Therapy and Comparative Criminology, 43*(1), 90–102. http://dx.doi.org/10.1177/0306624X99431009

Withers, L. (2001a). *Time together: A survival guide for families and friends visiting in Canadian federal prisons and the directory of Canadian organizations providing services to the families of adult offenders*. Ottawa, ON: Canadian Families and Corrections Network.

Withers, L. (2001b). *Waiting at the gate: Families, corrections and restorative justice*. Kingston, ON: Canadian Families and Corrections Network.

8 An Outreach and Support Program for Socio-economically Vulnerable Fathers

GENEVIÈVE TURCOTTE, GILLES FORGET,
FRANCINE OUELLET, AND ISABELLE SANCHEZ

As part of their ongoing efforts to reach out to and support at-risk fathers with a view to acting before child maltreatment problems arise, the members of Prospère again teamed up with their partners to run a new participatory action research (PAR) project: *Relais-Pères* (Relaying Fathers).[1] A research team monitored, documented, and analysed the program and its impacts over a period of thirty-one months between September 2005 and March 2008 (the reference period). This chapter summarizes the findings of our analysis, and sets out the successes as well as the problems encountered during the project.

Relaying Fathers: Basic Parameters

Relaying Fathers relies on the work of home visitors[2] and community development workers to (1) reach socio-economically vulnerable fathers in their natural milieu; (2) offer them ongoing, sustained involvement and support in various spheres of their lives – fathering, personal, co-parenting, socio-economic, and relational; (3) connect them with community resources if necessary; and (4) encourage their active participation in society. The ultimate goal of the program is to help men assume their role as fathers and encourage them to integrate into society in the interests of their children's welfare.

The program targets vulnerable fathers of all ages who have one or more children age five or under, whether living with them or not. As far as the concept of vulnerability is concerned, the program adopts concepts that borrow from the work of Castel (1994, 2003, 2009). The first notion we took from his work is that vulnerability occurs within a specific context: it must be seen as an effect of overall social dynamics that make some people fragile, such as job market imbalances that exclude ill-prepared employees, ever-increasing skill requirements, impoverishment of community social networks, and budget cuts affecting social policies and services. Inspired by the work of Castel and others (Long, 2008; Richmond & Saloojee, 2005), Relaying Fathers adopted a definition of vulnerability that incorporates three dimensions:

- *socio-economic*: financial instability, debt, and housing problems;
- *relational*: trouble accessing the mutual-aid system, formal services, and social participation, and lack of reference points and social relationship models, especially for the role of father; and
- *cultural*: lack of education, lack of integration into the host society.

Castel identifies vulnerability as an intermediate zone between integration and marginalization – or as disaffiliation at the junction of socio-economic instability and fragile social bonds. The fathers the program seeks to reach are in this intermediate zone, and the goal is to prevent their marginalization.

Relaying Fathers was established in four Montreal neighbourhoods by a dozen or so partners (representatives of community organizations, educators, social workers, and researchers) working together on a steering committee. As with the other programs developed by the Prospère team, the implementation and evaluation of Relaying Fathers was done from a PAR perspective (see Chapter 1). The original partners opted for a broad, open-ended framework, so that the project could be developed in the field, step by step, in a process involving everyone associated with it, and based on the needs of the fathers and their families and the realities of their specific situations. This type of research banks on "ways of doing things" that are gradually emerging from action in the field or, more specifically, from the constant interaction between action and critical thinking about the action. This interaction takes place within a process involving close, ongoing collaboration between researchers and field workers. The researchers, who were involved in the program from the outset, helped mobilize partners, seek funding, and recruit and train home visitors. In the experimentation phase, the researchers became actively involved in the steering committee, where their role was to (1) lead discussions; (2) observe, understand, formalize, and make visible what was happening in the field; (3) encourage critical thinking about action and implementation issues; and (4) provide support for setting up activities and producing annual reports. The field partners and home visitors were associated with research operations, and took an active part in developing data-gathering instruments, interpreting and validating results, and sharing and disseminating knowledge. All this was made easier by a history of successful collaboration and warm relations based on mutual respect and trust.

A variety of means were used to encourage critical thinking about the action. Items concerning developments in the fieldwork and research were on the agenda of the committee's monthly meetings. The research team offered its services to write detailed minutes of each meeting, to have an accurate record, approved at the following meeting, of changes in the intervention process, decisions on program implementation, and areas of consensus and controversy surrounding some implementation issues. Discussions were led by researchers, based on summaries of the cases analysed for the study. Group interviews were opportunities for in-depth collective thinking about actions as they were being developed.

One role of the research team was to evaluate the program implementation process and its impact on fathers. In the following pages, we outline our analytical and methodological perspectives, as well as the main results of our evaluation. We present the results in terms of our core research objectives – namely, to (1) produce knowledge on the best ways to support the involvement of socio-economically vulnerable fathers by formalizing the Relaying Fathers practice model; (2) identify the facilitators and obstacles in implementing these practices by analysing the context out of which the project emerged and the process of structuring the fieldwork (for example, partnership dynamics, recruitment methods, and support to visitors); (3) assess the program's ability to reach fathers in vulnerable situations; and (4) highlight the effect of the program on the personal, fatherhood, co-parenting, socio-economic, and relational dimensions of the experiences of a sample of fathers.

Evaluation of Relaying Fathers: Analytical and Methodological Perspectives

Experimentation with this type of outreach work was therefore accompanied by a study to evaluate the program implementation process and the project's outcomes. This was an innovative aspect of Relaying Fathers, as a review of social work with fathers revealed that few such programs have been put through a systematic evaluation process (Bolté,

Devault, St-Denis, & Gaudet, 2002; Dubeau, Villeneuve, & Thibault, 2011; Hoffman, 2011). We consider evaluation an integral part of the development of innovative programs designed by researchers and their field partners. This has two implications: first, data gathering is continuous, with evaluation taking a variety of forms, depending on the stage of development of the program; second, the knowledge produced at the various stages is reinvested into the program in some way, allowing for a fine-tuning of, or major changes in, the intervention process.

The Analysis Framework

The goal of the evaluation was to underscore the theory behind the program (Patton, 1990), that is, to highlight the relationship between the program implementation process and the program's impact on the target population, as the analysis framework in Figure 8.1 illustrates. The analysis framework assumed that innovative practices were being developed and implemented under the influence of: (1) situational variables; (2) the characteristics of the participants implementing it (that is, the partners and visitors) and of the organizations they represent; and (3) the dynamics of the partnership at work. By "impact of the program," we mean the changes perceived in the fathering, personal, co-parenting, socio-economic, and relational experiences of fathers throughout the program. Note that we use "impact" to signify that there is always an antecedent, at least an implicit one, to a result; it does not connote the idea of causality (Miles & Huberman, 1994). Assessing the impact of a program like Relaying Fathers poses a certain number of analytical and methodological challenges. The first challenge had to do with the researchers' obviously limited monitoring period: at the time of the second phase of data gathering, each of the fathers was at a different stage of the program and of his own journey. The second challenge involved structural factors liable to interfere with achievement of the objectives, despite sustained efforts on all sides. To overcome these challenges, our approach to evaluation assigned as much importance to the actions the fathers took to improve their situation as to the outcomes of those actions in terms of achievements or stages completed.

The Methodological Framework

To conduct an in-depth analysis of the relationship between the project process and its impact on fathers, the research team decided on

Figure 8.1. Relaying Fathers: The Analysis Framework for Evaluating the Project

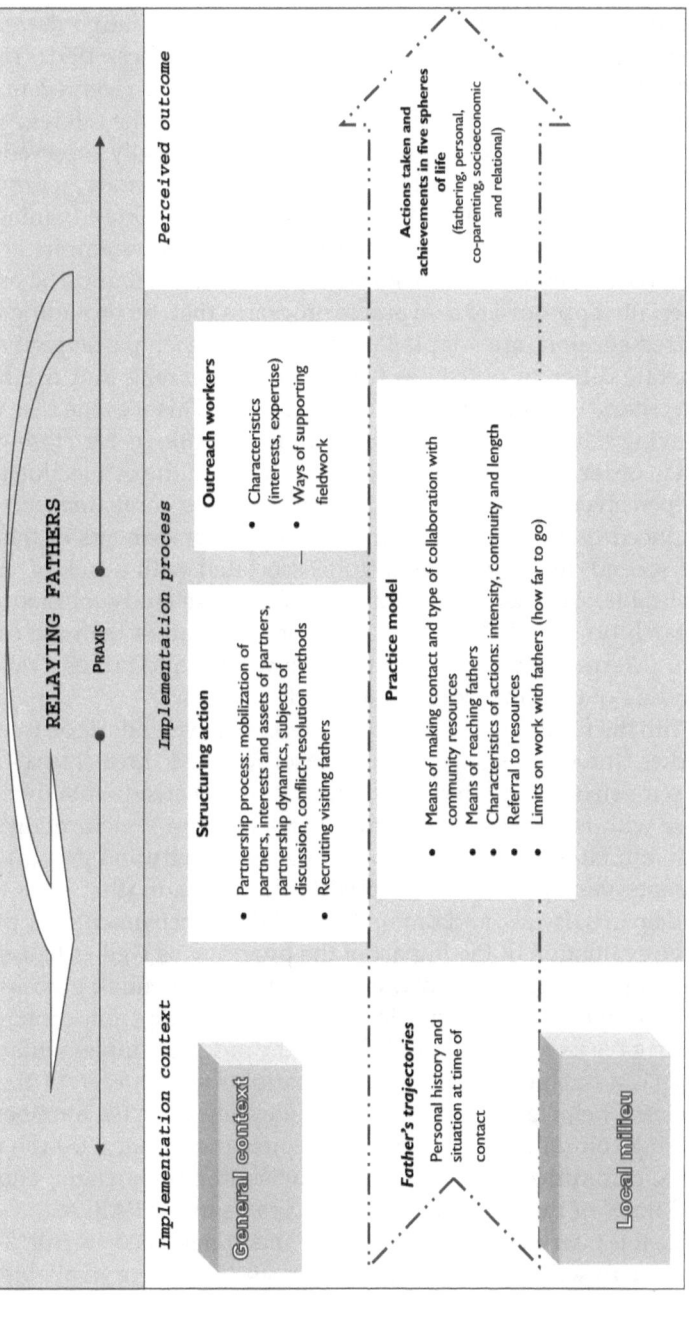

a strategy that focused on case studies and qualitative data analysis (Gagnon, 2005; Gerring, 2007; Huberman & Miles, 1991; Yin, 1994, 1998). In this study, a case refers to the support received in concert with the father's own path of change throughout the reference period. The method we used is a research strategy typically reserved for site studies, adapted to individuals. We opted for this strategy primarily to ensure consistency with the program's objectives. One advantage of the case-study method for our purposes is that it allows empirical investigation of a phenomenon in the setting in which it occurs. The method is especially appropriate to evaluate programs that, by providing individualized support, are adapted to the needs of each participant and that generate different outcomes for each one, meaning that fixed evaluation criteria cannot be applied (Patton, 1987). This was the case with the Relaying Fathers program. The method also allows for close observation in order, first, to determine, for each father, the connection between the perceived impacts of the program and the contextual factors that produced them – in particular, the various components of the project; and second, to identify the factors associated with a lack of impact, if applicable. Another relevant aspect of the case-study method is in the research process that favours "the discovery rather than the confirmation" (Merriam, 1988, p. 19) of new knowledge and brings a rich understanding of the dimension under study.

With the funding obtained for the research, we undertook twelve case studies (three per site).[3] For each case, we used three sources of data: (1) semi-structured interviews with visitors at two points during their work with fathers (eight months apart); (2) semi-structured interviews with four fathers; and (3) visitors' program activity and process records. The interview guide was adapted to the situation (that is, in terms of participants, issues, and time). We used these instruments for the qualitative evaluation of the impact of the program, as well as to assess program implementation and systematize the intervention process.

Along with the case studies, we also had data from other sources, which gave us a more general view of the program implementation process: (1) a socio-demographic information sheet on each of the fathers receiving help; (2) a four-part group interview with the members of the steering committee on various implementation issues; (3) the minutes of the committee meetings written up by the researchers; and (4) the field notes of the researchers as participants in the PAR.

All the interviews were recorded and transcribed in full. The data were analysed continuously as soon as they were available, which made it easier for the researchers and partners to learn more about each case, and to observe theoretical saturation of the data. The data were subject to a qualitative analysis based on condensation and presentation (Huberman & Miles, 1991). The concept of data condensation refers to the set of operations for transforming, categorizing, and relating data. Here, we used the analytical-memo method (Corbin, 1986; for details, see Turcotte, Forget, Ouellet, and Sanchez (2009): twelve memos were written as the interviews were conducted and, in order to deepen the analysis, were constantly revised to incorporate new data as they became available. The concept of data presentation refers to the development of tables that represent the fathers' situations at the beginning of the program, the case objectives, actions taken by the visitors and fathers, and the impacts as both parties perceived them. For the development of the analytical memos and the interpretation of data, we decided on a corroboration process based on discussions of interpretations by at least two research team members (Poupart et al., 1997). At several stages of the analysis, the results of the research were also reviewed and validated by members of the program steering committee and the visitors.

Observations on the Practice Model

One objective of the program evaluation was to produce knowledge on the best ways to support the involvement of socio-economically vulnerable fathers by formalizing the practice model implemented by Relaying Fathers. More precisely, the objective was to highlight "ways of being and acting," as well as concrete means (methods and techniques) used by the home visitors to achieve the program's objectives. This was a significant challenge because social work has fuzzy boundaries that are often hard to define and make explicit. We made it our mission to document and make visible the type of practice developed in this program. To do so, we drew on accounts of the actual experiences of home visitors with twelve fathers. In four cases, the visitors' descriptions were compared with the fathers' points of view. The researchers' attempt at formalizing the action was also reviewed by the partners and home visitors at steering committee meetings.

Through the analysis, five main features of the practice model developed in Relaying Fathers were identified: networking, outreach, a holistic view of the individual, ongoing involvement in the lives of the fathers, and a family perspective.

Networking

The parts of the job of the home visitors that were deemed to be absolutely essential by everyone associated with the project were to become known in the neighbourhood, to forge bonds with community resources, to promote the mission of the program, and to be visible in community activities and in public places to which fathers were likely to go. There were several networking objectives: (1) to become a stable reference point for vulnerable fathers in the community; (2) to provide several ways of reaching vulnerable fathers; (3) to improve work with fathers with a view to providing complementary services (and referrals to community resources, when applicable); (4) to create places and mechanisms to provide support for fathers' participation in society; (5) to help men see themselves as members of a community; and (6) to ensure a follow-up in the community if necessary at the end of the program.

Outreach Work

To reach vulnerable fathers and establish a bond of trust with them, the practice model adopted some of the distinctive features and principles of outreach work (Bastien et al., 2007; Thalineau, 2009):

- The work takes place within a defined geographic area. The organization responsible for the program at each site is well established in the community where the target population lives. The home visitors live in the neighbourhood or have close ties to it. Vulnerable fathers are reached and helped as much as possible in their natural milieu (such as at home, in a local café, or at a neighbourhood event), rather than in a controlled or institutional setting.
- The work takes place between people with something in common. It relies on recruiting male home visitors, who draw on their common experiences with the fathers – as men, as fathers, as divorcees, as immigrants – and share personal stories to initiate contact and start a dialogue. In addition, in three out of four neighbourhoods, the visitors were non-professionals.
- The work takes place within a close relationship environment. Strong personal involvement, an egalitarian relationship, being there for the father, and forging a bond of trust with the father lie at the heart of the work method that was developed in Relaying

Fathers. The challenge of establishing and maintaining trust is significant because the fathers have often experienced loss and isolation. They also often distrust institutions and feel disqualified from their role as fathers. Thus, throughout the program, four facilitators for creating and maintaining a bond of trust with vulnerable fathers were identified.

In addition to these principles, the project established some conditions that home visitors should follow in establishing their relationship with fathers:

- In their dealings with the fathers, home visitors should focus on their roles as men and fathers. This helps to establish an egalitarian relationship between them, which is a fundamental means of empowerment (Breton, 1994; Rappaport, 1987; Zimmerman, 1995).
- Home visitors should adopt a point of view that focuses on the fathers' experiences. In other words, they should start with what fatherhood means to these men, the role the men wish to play in their children's lives, their fears about fathering, and the obstacles with which they have to contend. To start a dialogue, visitors should try informal chats and listening attentively to the fathers' stories.
- Home visitors should accept the father as he is, without judging his past or present situation. This condition assumes that the visitor listens to the father's story respectfully and accepts it as true – that is, as representing reality as perceived by the father. It is especially important to make him feel that he is being taken seriously as a man and as a father. As Breton (1998) points out in a paper on the conditions of empowerment, this validation of the father's story becomes the means through which he gains his own voice and learns to use it to name his world. One of the fathers interviewed individually spoke of the importance of the non-judgmental attitude of the home visitor: "What I liked most about his way of working was that he never made any judgments, you know. 'Oh, you come from such-and-such an environment, that's no good for a kid.' No. He just told me that you don't always choose the road you take. There are circumstances ... I don't feel put down. I know I won't be judged."
- Home visitors should be easily available to the father. Visitors talked especially about the importance of doing concrete things to demonstrate their availability, by "giving it to them straight" and

being consistent – that is, by doing what they said they were going to do. When questioned about what worked best for them, the four fathers interviewed said that they benefited from feeling that someone was there for them, was interested in them, listened to them, and asked how they were doing. The use of strong expressions, such as "He's like a father to me," "He's kind of a role model ... the father I need in my life," and "All the fathers confide in him as a friend," is a good indication of the close relationships that develop between the participants.

A Holistic View of the Individual

To allow for the diversity and complexity of needs and roles, the home visitors adopted a holistic view of the individual that takes into account the various aspects of his life.

A WIDE RANGE OF OBJECTIVES
Adopting a holistic view of the individual means that a wide range of case objectives can be addressed. For each father visited, a number of objectives involving different spheres of his life were pursued simultaneously, depending on his own path and experiences. Help in the fathering sphere focused on three often-interrelated objectives. The first was to support the father in his intention "to be a good father." One father who had no father figure in childhood and who had just been given custody of his twenty-month-old child, with whom he had never lived before, described his needs to his visitor this way: "How do I invent myself as a father?" Behind the intention to be a good father, there is frequently a need to learn how to "take care of a child" – for instance, to decode the child's signals and communicate with him or her. For some, that also meant changing their way of life to accommodate the child. This was the case of a father who told us, "My goal ... was to stay away from drugs and alcohol, away from legal problems. I didn't want my son having anything to do with that." Another objective informed all the actions of home visitors in this sphere: helping the father become aware of his potential as a father, thus easing his anxiety about fathering. In some cases, the objective was to support the father as he sought recognition of his paternal rights.

In addition to direct support for the father's involvement with his child, which was the cornerstone of the program, many of the program's objectives involved addressing socio-economic problems, as the father-child relationship cannot be dissociated from the family's living conditions. The program's objectives included re-establishing the social bond, improving housing conditions, settling legal or social problems such as immigration status and child welfare reports, and providing help with entering the labour market.

MULTIPLE METHODS OF SUPPORT

To achieve these objectives, home visitors used a variety of methods. First, they offered individual assistance – active listening, information sharing, emotional support, and dialogue to raise awareness about fathering, drug and alcohol use, or way of life. Special attention was paid to helping fathers discover all the dimensions of fatherhood by showing that the father is not just a breadwinner.[4] In some cases, visitors provided some "handholding," demonstrating how to care for and stimulate the child, find a job, draw up a budget, or run a household. Home visitors used methods adapted to the interests and experiences of the fathers. They corroborated what surveys of practices have already shown: that it is important to plan activities that put the fathers to work in task- and action-oriented activities, rather than developing insight and expressing feelings (Bolté et al., 2002; Dubeau et al., 2013; Dulac, 1998, 2001; Forget, Devault, Allen, Bader, & Jarvis, 2005; Forget, Devault, & Bizot, 2009; Hoffman, 2011). Some of the activities were rather original, not to say unconventional; for instance, visitors used a car as a tool, seizing the opportunity afforded by providing a lift or doing mechanical work to start a dialogue with the father. Visitors also mentioned having informal discussions in a local café, at a hockey game, or during a stroll through the neighbourhood.

The Relaying Fathers home visitors also referred fathers to community resources in some situations – for example, if the father's problems were complex or if specialized help was required. In any case, the referral was personalized, and the visitor usually accompanied the father to appointments, especially if the father was seeking financial help or medical care, going to court, or meeting with various administrative authorities. In addition, home visitors sometimes engaged in mediation and advocacy. On some occasions, home visitors accompanied fathers to negotiations with government services or legal authorities to have certain rights recognized (especially those concerning access to the child), acted as mediators in helping to seek agreement in areas of tension between the two parties, and played the role of advocate to speed things along or attest to the father's progress and the involvement of a helper in his life. Often visitors also played the role of interpreter by going to appointments to make sure that the father understood the issues properly.

One of the unique features and great strengths of the program was, incidentally, its foresight in setting up the conditions necessary to restore the social bond, which many studies have shown is a prerequisite to citizen involvement. Home visitors did all manner of things to publicize neighbourhood resources, services, and activities; to encourage participation in recreational and cultural activities in the neighbourhood; and to create opportunities for meetings with other families and other fathers (for example, field days, camp weekends, family outings to museums, "guys' suppers," and father and child activities). To do so, they again focused on systematic physical accompaniment when dealing with community resources and activities. For the home visitors, these activities were also an opportunity to get fathers to relate to their children in a playful situation, to talk freely with other fathers about being a father, and to see other fathers interacting with their children. This excerpt from an interview with one father gives an idea of the type of activities that were organized to foster development of a social bond among some of the fathers in our sample.

> The visitor was telling me about activities, lots of activities that he did at Christmas, Easter, in the summer. There were parties in the parks. You know, I said to myself, 'Hey, that's going to be great for the kids. Someone who can help us go out as a family instead of staying home all the time.' So I said, 'OK, right, if you can help us with that, it would be great for me, you know.' At the same time, my kids could meet other families, and I could meet other fathers. Then other fathers could give me advice, too. You know, talking is great.

Intensity of the Intervention

Another characteristic of the practice model that was developed in Relaying Fathers was the intensity of the support provided fathers. The level of intensity was based on each father's needs, and was reviewed along the way so it could be changed as the situation changed. At first, contact was frequent, then the visits tapered off as the father progressed. The contact could also become more frequent in times of crisis or relapse, if the father agreed. For example, in the first five months of working with one father, the home visitor made twenty-six home visits, telephoned thirty-four times, and went to eleven appointments with him. In the months that followed, as the situation seemed to stabilize, the home visitor continued to stay in touch with the father through one telephone call and one visit a week. And the father called the home visitor whenever he was "worried or unsure what to do."

A Focus on Family and Co-parenting

The support work took a child-centred family approach. By adopting a vision that focused on the complementary roles of the father and mother, it sought to enhance the quality of the co-parenting relationship. Through negotiation and mediation, this involved working to improve the quality of the relationship between the spouses or ex-spouses, especially by encouraging clear communication on child-rearing issues.

Key Factors in the Success of the Program Implementation

To foster the development and implementation of its practice model, Relaying Fathers focused on four factors, each of which brought its own successes and problems: effective partnership, community support, recruitment of male home visitors, and clinical support.

Effective Partnership

Our analysis shows that Relaying Fathers established an effective partnership, which is one of the well-documented facilitators of innovative programs (Bilodeau, Chamberland, & White, 2002; Fawcett, Schultz, Watson-Thompson, Fox, & Bremby, 2010; Mishara, 2004). This partnership was founded, first, on a convergence of organizational, professional, and personal interests around the importance of reaching vulnerable fathers and, second, on strong relational capital, as the partners had worked together earlier on programs with positive outcomes. This relational capital meant that cultural obstacles to collaboration could be overcome quickly, thus facilitating the definition and sharing of roles and responsibilities, as well as fostering teamwork and collective efficiency. Throughout the process, the partners demonstrated their enthusiasm for the program, a willingness to share their clinical or scientific knowledge, and a commitment borne out by their steady attendance at steering committee meetings.

To foster the participatory process and involve all participants in critical thinking about the fieldwork and various research operations, the project partners decided from the outset to set up a steering committee on which they would all be represented. The committee was seen as a means for discussing practices and drawing on the experience and expertise of all the partners. It also made it possible to get oriented, to verbalize what united and divided the participants, and to share the rules and codes of ethics specific to the various professions represented. And it served as a forum for discussion and negotiation of key implementation issues. For the researchers, being on the steering committee greatly facilitated access to home visitors and fathers, who spoke about the practices being developed, lending detail and nuance to the interpretation of the program fieldwork.

The partners also took time to build cooperation by: (1) developing a common representation of the situation and the action to be undertaken consistent with all of their philosophies; (2) confronting their divergent values with respect to the conceptual basis of the practice model; and (3) getting to know one another and developing group solidarity. Moving from program design to implementation led to the discovery of some areas of divergence, which is only natural in the start-up phase of an innovative program such as Relaying Fathers (Bilodeau et al., 2002; Prilleltensky, Nelson, & Peirson, 2001). Yet, through their work on the steering committee and, more particularly, in the group discussions of major implementation issues, the partners were able to identify and acknowledge their differences and, above all, talk about them explicitly to reach compromises acceptable to everyone.

Community Support

One of the conditions essential to setting up our network was, of course, the willingness of community organizations to reach out to and support fathers. Over the months, both partners and home visitors noted that setting up a father-to-father program in their neighbourhood led the actors they dealt with to think about their own practices involving vulnerable fathers. They also observed an increase in referrals from health care services and community organizations, as well as greater cooperation in the organization of activities, such as home visits and family suppers. This change was first seen among the program partners. One partner, which had developed its expertise in mother-to-mother support, ended up incorporating male visitors not just into the organization, but also into the visiting mothers' everyday practice. Now, when the mothers meet fathers in difficulty on their home visits, they can refer them to their colleagues and discuss the place and role of the father. This cooperation between visiting fathers and mothers shows that the work of a male-female dyad is especially productive, as other fatherhood support programs have shown (Bolté et al., 2002; Dubeau et al., 2011).

Nevertheless networking was not accomplished without difficulty, and participant accounts highlight that alliances can be somewhat fragile. Clearly it is still hard to make room for fathers in services settings, and a number of factors converged to underscore the work that remains to be done to change the attitudes of social workers, institutions, and organizations around working with fathers. For one, initiatives to enhance children's welfare, particularly in health care services, are still associated with "maternal and infant health," as the members of the steering committee said in a group interview. Moreover, excessive workload and the discomfort mentioned by several people raised the issue of the ambiguity of services with regard to possible perceptions of fathers: Are they thought of as part of the problem or part of the solution?

Recruitment of Male Home Visitors: Successes and Challenges

From the outset, the partners were counting on hiring male visitors to take up the challenge of reaching vulnerable fathers, as the literature on work with fathers has repeatedly underscored the importance of men working with men (Bolté et al., 2002; Dulac, 2001; Forget et al., 2005); indeed, the program evaluation confirms that father-to-father work is essential. The home visitors often served as role models, as both men and fathers, to the fathers they supported. Their involvement fostered the development of a bond of trust with isolated men who otherwise had little inclination to seek out neighbourhood resources.

Paradoxically, male involvement is one of the biggest challenges of social responses to men's needs, and during the Relaying Fathers reference period, it turned out to be difficult to recruit male home visitors. Two explanations have been suggested. One is the small pool of potential male practitioners, as not many men are trained to help families and children. This example, which corroborates many other similar observations, should prompt decision-makers to find new ways to train and attract men to the helping professions. The second explanation has to do with working conditions. Our experience shows that such a program can function only if home visitors are paid suitably and enjoy the latitude required to meet fathers' needs. The issue of pay brings up questions of equity and resources, which are obstacles to changes in this area.

Clinical Support

One of the biggest strengths of the program was the support given to home visitors, who benefited from clinical supervision and received ongoing training, two elements often lacking in outreach programs. But everyone regretted the lack of a formal structure to facilitate the sharing of experiences and mutual support among the visitors. Thus, a remaining challenge of the program, as in other experimental work with fathers, is to set up formal mechanisms to encourage dialogue among home visitors. This is all the more important because working with fathers is new, and there are few existing guidelines.

Observations on Reaching Vulnerable Fathers

One objective of the program evaluation was to determine the project's ability to reach vulnerable fathers. Indeed, one of the biggest challenges was actually to reach fathers in difficulty. It is well known that men are less likely than women to seek help or advice when they are having problems (Dulac, 2001; Rondeau, 2004). When fatherhood is added to the situation, even fewer men seek support after their child is born, since attention is devoted to the mother and child.

Our data show that the program was a success in this respect. Over the reference period, home visitors helped close to one hundred fathers. The picture we got from the information sheets on eighty-one men filled in by home visitors (see Table 8.1) is of slightly older fathers, most of them (61 per cent) over age thirty, and the great majority (85 per cent) with at least one child under age six. Most (64 per cent) of these fathers were living with their wife (married or common law). The fathers were from a variety of ethnic and cultural backgrounds. Among the 43 per cent born outside Canada, a little more than half (56 per cent) were recent immigrants, having arrived within the previous three years.

Most of the fathers the program reached were struggling to various degrees with problems that made them vulnerable (Castel, 1994): economic instability, poor education or unrecognized qualifications, social

Table 8.1. Characteristics of Fathers Outreached by the Relaying Fathers Program

Characteristic		(%)
Age (years)	Under 20	5.0
	20–29	33.3
	30–39	50.0
	40 and older	11.7
Education	Did not finish high school	48.6
	High school (grade 11) or higher	51.4
Birthplace	Canada	57.0
	Outside Canada	43.0
Employment status	Employment assistance (welfare)	48.0
	Employment insurance	4.0
	Employed	42.0
	Student	6.0

Note: The data concern eighty-one fathers who received "significant" support, defined as at least three meetings. The portrait here does not take into account fathers who received services on an irregular basis.

isolation, lack of reference points and role models for fathering, and, for new arrivals, problems adjusting to the host society.

Socio-economically Unstable Fathers

Employment assistance (welfare) benefits were the main source of income for 48 per cent of the fathers, which put them below Statistics Canada's low income cut-off. Although 42 per cent had jobs, these were most often poorly paid and precarious positions. Economic instability (financial problems, debt, poverty), in fact, was one of the biggest problems home visitors reported, affecting 85 per cent of fathers the program helped. At the two sites where this information was gathered, visitors also reported that twenty-two of the forty-two fathers reached had housing problems when they joined the program.

Socially Isolated Fathers

In addition to having economic problems, a large proportion of the fathers (65 per cent) were socially isolated. For instance, they were unaware of community resources, had trouble accessing the mutual aid system and formal services, and received very little assistance from the informal social support system. Some accounts indicate that this type of problem is especially significant among recent immigrants.

Fathers with Relationship Problems

The third type of problem noted by the home visitors, and encountered by 46 per cent of the fathers, concerned married life and co-parenting: these problems include conflicts, tension, or trouble communicating with spouses or ex-spouses, and difficulty having custody or visitation rights recognized. Visitors also identified issues related to parenting skills among 44 per cent of the fathers with whom they worked. This category covers problems to do with a lack of reference points and role models for parenting and fatherhood, fathers' lack of confidence in their own parenting abilities, lack of awareness of attitudes and behaviours favourable to child development, and infrequent contact with the child.

Fathers Struggling to Adjust to the Host Society

The home visitors noted that many fathers born outside the country encountered problems integrating into their host society, including social isolation, difficulty having their qualifications recognized and finding a skilled job, and loss of identity reference points related to the redefinition of gender roles. The consequences of unstable employment are especially significant among immigrant fathers, for whom the role of breadwinner is fundamental to their identity, as we have seen above. For many men, difficulty finding a suitable job leads to psychological distress, which adds tension to his relationship with his wife and children.

* * * * *

The two interview excerpts below illustrate certain characteristics of the fathers reached by the project:

> I had no idea how to take care of a child. As far as I was concerned, he was just a pest I didn't want in the house. I'd just gotten out of detox, and I wasn't ready to handle it ... I needed to know how to react to my son, how to be a good father. I had no idea how to cope with a child. That was the main thing. That's what we worked on ... So, for me, it was really to have my son living with me in a healthy environment. I didn't want my two-year-old to wind up without a father because he was hanging out with criminals.

> Because we were isolated, we stayed stuck in our own little world, in a four-and-a-half-room apartment, watching TV. When the weekend came, we were looking forward to Monday ... We never went out. We were shut in. We never saw anybody. We didn't have many friends ... Now that I've met N. [visitor], I have someone to talk to. He was the only person I used to speak to in Canada, by the way.

What we can learn from this experience is that vulnerable fathers can be reached, but it takes time, energy, determination, and creativity. Although we cannot establish a causal link between those variables, visitors' accounts indicate that success in this respect depends on becoming rooted in the community, which is one of the great strengths and original features of the program. The home visitors developed close ties with health care services and local community organizations, which have been major sources of referrals.

The Relaying Fathers experience also confirmed what surveys of exemplary practices have often identified as a facilitator for reaching vulnerable fathers: the importance of reaching out to them in a meaningful context (Bolté et al., 2002; Forget et al., 2005). Reaching out might mean making contact directly with the father in an informal public place – 15 per cent of the fathers were reached this way. Most often, however, visitors took a number of steps to make contact once a father was referred to them. This was done by creating informal opportunities to meet and talk in the father's home, mainly by going along with the women working with the mothers, by going for coffee in a neighbourhood café, by asking for the father's help with a practical project, or by inviting him to a neighbourhood activity or sports event.

Lastly, it would not have been possible to make contact with vulnerable fathers if the program had not had one essential characteristic: committed, enthusiastic, and stable practitioners who gradually became role models in the neighbourhood.

Observations on the Impact of Relaying Fathers

Discussions with home visitors, the fathers themselves, partners, and researchers revealed that the actions of visitors had positive effects on the fathers they helped. The impacts concerned three main spheres of the fathers' lives: the fathering sphere, the social sphere, and the socio-economic sphere.

In the fathering sphere, both home visitors and fathers reported an improvement in the men's self-confidence as fathers and a lessening of a tendency to be anxious in that role. Furthermore, many of the fathers took steps to get closer to their children and improve their relationship with them. These steps took a variety of forms, depending on the case. Visitors observed that the fathers tended to take more time to play or do activities with their children in order to show their affection. Fathers reported learning how to care for, play with, and communicate with their children. Others took steps to achieve recognition of their paternity or their rights involving their child. Home visitors and fathers alike saw in these changes the results of their efforts to validate the role of parent and the pleasure of interacting with a child; the practical role modelling for fathers during home visits; and the practical support in dealing with institutions. In some cases, the effects in the fathering sphere were achieved by helping the father to focus less on his role as breadwinner and more on other aspects of his role. Here is what one father said about the changes his home visitor made in his life:

> He gave me a huge, huge amount of support. He gave me a ton of advice: how to show affection to a child, how to play with a child, how to stimulate children, how to get them to move. You know, he showed me all kinds of stuff ... He showed me how to do things. So I saw how he did it, then I did the same thing. That's why, right now, because of that man, I've really turned into a good dad ... Because at first, I had no self-confidence. And since then, I've gotten really good with the children.

It is clear from our data that the emphasis on accompanying the fathers in the study when they took part in activities and sought out community resources helped them break out of their social isolation. Among the indications of this were the fathers' greater awareness of community resources, greater willingness to make use of available services, and increasingly frequent participation in neighbourhood celebrations, family outings, and other activities organized in the community. Participation in recreational activities also facilitated the development of new socialization and support systems.

> When we met N., he invited us to a family activity at a community centre. We met other families. I met other fathers in the same situation as me. We even did something together. We went to the beach with the children – two days in a little hotel. I never would have thought it possible. We did

things as a family. We talked to other people, and that was great. It had an impact on me, on the life I have today. It encouraged me to live with my family. It helped me understand what it means to be a father, what a father's role in the family is.

The type of actions home visitors took also helped some fathers distance themselves from a negative social circle or dubious company. One father told us that his visitor had helped him "get out of the clubs" and "find the path I wanted to take."

We also observed that a number of fathers selected for the study took actions to improve their own and their family's living conditions, by going back to school or work, improving their housing, using food banks, managing their budget better, and reducing their debt. Because these actions involved three core aspects of fatherhood – breadwinner, family protector, and role model for the children – they also helped restore men's confidence in their fathering ability.

Conclusion

For many years, surveys of social work with fathers and more theoretical work on the same question have underscored the difficulty of reaching the most vulnerable fathers. The theme of Relaying Fathers – support for father involvement – and the highly marginalized target populations the project managed to reach made it especially innovative. The program was also innovative in terms of the characteristics of its practice model: applying the principles of action used in outreach work to a positive theme (involved fathering); taking a broad spectrum of actions to respond to the needs of vulnerable fathers; and accompanying fathers in their search for community resources if their problems were complex or they required specialized help. Lastly, the program was innovative through the ongoing involvement of a research team that evaluated the program and helped produce knowledge on the best ways to support the involvement of socio-economically vulnerable fathers by formalizing the practice model implemented by the program within a participatory action research framework.

Without constituting a definitive response to the question of how to reach and support the vulnerable fathers of young children, our evaluation of this program does provide useful information, first, for continuing the program among organizations and areas already participating in the trial and, second, for setting it up in other neighbourhoods. Although our evaluation method might require caution in the interpretation of data, continuous monitoring of the practices that were developed in Relaying Fathers has enabled us at the very least to propose a plausible hypothesis concerning the ways in which the impact is produced. The changes and development we observed in a small sample of fathers resulted from a set of factors that we have attempted to highlight in our analysis:

1 a context favourable to the implementation of such a project;
2 an effective partnership based on shared interests, a history of successful collaborative efforts, and a willingness to engage in critical thinking about practices and the research process;
3 partners who actively cooperated in the work by helping recruit home visitors, referring vulnerable fathers to the program, and promoting the importance of making room for fathers in their respective organizations;
4 committed, available, male practitioners well rooted in the community, who received training and continuous clinical supervision;
5 an approach that focused on outreach, steady involvement, response to fathers' immediate needs, and going with them to seek assistance from neighbourhood resources so that they could achieve something meaningful to them;
6 the willingness of the fathers to discover their fatherhood and the place they want to assume in the lives of their children;
7 the willingness of community family organizations to take over in cases of special needs; and
8 sufficient funding for the outreach work and research.

Our data corroborate what other qualitative researchers have found in Quebec (Allard & Binet, 2002; Anderson, Kohler, & Letiecq, 2002; Brown, Callahan, Strega, Walmsley, & Dominelli, 2009; Devault et al., 2008; Nelson, 2004; Ouellet & Goulet, 1998) – namely, that fatherhood can be a potential motivator of men in vulnerable situations and might spur them to get involved in society. The life stories we collected show that, although their situations might place limitations on their involvement with their children, these fathers also have great strengths, which home visitors were able to leverage – especially a serious motivation to assume their responsibilities and be better fathers – which was what prompted them to take action, in many cases successfully.

This hypothesis regarding the impact of Relaying Fathers will be retested at a later stage through an evaluation of the impact on a larger sample of fathers.[5] The program experience also shows that it will be important to continue developing and validating research instruments suitable for fathers. Lastly, since the ultimate goal of the program is to promote children's welfare, it will be important in the years to come to explore the impact of this support for fathers on their children's development, although this will require substantial funding.

NOTES

1 This research was made possible by a grant from the Groupe de recherche et d'action sur la victimisation des enfants and from the Montreal Public Health Department.
2 Non-professional male visitors are recruited to provide paid support to fathers in their neighbourhood, principally by means of home visits. Visitors receive basic training in helping fathers in difficulty and are supported by a clinical team. At one program site, visitors are professional community development workers. We refer to the program's practitioners as "home visitors" throughout the chapter.
3 Home visitors selected the twelve cases on the basis of the following criteria: (1) the fathers had to match the Quebec perinatal program's vulnerability indicators, be poorly educated, have an income below Statistics Canada's low income cut-off, or be a recent immigrant having trouble adjusting; and (2) the support provided had to be substantial enough for analysis, meaning there had to have been at least three home visits. The first twelve fathers (three per site) who met the criteria were selected. In actuality, the fathers received support for anywhere between three and twenty-four months during the reference period.
4 This type of action is particularly important for some unemployed fathers, notably newcomers to Canada, who are especially vulnerable to the effects of unemployment and financial instability on two key aspects of fatherhood: as breadwinner and family protector.
5 Funding for this evaluation has been received from the Social Sciences and Humanities Research Council of Canada.

REFERENCES

Allard, F., & Binet, L. (2002). *Comment des pères en situation de pauvreté s'engagent-ils envers leur jeune enfant? étude exploratoire qualitative*. Quebec City, QC: Régie régionale de la santé et des services sociaux de Québec.

Anderson, E. A., Kohler, J. H., & Letiecq, B. L. (2002). Low income fathers and "responsible fatherhood" programs: A qualitative investigation of participants. *Family Relations, 51*(2), 148–155. http://dx.doi.org/10.1111/j.1741-3729.2002.00148.x

Bastien, R., et al. (2007). Travail de proximité: matière à penser le social, la prévention et le politique. In E. Baillergeau & C. Bellot (Eds.), *Les transformations de l'intervention sociale: entre innovation et gestion des nouvelles vulnérabilités?* (pp. 73–95). Quebec, QC: Presses de l'Université du Québec.

Bilodeau, A., Chamberland, C., & White, D. (2002). L'innovation sociale, une condition pour accroître la qualité de l'action en partenariat dans le champ de la santé publique. *Canadian Journal of Program Evaluation, 17*(2), 59–88.

Bolté, C., Devault, A., St-Denis, M., & Gaudet, J. (2002). *On father's ground: A portrait of projects to support and promote fathering*. Montreal, QC: Université du Québec à Montréal, GRAVE-ARDEC.

Breton, M. (1994). On the meaning of empowerment and empowerment-oriented social work practice. *Social Work with Groups, 17*(3), 23–37. http://dx.doi.org/10.1300/J009v17n03_03

Breton, M. (1998). *Insertion: résultat concret de l'empowerment*. Toronto, ON: University of Toronto, Social Work Department.

Brown, L., Callahan, M., Strega, S., Walmsley, C., & Dominelli, L. (2009). Manufacturing ghost fathers: The paradox of father presence and absence in child welfare. *Child & Family Social Work, 14*(1), 25–34. http://dx.doi.org/10.1111/j.1365-2206.2008.00578.x

Castel, R. (1994). La dynamique des processus de marginalisation: de la vulnérabilité à la désaffiliation. *Cahiers de Recherche Sociologique, 22*(22), 11–28. http://dx.doi.org/10.7202/1002206ar

Castel, R. (2003). *L'insécurité sociale: qu'est-ce qu'être protégé*. Paris: Seuil.

Castel, R. (2009). Les ambiguïtés de l'intervention sociale face à la montée des incertitudes. *Informations sociales*, (152), 24–29.

Corbin, J. (1986). Coding, writing memos, and diagramming. In W. C. Shenitz & M. Janis (Eds.), *From practice to grounded theory: Qualitative research in nursing* (pp. 91–101). Menlo Park, CA: Addison-Wesley.

Devault, A., et al. (2008). Life stories of young fathers in contexts of vulnerability. *Fathering, 6*(3), 226–248.

Dubeau, D., et al. (2013). *Soutenir les pères en contexte de vulnérabilités et leurs enfants: des services au rendez-vous, adéquats et efficaces*. Report. Quebec City, QC: Concerted Action Program, Health and Social Service Department and Society and Culture Research Fund.

Dubeau, D., Villeneuve, R., & Thibault, S. (2011). *Être présent sur la route des pères engagés: recension québécoise 2009–2010 des modalités de soutien pour les pères*. Montreal, QC: Regroupement pour la valorisation de la paternité.

Dulac, G. (1998). L'intervention auprès des pères: des défis pour les intervenants, des gains pour les hommes. *PRISME, 8*(2), 190–206.

Dulac, G. (2001). *Aider les hommes... aussi*. Montreal, QC: Éditions VLB.

Fawcett, S., Schultz, J., Watson-Thompson, J., Fox, M., & Bremby, R. (2010). Building multisectoral partnerships for population health and health equity. *Preventing Chronic Disease, 7*(6), A118.

Forget, G., Devault, A., Allen, S., Bader, E., & Jarvis, D. (2005). Les services destinés aux pères, une description et un regard sur l'évolution des pratiques canadiennes. *Enfances, familles, générations*, Retrieved from http://www.erudit.org/revue/efg/2005/v/n3/012538ar.html

Forget, G., Devault, A., & Bizot, D. (2009). Des pratiques exemplaires pour soutenir l'engagement paternel. In D. Dubeau, A. Devault, & G. Forget (Eds.), *La paternité au XXIe siècle* (pp. 221–235). Quebec City, QC: Presses de l'Université Laval.

Gagnon, Y.-C. (2005). *L'étude de cas comme méthode de recherche: guide de réalisation*. Quebec City, QC: Presses de l'Université Laval.

Gerring, J. (2007). *Case study research: Principles and practices*. Cambridge, UK: Cambridge University Press.

Hoffman, J. (2011). *Father factors: What social science research tells us about fathers and how to work with them*. Peterborough, ON: Father Involvement Research Alliance, Retrieved from http://www.fira.ca/cms/documents/211/FatherFactorsFinal.pdf

Huberman, M., & Miles, M. B. (1991). *Analyse des données qualitatives: recueil de nouvelles méthodes*. Bruxelles, Belgium: De Boeck Université.

Long, D. (2008, December). *All dads matter: Towards an inclusive vision of father involvement initiatives in Canada*. Guelph, ON: Father Involvement Research Alliance. Retrieved from: http://www.fira.ca/cms/documents/176/April7.Long.PDF

Merriam, S. B. (1988). *Case study research in education: A qualitative approach*. San Francisco, CA: Jossey-Bass.

Miles, M. B. & Huberman, A. M. (Eds.). (1994). *Qualitative data analysis: An expanded sourcebook*. Thousand Oaks, CA: Sage.

Mishara, B. L. (2004). *Concertation entre décideurs et chercheurs pour le transfert des connaissances sur le suicide*. Montreal, QC: Université de Montréal.

Nelson, T. J. (2004). Low-income fathers. *Annual Review of Sociology, 30*(1), 427–451. http://dx.doi.org/10.1146/annurev.soc.29.010202.095947

Ouellet, F., & Goulet, C. (1998). *Être père en milieu d'extrême pauvreté*. Montreal, QC: Direction de santé publique de Montréal-Centre.

Patton, M. Q. (1987). *How to use qualitative methods in evaluation*. Newbury Park, CA: Sage.

Patton, M. Q. (1990). *Qualitative evaluation and research methods* (2nd ed.). Newbury Park, CA: Sage.

Poupart, J., et al. (1997). *La recherche qualitative: enjeux épistémologiques et méthodologiques*. Montreal, QC: Gaétan Morin.

Prilleltensky, I., Nelson, G., & Peirson, L. (2001). *Promoting family wellness and preventing child maltreatment: Fundamentals for thinking and action*. Toronto, ON: University of Toronto Press.

Rappaport, J. (1987). Terms of empowerment/exemplars of prevention: Toward a theory for community psychology. *American Journal of Community Psychology, 15*(2), 121–148. http://dx.doi.org/10.1007/BF00919275

Richmond, T., & Saloojee, A. (2005). *Social inclusion: Canadian perspectives*. Blackpoint, NS: Fernwood.

Rondeau, G. (2004). *Les hommes: s'ouvrir à leurs réalités et répondre à leurs besoins*. Report of the Working Committee on Men's Health. Quebec City, QC: Ministère de la santé et des services sociaux du Québec. Retrieved from http://publications.msss.gouv.qc.ca/acrobat/f/documentation/2004/04-911-01rap.pdf

Thalineau, A. (2009). L'intimité et l'injonction à l'autonomie dans le travail social de proximité. *Nouvelles Pratiques Sociales, 21*(2), 124–136. http://dx.doi.org/10.7202/038966ar

Turcotte, G., Forget, G., Ouellet, F., & Sanchez, I. (2009). *Le projet Relais-Pères: analyse d'une pratique innovante pour soutenir l'engagement paternel et l'insertion sociale de pères vulnérables dans quatre quartiers de Montréal*. Montreal, QC: Centre jeunesse de Montréal - Institut universitaire.

Yin, R. K. (1994). *Case study research: Design and methods*. Beverly Hills, CA: Sage.

Yin, R. K. (1998). The abridged version of case study research: Design and method. In L. Bickman & D. J. Rog (Eds.), *Handbook of applied social research methods* (pp. 229–259). Thousand Oaks, CA: Sage.

Zimmerman, M. A. (1995). Psychological empowerment: Issues and illustration. *American Journal of Community Psychology, 23*(5), 581–599. http://dx.doi.org/10.1007/BF02506983

9 Knowledge Transfer: Moving Evidence into Practice

GILLES FORGET

A review of Prospère's achievements would be incomplete without an appraisal of the final steps of the research process: the transfer of knowledge, or the dissemination, adaptation, and use of the research results. Many organizations argue that research results should further knowledge and directly influence policies, programs, practices, attitudes, and beliefs (Centraide of Greater Montreal, 2000; Quebec, 2006; SSHRC, 2009). In previous chapters, the authors discussed tools and techniques used to disseminate research results. In this chapter, I present tools and techniques that specifically address knowledge transfer, an essential part of participatory action research (PAR). In particular, I outline a framework for knowledge transfer projects and an analysis of such projects according to target populations. Knowledge transfer is a complex process, and one that funding agencies are increasing requesting. Here I give examples of the knowledge transfer projects – from training programs to performance arts initiatives – that Prospère has developed with the collaboration of various partners.

A focus on knowledge transfer is not new – indeed, Huberman (1994) ascribes the first inquiries into this technique to as early as the mid-1930s. At that time, as Huberman and other authors point out, research results would drive development, change, innovation, and social transformation using the linear research–development–dissemination model. This process would follow a series of logical steps from the beginning of the research process to the dissemination of the results among the target markets, which would then adapt and integrate the results into their practices (Gélinas & Pilon, 1994). Experience has shown, however, that this process does not necessarily lead to an adaptation of the results or to changes in public policies, programs, or practices. Consequently, researchers have tried to gain a better understanding of the elements that foster the adaptation and use of research findings. Various terms are used to designate this area of research: co-construction, exchange, translation, dissemination, and knowledge deployment, and knowledge transfer (Graham et al., 2006). Some of these terms emphasize process, others emphasize use, but all refer to the dissemination of research results and to the validation of their use.

A Reference Framework

When the Prospère team started to disseminate its research results, three perspectives guided the adoption of a reference framework for knowledge transfer: knowledge application, knowledge mobilization, and results validation.

Five principal models characterize the knowledge application perspective.[1] In the technological model, the use of knowledge is driven by decision-makers' needs and expectations. The economic model, which is close to the technological model, is also driven by users' needs, but adds the element of the furtherance of knowledge to the equation. In the organizational interest model, knowledge is disseminated and used insofar as it is in line with the organization's priorities. The dissemination model's main focus is the researchers' efforts to make the results more accessible by presenting them in plain, non-technical, language. Finally, the interaction model combines the principal elements of the other models – users' needs and expectations, organizational priorities, and the researchers' goal to reach a wider audience – and links all the elements together to measure and understand how the transfer is accomplished.

The knowledge mobilization perspective[2] emphasizes the development of new knowledge transfer tools using exchanges between researchers and user teams. In this perspective, nine variables are grouped in three main dimensions: process, means, and deployment. The process is characterized by (1) the conditions prevailing when a project is launched; (2) the exchanges between researchers and users; and (3) the mechanisms adopted to make decisions and circulate the information. The means to ensure knowledge transfer are defined by the characteristics of the target audience, the resources available, and the medium chosen. Finally, the deployment is contingent upon the decisions made to ensure dissemination of the results, evaluation of the operation, and feedback to the partners.

The validation perspective was inspired by the industrial research model, which was applied in the context of social innovation. Here, knowledge transfer is viewed as a chain of events that determines the use of the results, the unfolding of the research steps, and the interaction between researchers and users. In this respect, these elements are integrated into the first two perspectives, which divide the knowledge transfer process into steps based on the relationship between researchers and users. In addition, however, the validation perspective defines two transfer zones for the adaptation and use of results: proximal and distal.

To conclude that the validation of a research project has generated social innovation, one must first ascertain that the results have been successfully adapted by the targeted users (*proximal transfer*), whether or not the users participated in the project design. One must then ascertain that the results have been successfully disseminated (*distal transfer*), a process which reaches multiple users in other sectors and maximizes social impacts (Beaudry, Régnier, & Gagné, 2006, p. 3).

Prospère's knowledge transfer strategies can be described and analysed using five dimensions within these three perspectives. The first dimension is the context, which includes both the socio-political environment and the more specific research context. This dimension underlines the importance of the context in both the knowledge application and knowledge mobilization models. The second dimension covers knowledge from the research results and from other sources. The element that links the three perspectives, the interaction between researchers and actors, constitutes the third dimension. The fourth dimension examines the techniques used to transfer the knowledge and its appropriateness to the needs and expectations of the target clientele. Finally, the dimension of *proximal* and *distal transfers* serves to qualify the use of the knowledge and describes the outcome of the knowledge transfer process. This dimension is apparent in three ways: changes observed, new roles adopted, and the suggested use of the proposed knowledge. The knowledge transfer schema shown in Figure 9.1 illustrates this reference framework, and includes some variables associated with the chosen dimensions. It should be noted that this is a dynamic process that requires a two-way interaction between researchers and users at every stage (Lemire, Soufrez, & Laurendeau, 2013).

I begin by summarizing the general context in which the Prospère team was established from the perspectives of both the research and the father involvement issues; I then describe some of the knowledge

Figure 9.1. Knowledge Transfer, an Analytical Perspective

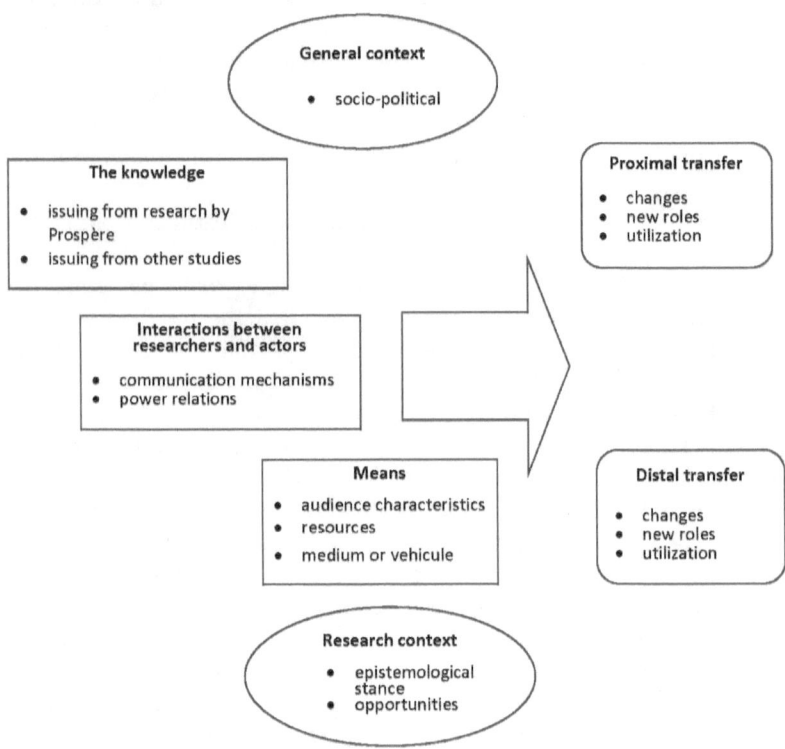

transfer strategies and activities. The strategies are grouped according to four target clienteles: at the local level, decision-makers, practitioners, and the general population; and, at a broader level, the scientific community. After presenting available evaluation data, I conclude with comments on the conditions that facilitate or hinder dissemination, adaptation, and use of the knowledge generated by social research.

The Context

The projects described in the preceding chapters were carried out in a socio-political context appropriate to the development of research on father involvement, and favoured an increased emphasis on the father's role and place in his children's lives in the development of public policies and programs. This favourable environment facilitated the creation of the Groupe de recherche et d'action sur la victimisation des enfants (GRAVE, Action and Research Group on Child Victimization) in 1993. Concurrently, Quebec provincial policies for the support of families were strengthened, and the Conseil québécois de la recherche sociale (Quebec Council of Social Research) – today known as the Fonds québécois de recherche sur la société et la culture, FQRSC (Quebec Research Fund on Society and Culture) – was instituted. Besides supporting research groups, thereby ensuring a critical mass of researchers, encouraging the advancement of disciplines, and providing stable triennial funding, this program identified knowledge transfer as a vital need, leading to an additional incentive to carry out new work in this area. At the same time, researchers expressed a desire to change their dissemination methods. Moving away from the publish-or-perish principle that prioritizes the publication of as many peer-reviewed papers as possible, they wanted to direct their research results towards other targets, using new vehicles. This desire for a change in direction was all the more timely since Canadian research policy philosophy was moving from "publish or perish" to "go public or perish," compelling researchers to justify their government grants by making their results more accessible (Renaud, 1999). The emphasis in public programs on the importance of knowledge transfer was reiterated in a Quebec government policy paper on science and innovation, which included the strengthening of knowledge translation mechanisms among its three main objectives (Quebec, 2006). This motivating context was further enhanced by the increased attention of decision-makers to research results and by the pressure on services agencies to put evidence-based programs into place. Finally, as mentioned previously, the PAR approach relies on two elements that foster knowledge transfer: close and sustained exchange between researchers and users, and ongoing reinvestment of the knowledge acquired during the implementation of the project.

The Scientific Community

The dissemination of research results to the scientific community relies mainly on the publication of articles in local, regional, national, and international journals.[3] The scientific community uses this knowledge as a reference in studies and publications and as a topic of discussion among scholars about its validity and significance in their respective fields of study. Some of Prospère's studies are good illustrations of knowledge transfer in this arena. For example, the publication of an article by our colleague Daniel Paquette (2004) on "fathers' specific functions" in the US journal *Human Development* was followed by comments by a well-known researcher in the field of fatherhood studies (Tamis-LeMonda, 2004).

One of the primary research team's responsibilities is to ensure the continuous training of the emerging generation. GRAVE-ARDEC (Alliance de recherche pour le développement des enfants dans leur communauté), along with other research teams, thus supports the training of young researchers and introduces them to the dissemination of research results through their biannual colloquium. For Prospère members, this forum was the first opportunity to present and exchange information and receive feedback on the development, implementation, and evaluation of their PAR projects to promote father involvement. Regional, provincial, national, and international scientific conferences provided further opportunities for the dissemination of research results to the scientific community.

In addition to the biannual colloquium held by GRAVE, grants from Health Canada for the research project *Sur le terrain des pères* (Involving Fathers)[4] (Bolté, Devault, St-Denis, & Gaudet, 2002) enabled the organization of the first national symposium on the role of fathers. This event brought the research team into contact with the larger scientific community, decision-makers, and the general public. The two-day symposium comprised three main sessions. The first involved managers and practitioners working on projects on best practices identified by Involving Fathers, and provided the opportunity to exchange ideas on actions required to implement father involvement initiatives. In the second session, the general public was invited to listen to participants' viewpoints from the family, social, educational, and trade union spheres concerning the paternal role in Quebec society. The third session, in an academic conference format, was held within the framework of the 2000 edition of Quebec's Journées annuelles de santé publique (Annual Public Health Days), during which experts from Quebec, elsewhere in Canada, and the United States presented and discussed the results of their fathering research and its effects on children's health and well-being. At this venue, workshops were conducted to inform participants about ongoing initiatives to support child development and promote father involvement (see Forget, 2001).

The scientific conferences organized by the team also supported the action plans in the Prospère PAR project, which aimed to promote father involvement in two socio-economically vulnerable Quebec communities (see Chapters 3 and 4). To promote the project among local decision-makers and the general public in Pointe-Calumet, a semi-rural township northeast of Montreal (site A), the steering committee organized a one-day event at the local community centre to reflect on fatherhood. The program began with a meeting with the members of the project steering committee and world-renowned fatherhood expert Michael Lamb. After hearing a presentation of the theoretical basis of the Prospère project and the plan for its local implementation, Dr Lamb addressed the aspects he considered essential to its success. The presence of this highly respected researcher and his interactions with the members of the steering committee helped convince local decision-makers of the importance of carrying out a project to promote fatherhood involvement in their community. In the afternoon the research team presented the project to practitioners in the area, and in the evening an "improv" show on the theme of fatherhood was performed in the jam-packed community hall. The show, developed by Quebec actor Robert Gravel and inspired by the Ligue nationale d'improvisation (National League of Improvisation), pitted a team of practitioners from the steering committee against a team of local decision-makers, including the mayor of the township. The teams had to improvise short scenes relating to the role and place of fathers. The researchers' support in mobilizing the community took other forms at site B, a low-income inner-city neighbourhood in the Rosemont borough of Montreal. As part of the activities organized for Family Week, the researchers presented their views on father involvement and its effects on children's health and well-being.

The Decision-Makers

The research carried out by Prospère underlines the importance of policies and programs to promote fathers' involvement with their children. If the knowledge stemming from research and from institutional and community partners leads to avenues for action, how should this knowledge be communicated to persuade decision-makers to integrate it into policies and programs for fathers and families? Although Prospère's actions have been relatively modest in scope, they nevertheless have had an influence on public policies, programs, and publications.

Policies and Programs

When the knowledge transfer process began, the need to focus on fathers and father involvement had already been emphasized in the report *Un Québec fou de ses enfants* (A Quebec Crazy for Its Kids) (Quebec 1991) and given priority in the Quebec government's five-year public health policy statement through the following directive: "All prenatal and early childhood programs must systematically include a component dealing with the importance of the role of fathers and their involvement with their children" (Quebec, 1997, p. 39). The fact that the results from Prospère's research were used in the design of several public programs following this directive can be attributed largely to the presence of institutional researchers on the team. The results of Prospère's studies led to the establishment of a long-term province-wide program called Services intégrés en périnatalité et en petite enfance (Integrated Perinatal and Early Childhood Services) and, more generally, to specific father involvement interventions in activities, programs, resources, and family services in Quebec and elsewhere.

A Consultation

Few policies deal specifically with fathers, even though practitioners' expectations regarding fathers are heavily influenced by public policy. A review of men's health and well-being and of their perceptions of available services, entitled *Les hommes: s'ouvrir à leurs réalités et répondre à leurs besoins* (Men: Understanding Their Realities and Meeting Their Needs) was submitted to Quebec's Ministère de la Santé et des Services sociaux (MSSS, Ministry of Health and Social Services) by a working committee led by Gilles Rondeau (2004). The authors suggested that intervention paths should include activities targeting fathers. As is customary when a report on the population is submitted, the MSSS held hearings to solicit input from groups and individuals concerned. The members of the Prospère team prepared and submitted a paper urging that the approach to fatherhood be broadened to include aspects other than the assistance provided to separated and divorced fathers. The paper recommended health and social services for fathers, ranging from the promotion of father involvement to the support of vulnerable fathers. Prospère's arguments can be summarizes as follows:

- *promote the father image*: according to the needs and services assessment carried out in collaboration with community partners,

actions should first aim to raise awareness of the importance of the father's role;
- *support involvement among fathers in general*: promoting the co-parenting model is the best way to stress the need for negotiation and the benefits of the participation of both parents in their parenting roles; in addition, when obstacles arise during this process, it is strongly recommended that parents be referred to a mediator;
- *provide intensive support for the most vulnerable fathers*: since the father's behaviour directly affect his health and well-being and those of the mother and children, specific actions should target vulnerable fathers to help them modify their life habits, such as by going back to school or finding a steady job, and to provide guidance in their co-parenting efforts;
- *create father-friendly environments*: father-friendly meeting places, resources, or public venues are rare, so it is important to provide this type of environment in order to reach fathers during their daily routine and to make existing practice/service environments more responsive to their needs.

The Performance Arts: An Entertaining Knowledge Transfer Strategy

A theatre initiative about fathers was developed as an intervention method to transfer knowledge to decision-makers. Intervention theatre, forum theatre, or action theatre are forms of theatrical expression that have long existed in Quebec and elsewhere, and have been used in health-promotion activities to address topics such as suicide, HIV/AIDS, and so on. The script is usually discussed with the promoter who wishes to communicate a message. The resulting presentation is quite short, and uses accessories and a production format that can be transposed easily to a variety of public venues. Besides playing their roles, the actors encourage audience members to participate.

A play, *Les pères et les services, deux solitudes* (Fathers and Services: Two Solitudes), was created by TAC Com[5] to raise awareness among decision-makers and practitioners about the importance of the role of fathers in the family unit and the need to upgrade the level of services to fathers. The twenty-minute play features two fathers talking while on their way to work. Their conversation is the leitmotiv of short scenes illustrating the interaction between fathers and various services providers. In one scene, a father answers several telephone calls after he and the mother return home with their newborn. Most of the callers ask only how the mother and the child are doing, but the pharmacist also asks, "And what about you? How do you feel?" – showing that he cares about the father's well-being as well.

The play was performed during Quebec's Annual Public Health Days at a dinner attended by registered participants. The organizers' assessment of the event was extremely positive. The play was subsequently presented at the launch of the *Pères en mouvement, pratiques en changement* (Changing Fathers, Evolving Practices) training program to an audience of organizations funded by Centraide of Greater Montreal. In the evaluation forms filled out by fifty-two of the ninety-seven audience members, the majority of respondents indicated that the play was an effective public awareness tool that directly addressed their daily reality; moreover, the results showed a satisfaction rate of over 92 per cent regarding this segment of the launch. The respondents also remarked that the play encouraged them to reflect on fatherhood, to participate actively, and to dismiss some of their preconceived ideas regarding fathers. There have been several other presentations of the play, and it is included in the theatre company's catalogue for booking purposes.

Prospère's knowledge transfer strategies also included other stage performances – namely, the *Su-père Show* (Super Show) and *La Grande permission* (The Great Permission). The Super Show was organized to be presented during the one-day event devoted to the review of the progress of the provincial deployment process of Changing Fathers, Evolving Practices. With the participation of the team's Montreal partner, the Regroupement pour la valorisation de la paternité (RVP), the idea became reality in a ninety-minute production that also served as a fundraising event for the RVP's activities. A member of RVP, who is also a well-known artist, acted as master of ceremonies for the show, and emphasized the value of fatherhood. The participants delivered excerpts from a play about the male status, speeches, and humorous monologues on the fatherhood topic, and sang songs about fatherhood. All guest actors performed on a *pro bono* basis. A sequel to the Super Show was created five years later.

Using the performance and media art fields, Prospère's team also produced The Great Permission[6] as a celebration of the completion of the team's ten-year research activities and as an opportunity to express its appreciation to all the partners. After opening remarks and speeches, participants were urged to peruse the tools produced by Prospère and its various partners. The highlight of the evening was the presentation of an original slideshow on the theme of fatherhood by Alain Bissonnette, a local artist. For the finale, a few of the more talented members of the research team gave voice to a memorable medley.

The Practitioners

The results of the field study to assess existing services at the two pilot sites of the Prospère project (Forget, 1995) revealed what remained to be done to raise awareness about father involvement among practitioners and to furnish them with the appropriate tools to reach fathers and respond to their needs. In this pre-intervention analysis, it was found that the proposed initiative to promote father involvement led services professionals in these communities to ask questions. It was also found that existing services were directed almost exclusively at improving the well-being of mothers and their children. These findings, correlated with the results of other Prospère studies and other emerging knowledge in the field, quickly led researchers to determine that the training of practitioners is an essential part of knowledge transfer.

Changing Fathers, Evolving Practices

The training program, Changing Fathers, Evolving Practices, was and remains an important activity aimed at translating *knowledge, know-how*, and *knowing-how-to-be* among practitioners. The training program was disseminated to services providers from various sectors in Montreal, in the province of Quebec, in the rest of Canada, and in France.

The program, designed to be co-conducted by a man and a woman, can be administered in a variety of formats. A training manual provides a detailed description of procedures in the sessions, but trainers can adapt the program to the characteristics of the territory and to their own particular competencies. Every trainee receives a guide for each workshop that outlines the day's schedule, explains the activities, and summarizes the main points to be presented. The trainees' guide also contains a list of bibliographical references, tools, and websites that can be consulted to supplement the training sessions. The training program is designed to bring together partners located in the same territory whose work is related to father involvement, and it strives to reach as many male practitioners as possible. The objectives of the training program are to:

- encourage a better understanding of the importance of father involvement;

- develop concrete intervention avenues to promote practices that provide more attention to fathers;
- foster father-friendly services and organizations; and
- disseminate concrete tools to develop local cross-sector action.

The content of the training program is based largely on knowledge produced by the research carried out by Prospère. It focuses on the father's role and on the definition and dimensions of father involvement. Obstacles and solutions with regard to the progressive integration of fathers as a targeted clientele in services and organizations are also main topics. Finally, the program identifies common elements among best practices. The content is also inspired by the results of studies on the effects of father involvement on children's developmental outcomes, the evolution of fatherhood through the ages, data on new family realities, fathers' expressed needs, and the main strategies to reach fathers. The training has adapted adult education techniques to draw on learners' experiences, teamwork, and dialogue between trainers and trainees. The sharing of local experiences might include the testimony of a practitioner from the region. Finally, during breaks in the training sessions, participants are invited to peruse the display of texts and practical tools set up by the trainers. These items include the principle theoretical writings on which the training program is based, several tools developed by Prospère and its partners, and other tools added during the training process. All of the above are resources provided to stimulate reflection and action among the trainees.

The training program was drawn up in several stages (Ouellet & Forget, 2003b). The validation of Prospère's research results by practitioners from three communities – a city in an outlying region, a semi-rural community, and an inner-city neighbourhood – was made possible by the financial support of Montreal's Agence de la santé et des services sociaux (Health and Social Services Agency) and the MSSS. The validation process relied on the participation of fifty-six practitioners in these three communities, who were working in institutional, community, and other services networks concerned with the role of the father. Their comments were taken into consideration, and the content was finalized for use in the provincial deployment of the training program, which involved forty-nine future trainers from eleven Quebec regions and from Montreal (including staff members from fourteen of the then twenty-nine Centres locaux de services communautaires in that city).

The Deployment of the Training Program

In Montreal, with the help of a federal grant from the Community Action Program for Children (CAPC) and in collaboration with a family agency (Station familles de Montréal), six free training sessions were given to practitioners working in organizations supported by the CAPC.

Following the first six sessions, the deployment continued, thanks to the participation of the umbrella organization, Centraide of Greater Montreal. Centraide entered into a partnership with Montreal's Agence de la santé et des services sociaux, through which services providers from organizations supported by Centraide received the training free of charge. This partnership also made possible the development and validation of a workshop entitled *Migration and Fatherhood*, since both institutions shared the same main focus. Centraide asked an independent researcher to evaluate the adaptation and use of the training program (Venet, 2006). The evaluator followed and documented every stage of the program, and assessed its impact on the organizations and on the providers' services; she also led an advisory committee made up of representatives of the partner organizations. The evaluation had four general objectives: (1) to draw a profile of the organizations and the services providers who benefited from the training program; (2) to evaluate changes in the practices of services providers who had undergone the training; (3) to evaluate changes in the organizations whose members had undergone the training; (4) to present a few examples of networking.

The evaluator's analysis was based on assessment charts and a questionnaire (the first part of which was completed during the training and the second part a few months afterwards), as well as on interviews with thirty-six managers and practitioners of various organizations after they had undergone the training. Table 9.1 summarizes the principal findings of the evaluation. The evaluator concluded: "The effects noted were positive and fulfilled the stated expectations of the Changing Fathers, Evolving Practices training program."

In Quebec, the provincial deployment of Changing Fathers, Evolving Practices was carried out by Prospère's team members together with the practitioners who provided training to the facilitators. In total, some one thousand practitioners from twelve of Quebec's sixteen administrative regions benefited from the two-day training session. For example, a male-and-female team from the Lanaudière region that had undergone

Table 9.1. Summary of the Evaluation of Changing Fathers, Evolving Practices

---

The reference framework

In almost all the organizations:
- there are fathers benefiting from services;
- no discrimination towards mothers/fathers is seen at first contact (in terms of the premises, welcome by services providers, the information given);
- fathers are invited or sought out to join in family activities, special events, and outings, and when they do not, services providers try to find out why.

In most of the organizations:
- fathers increasingly are present;
- fathers are taken into consideration as much as mothers (regarding information concerning them, involvement in activities, follow-up regarding their children);
- services providers are encouraged to draw fathers into active participation, and are given information and support when called on to implement father involvement initiatives.

In a few of the organizations:
- services providers make sure they reach fathers as well as mothers (in-home visits), and transmit information directly when the parents are separated;
- fathers are prioritized, and specific means are employed to reach them (through customized approaches and activities, availability of staff, especially male services providers, designated to work with fathers);
- fathers participate in decision-making.

The changes
- only 4 out of 22 practitioners said that no changes had taken place after the training;
- 10 practitioners said the changes introduced were directly due to the training.

Among practitioners	*In the organizations*
- the approach has become more specific, and more practitioners solicit fathers and try to determine the reasons for their lack of participation; - communication with fathers has improved; - services providers have become more vigilant and aware of fathers' needs.	- fathers are present in greater numbers (but are still in the minority compared to mothers); - a common vision occasionally has been developed; - the promotion of activities has been adapted to target fathers; - the scheduling of activities has been changed to be more accessible to fathers; - some administrative changes were introduced; - there are more male services professionals in organizations; - in some organizations, there is a willingness to engage in projects related to fatherhood through joint action groups and programs with neighbourhood organizations.

Obstacles hindering change
- regular programming already overloaded;
- lack of time and flexibility in schedules;
- lack of financial and human resources;
- scarcity of male services professionals;
- absence of fathers in the organization, implying the need for customized strategies to reach them;
- personal resistance by some services professionals (including those who had received training);
- lack of open-mindedness in some organizations.

a train-the-trainer program at the beginning of the deployment process conducted six training sessions, reaching 130 practitioners. Sometime after the presentation of the program, this team, with the assistance of a university researcher, evaluated its impact (Ferland, 2004) by means of evaluation questionnaires completed by sixty-eight service professionals (53 per cent of the trainees). The services professionals indicated that they had become more aware of the needs of fathers and felt better equipped to support them in their efforts to exercise their parental role and functions. They also identified changes in the organizations, such as the greater availability of male services providers, the development of father-friendly tools, increased access to documentation on fatherhood, improvements in the facilities used by fathers, the creation of working committees, and an increase in the number of joint action initiatives.

At the provincial level, a study on the support of parents offered by community resources serving Quebec families (Lemieux, Charbonneau, & Comeau, 2005) emphasized the benefits of the training program. The authors noted that the awareness-raising component of Changing Fathers, Evolving Practices had produced positive results: "Perhaps due to the awareness effect of this activity ..., the subject of fathers seemed to be a central concern in all the regions we visited" (p. 27).

ELSEWHERE IN CANADA

During the provincial deployment of Changing Fathers, Evolving Practices, Prospère's relationship with one of the originators of the federal project *My Daddy Matters Because...*[7] led to the adaptation of the Quebec training program to the English-language version (Ouellet & Forget, 2003a). The validation process for the English-language version was done in three training sessions offered in collaboration with local trainers in Charlottetown, Prince Edward Island, and in Abbotsford and Vancouver, British Columbia. The evaluation of the English-language adaptation was as positive as the original version, but some minor revisions were made following this validation process, particularly in the illustrative examples. The last session to train local trainers took place in Kelowna, British Columbia. The BC Council for Families received a grant from the Public Health Agency of Canada to deploy the training program across that province. The evaluation of four of these training sessions submitted to the Public Health Agency (Sundstrom, 2005) indicated a very high level of satisfaction among participants, and recognized a significant knowledge transfer – particularly regarding cross-sector actions to promote father involvement and practical new information on interventions targeting fathers. Some of the participants also took part in post-training actions, including a media campaign to raise public awareness of the importance of the father's role. The BC Council for Families subsequently received additional funding to hold more training sessions.

IN FRANCE

APPROCHES (Agir pour la promotion de la citoyenneté des hommes et de leur santé), in collaboration with Montreal's Agence de la santé et des services sociaux and with the support of GRAVE, proposed the deployment of Changing Fathers, Evolving Practices in France.[8] Following the training session, fifty-eight practitioners in the Bouches-du-Rhône and Var regions were asked to evaluate the program. Both the quantitative and qualitative results clearly indicated that the main objectives of the program had been attained – that is, it raised awareness among the practitioners, stimulated their desire to act, encouraged networking, and was useful to them in their daily tasks in supporting fathers to exercise their parental role.

Adapted to the French context, the basic training session was presented in six three-hour workshops, co-conducted by a male and a female trainer, and involved fifteen services professionals from the same community but who worked in different sectors. The majority of the participants were men. The social and health data of the program content were updated and adapted to the French context. A third day was added to the initial training session to include a workshop on fatherhood and the migration process. From this workshop, the international versions of the trainer manual and the participant guide were edited (Forget, Bizot, & Ouellet, 2006).

The training of future trainers began in Marseilles with the support of the regional health and social services agency (the Direction départementale des Affaires sanitaires et sociales des Bouches-du-Rhône) and the national (cross-sector) family service agency (the Délégation interministérielle à la famille). The training program was divided into three main stages. The first, *self-training*, required that the participants read the manual to gain a basic knowledge of the material. The second stage, *co-training*, comprised three phases: a look at the overall contents and presentation techniques; the pairing of the future trainers with workshop leaders in joint activities; and a critical review of the previous phase, in which the participants identified and analysed difficulties they might have had in carrying out the activities. Finally, the third stage, *hetero-training*, depended on the training given by the facilitator-trainer duo during the basic sessions. At the end of this process, the future trainers were capable of training practitioners in their respective regions without further guidance. The promotion and dissemination of the Changing Fathers, Evolving Practices training program has continued in France.

Community Mobilization

Analysis of knowledge transfer often omits an element that is at the heart of the interaction between researchers and actors. I am referring not to the adaptation of research results to influence policies, programs, and practices, but, rather, to the use of the results to spur and support community mobilization. As described previously, Prospère employed several strategies to reach the latter goal.

A newsletter, *Double V voisinage* (Double N Neighbourhood), was one of several tools developed within the framework of the Prospère PAR project to promote father involvement and to mobilize actors. Approximately one hundred copies of the newsletter were printed and distributed to all the decision-makers and services professionals at the two participating sites. Each issue focused on a specific aspect of the research. The first issue was titled "The role of the steering committee: An urgent issue for discussion," and dealt with the interaction between the different organizations involved in the project and between researchers and actors. Subsequent issues of the newsletter presented results of the project evaluations.

The actors at the sites also used the knowledge gained during the Prospère project to develop knowledge transfer tools. The fathers of Pointe-Calumet (site A) and the surrounding area were mobilized to raise funds to produce a booklet to accompany the *Dessine-moi un papa* (Draw Me a Daddy) exhibition (Forget & Gariépy, 1997). The knowledge transferred to fathers and mothers visiting the exhibition was reinforced when they took the booklet home and used the ideas and activities presented in it to interact with their children. Actors at site B, the Montreal neighbourhood of Rosemont, produced a poster and a leaflet containing a questionnaire for parents to complete. Parents then could compare their answers with those of the four hundred fathers and mothers who completed the questionnaire used in the family survey of the field study. The questions were also used to create a game based on the popular TV game show, *Family Feud*, where two teams challenge each other's knowledge of today's behaviour of fathers and mothers.

The Population: Fathers, Mothers, and Children

The purpose of Prospère's research projects is first and foremost to improve the health of the general public. Of course, achieving this goal is contingent upon policies, programs, and practices of services providers, but above all it is dependent on the general population's values, attitudes, and behaviours. Therefore, several of Prospère's knowledge transfer strategies directly targeted the family unit: fathers, mothers, and children.

Draw Me a Daddy: A Travelling Exhibition

After reaching a consensus regarding their vision of the problem (the low level of father involvement in the community) and its solution, the steering committee at site A set out to implement its first yearly action plan. As the committee included representatives from the educational field, the idea of an association with the township's primary school seemed a natural choice. To do this, the teachers of kindergarten and grade one classes requested during the art period that their pupils "draw a Daddy." More than 150 drawings were collected from children between five and seven years old. The huge potential of this material was immediately apparent, but the real question, reflecting the steering committee's primary goal was: "How could the drawings be used to raise public awareness of the importance of the role of fathers?"

The strength of a team depends on the sum of its assets, and bringing actors together also brings networks together. Thus, a Prospère team member contacted one of his acquaintances, a community museologist,[9] requesting a bid for organizing and disseminating a travelling exhibition that would be called *Dessine-moi un papa* (Draw Me a Daddy). In her bid, she described the objectives of this tool this way:

> The committee promoting the *Initiative Place-O-Pères* [A Place for Fathers] project in Pointe-Calumet wishes to organize an exhibition illustrating fathers' involvement with their very young children, which, at the same time, will promote the social and community actions being carried out in this sense. The holding of this exhibition is a component of the action plan

of the promotion committee, an initiative by Prospère ... The objectives of the exhibition are to raise public awareness regarding the importance of fathers in their children's lives, and to draw attention to the Place for Fathers Initiative in Pointe-Calumet.

The exhibition comprised eighteen panels of texts, photographs, children's drawings, and other illustrations, combined with two-dimensional graphics that gave the finished product greater appeal. Parents and children visiting the exhibition could play parent-child games; they also had access to a software program that allowed fathers to evaluate their degree of involvement with their children by comparing their answers with those of the fathers interviewed in the evaluation of the Prospère project. The exhibit was designed to be easily moved and installed in any public facility with an exhibition space of 1.86 square metres or more. Two host-animators were responsible for setting up the exhibition and welcoming visitors.[10] Along with the staff of Muséobus, a mobile museum, local members of the steering committee were trained to welcome and inform visitors to the Draw Me a Daddy exhibition.

The exhibition content was based primarily on the knowledge emanating from Prospère's PAR project at the two pilot sites. The project was explained and father involvement and its principal dimensions were defined. As an example, a panel entitled *A Father in Interaction*, illustrated by the children's drawings addressing this particular dimension, included the following text:

> A father in interaction means that the father is present for his child. "Present" is defined by the time spent in interaction with the child or, in other words, the time that the child is convinced that his/her father is available and accessible. This dimension of father involvement is at the heart of the father's role. The emphasis is on the father's psychological or physical presence in his child's life rather than simply on his function of breadwinner, the role solely valued in the past. Direct contact with the child is important when carrying out childcare tasks and activities such as: playing hockey, visiting a museum, talking about school, dressing and feeding the child, watching the child play and answering his/her questions.

Presented for the first time at site A, in the centre of Pointe-Calumet, the Draw Me a Daddy exhibition was immediately hailed as a unique community mobilization tool. The tool's relevance and quality were given recognition by the Ministry of Health and Social Services, which provided a $25,000 grant to support its province-wide dissemination. In the following eighteen months, the exhibition was displayed for periods of forty days or more in twenty-seven districts throughout Quebec. According to an approximate count by the host-animators, an average of 165 fathers, mothers, and children attended each display. This number did not include the 30,000 visitors to the Parents and Kids Fair in Montreal, where the Draw Me a Daddy exhibit was displayed twice. Although a subsequent funding request for wider circulation was turned down, the exhibition continues to be disseminated by the Family Service Centre in Pointe-Calumet, but in a more limited manner.

At site B, in Rosemont, the steering committee was inspired by the success of the Draw Me a Daddy initiative and created a similar tool, but with different content and dissemination vehicles. Primary school representatives of the site B steering committee helped to obtain the participation of local schools. The teachers at site B asked their pupils to draw a situation they had experienced with their own father. A committee chose twelve of the drawings, one for each month, for use in a calendar highlighting the activities promoting father involvement. The calendar, edited and printed with the financial support of local businesses, featured a monthly maxim addressing the importance of the father's role and also presented certain research results.

The Doorknob Hanger

As part of the same PAR project, Prospère developed a series of doorknob-hanger cards called *Accroche-père* (Attract Fathers) bearing catchphrases highlighting fathers' roles, for distribution at regular intervals to all the households at the two pilot sites. The cards' main function was to attract fathers and prompt them to invest more time and effort in family life. Each card measured 215 × 105 mm, with a hole cut out to fit it over the doorknob. To maximize the tool's impact, the dissemination extended over an eight-month period and involved the distribution of a new card every month. This strategy ensured regular and repeated exposure, thus increasing both the understanding and retention of the information. The doorknob hangers transmitted the knowledge gathered in the family survey performed during the field study of the Prospère PAR project and in the interviews that were the basis of a doctoral thesis on fathers' mental health (Dufour, 2001).

From the beginning, certain parameters were defined to ensure the logical progression and reinforcement of both the form and the content of the doorknob-hanger messages. Various fathers' statements and sponsoring entities' logos from site A or site B were printed on the front of the cards. The reverse side contained information on a theme addressed in the family survey, together with the survey results and results of other research studies on the same subject. Lastly, a section on the back of the cards listed the current activity schedule in the local action plans. Particular attention was given to the visual presentation of the doorknob hangers to make them attractive and inviting for their target audience. The eight themes were: fathers' involvement and presence in their children's lives, fathers' sense of parental competence, balancing work and family life, disciplining children, couples' relationships, three father profiles, fathers and the community, and the father-child relationship. Although the main subjects were the same at both sites, the specific texts varied according to the data gathered in each community.

This eight-month knowledge transfer operation was evaluated in two ways. First, university students associated with the research project carried out interviews with 285 fathers and mothers at the two sites. In the first part of the interview, parents were asked if they were aware of the doorknob hangers, if they had read them, and whether they found the messages relevant. The second section of the interview concerned only the project target clientele – that is, the parents of children under age six. After answering the questions in the first section, these fathers and mothers were also asked if the tool had generated discussions and, if so, which topics were discussed. They were also asked if they knew about the father involvement initiative taking place in their community. The results (GRAVE-ARDEC, 1999) showed that approximately half the interviewees were aware of the contents of the doorknob hangers. This proportion increased to 60 per cent among fathers and 57 per cent among mothers of children under age six. Approximately two-thirds of these parents, representing a little over half of all the parents interviewed, had read the doorknob hangers and 87 per cent of them had found the contents relevant or very relevant. Half of the fathers and mothers were aware of the project.

The second evaluation of the tool was based on the post-intervention inquiry. The analysis revealed that 86 per cent of the fathers who said they had read the doorknob hangers were aware of the project compared with only 22 per cent of those who did not recollect receiving the hangers. Overall, the campaign reached its intended audience, as 70 per cent of the parents of children under age six had read the doorknob hangers compared with only a quarter of the parents of older children.

The evaluated effectiveness of this medium led to its repeated use. Taking advantage of the association with the national project, *My Daddy Matters Because...*, the doorknob hanger was presented to a community-based organization in British Columbia[11] that was looking for an original way to publicize its services. In adopting the tool, the organization created a series of four doorknob hangers addressing poverty, daycare, housing needs, and the importance of volunteering. Although our respective objectives differed, it was gratifying to learn that the tool had been useful elsewhere for the purposes of knowledge transfer and the promotion of an organization's services.

A Review of Knowledge Transfer

The review of Prospère's experiences provided an occasion for the team and its partners to reflect on knowledge transfer.[12]

A Favourable Context, with Some Resistance

As was evident during the evaluation process, the general research context facilitated knowledge transfer. The interests of the scientific community, practitioners, and the general public were taken into consideration while discussing the role and place of fathers, which ensured a greater receptiveness and sustained support from all actors. The team was continuously encouraged by social sponsoring bodies to innovate and share the results of their work with the various clienteles concerned with the promotion of father involvement. The participation of all the partners remained stable throughout the research period and even continued afterward. Last but not least, the public was on hand at the various scientific and public events encouraging knowledge transfer. Different government departments were equally receptive to Prospère's initiatives, integrating some of the initiatives into their own programs. Although funding for knowledge transfer remains at a relatively low level compared with the amounts dedicated to research and intervention, most of the experiences described above received the required funding.

The research context is not exempt from tensions. Resistance exists within the scientific community among advocates of feminist, masculinist, or gender-differentiated research. It is also reflected in the wariness towards the promotion of fatherhood initiatives of decision-makers who might not wish to appear to support advocacy for fathers' custody rights.[13] That the vast majority of practitioners working for associations or institutions in the family, health, and social services sectors – where entrenched attitudes or practices might prevail – are female makes it occasionally difficult to introduce new practices concerning fathers. Finally, the evolution of social attitudes in the general population is a gradual process, and evidence-based results are not instantly transformed into new parenting practices. Unfortunately, the daily newspapers still remind us of the abuse suffered by children, as well as the deplorable living conditions of too many parents – fathers and mothers alike.

The context of the research facilitated knowledge transfer in three principal ways. First, the repeated renewal of funding allowed the Prospère team to continue its research on the knowledge transfer component and enabled the search for new partners. Second, the choice of participatory action research as an epistemological and methodological position clearly influenced the research process, encouraging knowledge exchange, critical review, and ongoing questioning by both users and researchers. The interdisciplinary nature of the project and the methodological approach adopted by Prospère allowed the triangulation of data and observations, the multiplication of analyses, and the production of rigorous and nuanced knowledge. Finally, the fact that the team was composed of university and institutional researchers facilitated knowledge transfer through access to multiple networks and to some actors who are in a position to influence practices and parenting models.

This functioning mode is not without challenges for research teams: it requires that researchers negotiate among themselves when contradictions arise and that they disseminate all the gathered knowledge, not only the results of their personal research. This mode is also dependent on aligning individual goals and institutional expectations. A sense of humour, mutual respect, acceptance, and assistance are the necessary teamwork qualities that indisputably facilitate knowledge transfer.

The Varying Nature of the Clienteles' Interests

The means adopted constitute an intrinsic part of the knowledge transfer process. Our experience has shown that the means must be based on a needs analysis, be accessible, address as many audiences as possible, have the necessary financial support, and meet quality criteria. Even when these conditions are met, the effectiveness of knowledge transfer largely depends on the attention paid to and the benefits received by the various concerned clienteles. To expect immediate results after reaching the targeted population is a dream. Influencing social attitudes, policies, and programs takes time. It might be precisely because results are not immediate that social research objectives appear difficult to attain. Research and social action are a shared responsibility, and each actor is bound by different obligations. As to the complexity of the research objective itself, successful knowledge transfer is contingent upon multiple factors requiring an array of means broad enough to take into account all the nuances inherent to the individual, social, and political aspects of fatherhood. In addition, the development of knowledge translation tools requires adequate means and competencies. Network interchanges facilitate the development of dissemination tools using outside resources' competencies. However, throughout the process, the researcher remains responsible for keeping an eye on the message and, therefore, has the time-consuming duty of taking part in all stages of the production of the knowledge transfer tool.

Beyond the traditional means of knowledge transfer used by the academic community (communications, publications, reports, conferences), the Prospère team developed a variety of new dissemination strategies, ranging from the use of performance arts to direct advertising techniques to reach the general public at home. As the evaluation process has shown, these initiatives were well received by the target audiences. The diversity and array of the means used appear to be two key ingredients of a successful knowledge transfer strategy.

Interactions with the Actors: Partners and Relational Capital

Another key element in the use of research results is what Huberman (1994) calls sustained interactivity, which comprises the ongoing interactions between researchers and users and the mechanisms set up to support these interactions. This important element is discussed in the literature on knowledge application. In his interaction model, Mishara (2006) uses the concept of relational capital, defined as the relationship of trust that grows between the researcher and the user during a series of interactions. These interactions are facilitated by relatively complex exchange mechanisms, from the simple transmission of information to personal contact. Relational capital is influenced by several conditions.

In Prospère's experience, the conditions that should be present when a PAR project is set in motion are the identification of influential partners in the community, a convergence of interests, and the negotiated establishment of a clear consensus regarding the reference framework among all partners. Once the project has begun, development of relational capital includes a sustained investment in human, technical, and financial resources to ensure that the planned research and actions are properly carried out, together with free-flowing communications and the sharing of successes. In the end, the quality of a PAR project depends on ongoing dialogue, openness to feedback, and the integration of the resulting changes and solutions. The efforts made to maintain successful relations among partners and collaborators throughout the research project should also extend to knowledge transfer activities as an additional area for sharing recognition/appreciation and action. The relational capital evident in the experiences undoubtedly reflects the cohesion among the members of the research team established before the start of the project.

A number of difficulties can undermine relational capital. The mobility of team members, political or structural reorganizations, compartmentalization of the research and practice environments, and breakdowns in communication mechanisms are among the elements that might transform the initial framework and that must be monitored, reviewed, and renegotiated. The presence of a resource person specifically mandated to guide and encourage this interrelational make-up is an important contributor to the structure and cohesion of a team and leads to a successful knowledge transfer process.

The Appropriation, Use, and Construction of Knowledge

Knowledge evolves and is constructed throughout its appropriation and use. This can be seen in the transformation made to the means of appropriation by those wishing to translate the knowledge. This process was apparent in the way the trainers in the Changing Fathers, Evolving Practices program adapted knowledge to the realities of their regions, making use of their individual experiences and competencies. Cultural adaptation, through the integration of the characteristics of targeted territories, is another example of the transformation of the means of appropriation. In several of Prospère's knowledge transfer strategies, the means of knowledge appropriation was adapted by partners at the pilot sites who produced their own tools, by trainers who developed their deployment techniques, and by researchers who were creative in the dissemination of the results. This movement presupposes respect for one another's abilities, an emphasis on the value of competencies, and openness to the diversification of knowledge in social research.

Ultimately, each research project is carried out with the hope that the results will be used to change both attitude and public policy, or to validate decisions already taken (Reardon, Lavis, & Gibson, 2007). In Prospère's case, the successful achievement of this objective depended on mobilizing the partners to use the knowledge, and was measured by the extent to which the knowledge was transferred to targeted clienteles through either proximal or distal transfers. Prospère's experiences gave researchers the opportunity to observe the different ways in which particular knowledge transfer strategies can be carried out. In several instances, the results initially were shared with the first users, the partners at the sites, and the practitioners. This initial proximal exchange allowed researchers to validate the knowledge and to determine which portion should be retained. The partners then used these elements in other contexts and forms, as illustrated by the posters and other tools developed at site B. Pursuing their dissemination efforts, the researchers reached audiences on a regional scale through the travelling exhibition; on a provincial scale through the play; on a national scale through the symposium; and on an international scale through the training program. These experiences brought out the crucial nature of the partners' constant support, their participation in selecting the most relevant knowledge, and their collaboration in the dissemination efforts.

Challenges and Outlook for the Future

This review has allowed one to point out the Prospère team's successes and to identify the conditions that facilitate knowledge adaptation, use, and transfer, but it also underlines certain difficulties and challenges in this field. It appears much easier to mobilize proximal partners directly involved in the action than political and institutional partners, who are subjected to various influences and constraints. The major challenge remaining in promoting father involvement is to find the best way to gain the support of decision-makers.

A reflection on knowledge transfer would not be complete without a glimpse at the perspectives likely to contribute to its renewal and further development. Unless a greater effort is made to foster and encourage knowledge transfer, social research funding for it might dry up.

Prospère benefited from financial support, but more than once the team was forced to knock on a number of doors to obtain the necessary financial resources to complete the research process and to ensure the dissemination of the results. Funding bodies support knowledge transfer to the scientific community by earmarking a portion of research grants for the dissemination of results at academic conferences, but these amounts might not be sufficient to reach the population at large and to develop innovative practices in results dissemination.

This reflection brings one to the difficulty of reconciling research, action, and dissemination. For this reason, researchers are approached by knowledge brokers whose task is essentially to translate the knowledge and disseminate it among the targeted clienteles. The addition of this actor to the process might make perfect sense, but it should not exempt the researcher from his or her own responsibility regarding knowledge transfer.

The question of responsibility leads one to a necessary discussion of the ethics of knowledge transfer. The scientific community has established rules concerning the protection of participants in social research projects and the use of personal data, but what about the appropriation and use of the results of these projects?

The interactions among partners – that is, the relational capital – remain at the heart of this process. These interactions must be guided by values that include mutual respect and recognition. Intellectual property is one of the elements that should enter into negotiations between partners. But how can researchers ensure that each person's efforts will be given due recognition?

In the end, reviewing these experiences takes one to the subject itself: the father's role in child development. An element that shone forth in the knowledge transfer process was the public's unflagging interest in discussing fatherhood and exploring its limits, and in reflecting on the conditions needed to understand fatherhood better and to take action. Let us hope that, for the health and well-being of our society, this interest will continue to grow.

NOTES

1 This explanation is based on reflections on knowledge application by Brian L. Mishara and the team at the Centre de recherche et d'intervention sur le suicide et l'euthanasie (Research and Intervention Centre on Suicide and Euthanasia).

2   The notion of knowledge mobilization was introduced by Peter Levesque at the Father Involvement Research Alliance congress held in Toronto in May 2005.
3   For a selection, see http://www.unites.uqam.ca/grave/pages/recherche.php.
4   *Involving Fathers*, Project No. 6786–15–1998–1120026, Community Action Program for Children and Canada Prenatal Nutrition Program (CAPC/CPNP) National Projects Fund, Health Canada.
5   Online at http://www.taccom.ca.
6   This event took place at the cabaret Le Lion d'Or, Montreal on 19 November 2003.
7   "My Daddy Matters Because...," Project No. 6786–15–2002–4550009, CAPC/CPNP National Project Fund on Fathering, Public Health Agency of Canada.
8   The description of the deployment of the program in France is taken from the information sheet distributed to participants attending the presentation at the Paris city hall (Bizot & Forget, 2007).
9   The museologist, Odette Gariépy, was at that time director of Muséobus, a mobile museum in the Montérégie region. She has been an active participant in the development of the new community-based social tendency in museology.
10 A demonstration model of the exhibition was made for presentation at conferences and other events outside the community, including an international conference in Berne, Switzerland, in 1998.
11 The British Columbia project was called RAISE, and was created in 2006 by Abbotsford Community Services, Abbotsford, BC.
12 The last seminar held by GRAVE-ARDEC was called "Sharing Knowledge on Knowledge Translation: A Reflection on Knowledge Dissemination in Community-based Initiatives, *Prospère; 1, 2, 3, Go!*; and *Mères avec pouvoir*," Université du Québec à Montréal, Montreal, 17 May 2007.
13 The very mention of the term is enough to raise hackles in the discussion surrounding the father-child relationship.

REFERENCES

Beaudry, D. N., Régnier, L., & Gagné, S. (2006). *Chaîne de valorisation de résultats de la recherche universitaire recelant un potentiel d'utilisation par une entreprise ou par un autre milieu*. Quebec City, QC: Conseil des sciences et des technologies.

Bizot, D., & Forget, G. (2007). *Une formation pour transférer les connaissances et favoriser l'implication des pères dans la vie de leurs enfants*. Paris.

Bolté, C., Devault, A., St-Denis, M., & Gaudet, J. (2002). *On father's ground: A portrait of projects to support and promote fathering*. Montreal, QC: Université du Québec à Montréal, GRAVE-ARDEC.

Centraide of Greater Montreal. (2000). *Building caring communities and supporting their ability to act*. Montreal, QC: Centraide of Greater Montreal.

Dufour, S. (2001). *La santé mentale des enfants de milieux défavorisés: conceptions, pratiques et profils de pères* (unpublished doctoral dissertation). Université du Québec à Montréal, Montreal.

Ferland, L. (2004). *Intervenir auprès des pères... préoccupations d'intervenants*. Joliette, QC: CLSC–CHSLD d'Autray, Joliette.

Forget, G. (1995). *Un modèle communautaire de soutien à l'engagement paternel: analyse du milieu à Pointe-Calumet*. Montreal, QC: Direction de la santé publique de Montréal-Centre.

Forget, G. (2001). *Involving fathers: Proceedings of the first national symposium on the place and role of fathers*. Montreal, QC: Direction de la santé publique de Montréal-Centre.

Forget, G., Bizot, D., & Ouellet, F. (2006). *Pères en mouvement, pratiques en changement, édition internationale: guide du formateur et guides des participants (nos 1–6)*. Montreal, QC: Direction de la santé publique de Montréal-Centre.

Forget, G., & Gariépy, O. (1997). *Dessine-moi un papa* (exhibition guide). Montreal, QC: Direction de la santé publique de Montréal-Centre.

Gélinas, A., & Pilon, J. M. (1994). Le transfert des connaissances en recherche sociale et la transformation des pratiques. *Nouvelles Pratiques Sociales, 7*(2), 75–91. http://dx.doi.org/10.7202/301278ar

Graham, I. D., et al. (2006). Lost in knowledge translation: Time for a map? *Journal of Continuing Education in the Health Professions, 26*(1), 13–24. http://dx.doi.org/10.1002/chp.47

GRAVE-ARDEC (1999). *Les accroche-portes de CooPère Rosemont: quelques résultats d'une petite enquête*. Montreal, QC: Université du Québec à Montréal, Groupe de recherche et d'action sur la victimisation des enfants-Alliance de recherche pour le développement des enfants dans leur communauté.

Huberman, A. M. (1994). *Qualitative data analysis: An expanded sourcebook* (2nd ed.). Thousand Oaks, CA: Sage.

Lemieux, D., Charbonneau, J., & Comeau, M. (2005). *La parentalité dans les organismes communautaires pour la famille*. Montreal, QC: INRS Urbanisation, culture et société.

Lemire, N., Soufrez, K., & Laurendeau, M. C. (2013). *Facilitating a knowledge translation process: Knowledge review and facilitation tool*. Quebec City, QC:

Institut national de santé publique du Québec. Retrieved from http://www.inspq.qc.ca/pdf/publications/1628_FaciliKnowledgeTransProcess.pdf

Mishara B. L. (2006). *Vérification d'un modèle d'application des connaissances en prévention du suicide.* (unpublished).

Ouellet, F., & Forget, G. (2003a). *Changing fathers, evolving practices, trainer and trainees guide (1–4).* Montreal, QC: Direction de la santé publique de Montréal-Centre.

Ouellet, F., & Forget, G. (2003b). Pères en mouvement, pratiques en changement: une formation pour favoriser le transfert des connaissances. *Reflets, 9*(2), 222–240. http://dx.doi.org/10.7202/011099ar

Paquette, D. (2004). Theorizing the father-child relationship: Mechanisms and developmental outcomes. *Human Development, 47*(4), 193–219. http://dx.doi.org/10.1159/000078723

Quebec (1991). Un Québec fou de ses enfants : rapport de travail sur la santé des jeunes. Quebec City, QC: Ministère de la Santé et des Services sociaux, Direction des communications.

Quebec. (1997). *Priorités nationales de santé publique 1997–2002.* Quebec City, QC: Ministère de la Santé et des Services sociaux.

Quebec. (2006). *Un Québec innovant et prospère: stratégie québécoise de la recherche et de l'innovation.* Quebec City, QC: Ministère du Développement Économique, de l'Innovation et de l'Exportation.

Reardon, R., Lavis, J., & Gibson, J. (2007). De la recherche à la pratique: guide de planification du transfert des connaissances. Saisir et Agir, 1.

Renaud, M. (1999). Rendre public ou périr. *Interface, 20*(5), 38–39.

Rondeau, G. (2004). *Les hommes: s'ouvrir à leurs réalités et répondre à leurs besoins.* Report of the Work Committee on Men's Health. Quebec City, QC: Ministère de la Santé et des Services sociaux. Retrieved from http://publications.msss.gouv.qc.ca/acrobat/f/documentation/2004/04-911-01rap.pdf

SSHRC (Social Sciences and Humanities Research Council of Canada). (2009). *SSHRC's knowledge mobilization strategy.* Ottawa, ON: SSHRC.

Sundstrom, J. (2005). *Changing fathers, evolving practices training summary 2005.* Vancouver, BC: Council for Families.

Tamis-LeMonda, C. S. (2004). Conceptualizing fathers' role: Playmates and more. *Human Development, 47*(4), 220–227. http://dx.doi.org/10.1159/000078724

Venet, C. (2006). *Effet de la formation Pères en mouvement, pratiques en changement sur les participants et les organismes.* Montreal, QC: Centre de formation populaire.

Conclusion
Fathering: New Paths, Future Possibilities

ANNIE DEVAULT, GILLES FORGET,
AND DIANE DUBEAU

Most of the enormous changes to the family, although they began to take shape long ago, have occurred within the past thirty years. Some have experienced these changes as catastrophic, but it has been a fascinating journey for those observing the family's capacity for adaptability and survival. The fathers of today still refer to father models incarnated by men from an era when gender roles and, consequently, parental roles were clearly differentiated. Present-day expectations of fathers are much more diversified and complex. As well as being providers, fathers are expected to be emotionally available to their children and to guide them, participating actively in their education. As observers of the evolution of the family have remarked, this is the first time this has happened in the Western world. As researchers of the Prospère team, we have been front-row observers of this veritable social laboratory of new paternal (and maternal) practices, in which fathers are acting as the pioneers and inventors of contemporary fatherhood.

When deciding which of the Prospère studies on fathering and father involvement would be included in this book, we focused on two aspects: the situation of fathers in contexts of vulnerability, and the practice of participatory action research (PAR). The investigation of the fathers' experiences brought a better understanding of fatherhood as experienced by young, undereducated, poor, and excluded fathers, including those who have served prison sentences, opening the way to preventing the social exclusion of this part of the population. The second focus was methodological, with its emphasis on the PAR approach that, although it might be less known or less used by the scientific community, is particularly rich. This method is well suited to the current state of research on fathers in contexts of vulnerability, as it is often applied when exploring previously unstudied topics. Furthermore, as mentioned in Chapter 1, the distinguishing characteristic of PAR is its receptivity to actors and their inclusion as full participants in the research process. This was not the case in the past, when much of the literature on fathers and fathering was based on mothers' accounts. Although this way of conducting research on fathers is much less frequent today, there is still a need to give greater consideration to fathers' points of view, particularly of those living in contexts of vulnerability, in order to advance knowledge and to adapt intervention intended for them. Participatory action research is all the more appropriate in this sense, as the PAR process is constructed from the experiences of the actors involved in the project. Furthermore, research on the practices that support fathers (Devault, Gaudet, Bolté, & St-Denis, 2005) shows that an intervention framework is effective when fathers feel that they are listened to, are active, feel appreciated, and share in making decisions about the nature of father involvement activities and about the way they are carried out.

In retrospect the structure of this book reflects the two aspects we have chosen to emphasize. The first chapter presented the theoretical and conceptual bases of the PAR approach, pointing out its inherent strengths and potential shortcomings. Chapter 2 outlined the theoretical models and empirical research with which we established our definition of father involvement, adopting a constructivist ecological approach and a comparative perspective that allowed a triangulated analysis. In the six subsequent chapters (3 to 8), we described a number of Prospère's PAR projects designed to support father involvement in collaboration with practitioners in the field. The writing of these chapters allowed us to take an in-depth look at certain methodological dimensions of our evaluation of the effects of the interventions. Finally, Chapter 9 outlined the process of knowledge transfer that took place within the research team, showing the importance Prospère gave to the dissemination of its research results and innovations. To conclude this volume, we look at the future of modern fatherhood: how it will evolve, how it should be studied to arrive at a better understanding of it, and which actions should be taken to give it value and support.

Observations on Fatherhood to Guide the Advancement of Knowledge

Redefining Fatherhood Means Redefining Motherhood

The subject of father involvement affects us all, as men or women, as conjugal partners, as fathers or mothers. It follows that a discussion of the qualities of a good father inevitably leads back to a discussion of what makes a good mother. The demands articulated by the feminist movement are at the heart of the issues that bring men and women to the same table. The diversity of positions, often accompanied by strong feelings, must be acknowledged, but it is indisputable that the only solution is a frank and open discussion between men and women regarding the best interests of children. The PAR projects described in this book are good illustrations of the ways these issues can be addressed. The family approach used when drawing up the action plans to promote father involvement in the two communities, the dissemination of information on co-parenting, the family mediation offered to young fathers in the socio-professional organizations, and intervention targeting the partners of socially excluded fathers all clearly stem from the understanding that support for father involvement cannot be effective without including fathers' conjugal partners and their children's mothers. The personal testimony of fathers confirms that the evolution of fatherhood is interlocked with that of motherhood. But, are mothers willing to accept and encourage the new father involvement in all its dimensions? Or is it still too often the case that fathers are perceived as being "involved" with their children only when they act like good mothers? And what about the situation of fathers following a conjugal break-up, when they are seen simply as providers by some mothers and as actors in the judicial system? On this front, there has been a certain evolution in the courts: recent statistics compiled by the Quebec Ministère de la Justice in 2001 and 2010 show that shared custody arrangements in families receiving child support rose from 7 per cent of such families in 1997–98 to 21.5 per cent in 2009. This increase is an encouraging sign for divorced or separated fathers with respect to access to their children. In addition, the greater participation of women in the labour force has created stronger pressure on fathers to take on a more equitable share of family responsibilities. This is further evidence of the interdependence of the evolution of the paternal and maternal roles, as Silverstein

(1996) reminds us in an article that looks at fatherhood from a feminist viewpoint. In their struggle for equity in the workplace and in the family, should women not encourage men to assume more responsibility in the domestic sphere and play a greater part in the emotional and physical care of the children? On the other hand, women need to reassess their own place in the domestic sphere and relinquish at least some of the space and responsibilities that accompany this role traditionally reserved for mothers.

Encouraging Fathers of All Social Settings to Be Available to Their Children

There appears to be consensus in the new conceptualization of father involvement in the development of the relational family. In North America, in any case, a large number of social actors now advocate a more equitable division of parental roles and family work between men and women. Although the promotion, support, and reinforcement of this new family dynamic unquestionably have resulted in the improved well-being of children and their families, the establishment of a new normative framework has engendered additional forms of exclusion that can even result in the breaking off of the father-child relationship. Thus the new definition of fatherhood potentially constitutes a kind of tyranny towards those who might not have what it takes to meet the expectations that have been set. All fathers do not have equal access to this new way of being a father. These fathers might sense the gap between the redefined social norms and their inability to fulfil them from a cognitive or behavioural point of view. Also, some fathers might be excluded from this type of fatherhood because they are economically or culturally disadvantaged, or because they have limited or no contact with their children. These situations applied to many of the fathers who participated in the studies presented in this book: young fathers, fathers who have served prison sentences, separated fathers, and fathers living in poverty. Such categories are not mutually exclusive – fathers might fit several of them simultaneously or sequentially. Nevertheless, most of the authors who have examined these paternal realities in North America and Europe have found that fathers are rarely against these changes. Rather, it is the conditions required to institute the changes that are unfavourable. Therefore, to support men in this unprecedented process of parental socialization, a multiplicity of social and political actions should be put in place to foster a socially inclusive perspective of fatherhood. Particular attention should continue to be paid to the evolution of the social responses to the question of promoting, supporting, and strengthening father involvement. The same applies to the analysis of social policies that do or do not contribute to supporting fathers' involvement with their children.

Creating Father-Friendly Environments

Creating environments that are more receptive to fathers, that reach out to them and welcome and support them, particularly fathers in contexts of vulnerability, has always been a central concern of Prospère's research and actions. Viewing fatherhood from an ecological point of view implies the acknowledgment of the influence of several different systems. Thus, despite the considerable influence of male socialization on the evolution of fatherhood, social environments also play a major role in the transformation of the role and place of fathers. Besides the specific initiatives to reach vulnerable fathers in these PAR projects, further efforts should be made to reach them in other environments, through youth protection services, community organizations for immigrants, or community recreation associations.

Employment is a central element of the male world, and this also applies to fathers with low educational levels. Indeed, a man's work traditionally was seen as a gauge of his masculinity (in terms, for example, of his success, competence, or accomplishment), and many men still measure their personal worth by their work (Pleck & Sawyer, 1974). Yet present-day conditions have made access to jobs difficult for men. According to Castel (1994), employment opportunities have decreased due to the precariousness of jobs, increasing demand for more highly specialized skills, and economic crises and globalization, all factors that have led to the exclusion particularly of those with low educational levels. We also know that marginalization is caused not only by unemployment, but also by the subjective feelings it brings, such as isolation, powerlessness, and a negative self-image. Our studies have shown that many vulnerable young fathers view their inclusion in the workforce and the sense of dignity this gives them as the first steps in the process of becoming more involved with their children, just as the importance given their involvement in their children's development becomes a springboard towards social inclusion. Moreover, as Dienhart and Daly (1997) have pointed out, beyond men's choices regarding work, we should question Western values that overrate criteria of economic performance compared to family and parental commitments, particularly in the case of men.

Despite undeniable advances in this area, there is still much work to be done so that services will reach out to fathers and encourage them to increase and maintain their involvement with their children. Two salient findings in our ongoing research on fatherhood deserve mention here.

The first is the precariousness of specific support services for fathers. In Quebec, as in the rest of Canada, the funding provided to target fathers is minimal. In most cases, organizations wishing to set up activities, services, programs, or resources for fathers are obliged to adapt existing programs with no increase in funding. If, as studies have repeatedly shown, letting fathers know they are welcome in family activities does not necessarily convince them to join in, how can we hope they will become more involved with their children when social services still strongly associate children's health and well-being with the support given to mothers? It is unfortunate that inaugurating or adapting services for men is seen as a threat to the availability of services for women, as if offering one excluded the other. As we have reiterated throughout this book, with the heavy demands and responsibilities of life in present-day society, both men and women need support in exercising their parental roles, and the services offered to mothers do not always correspond to fathers' needs. Although our observations mainly concern organizations, the lack of funding for activities for fathers is just as conspicuous in government services. Here again, services for the family are ostensibly accessible to fathers as well as to mothers, but the physical availability of both parents is not taken into account. For example, how many interventions targeting parents of newborns are scheduled at times when fathers are at work?

The second finding that we wish to highlight here is the importance of intervention by men for men – from father to father – which emerged repeatedly in all our PAR projects as a condition for success in intervention to support fathers. This condition is difficult to put in place, however, due to the structural obstacle of the lack of male practitioners in the services professions in general and, more acutely, in community-based organizations that support the family. In the first case, changes should be made in several areas, from the recruitment of students to the content of the programs in these professions, if we want to re-establish a gender balance among the men and women who will support the fathers and mothers of tomorrow. In the latter case, better salary conditions in community work are essential to be able to recruit and keep dedicated services providers trained specifically in interventions aimed at fathers.

The Political Dimension of Fatherhood: The Father as Citizen

The initial reflection of the research team focused on the definition of father involvement. Like several other researchers in this area, we wanted to go beyond the traditional provider dimension to include the quality and quantity of the time fathers spend with their children, the emotional dimension, and the evocation dimension – that is, the relationship that exists between father and child even when they are apart. Continuing this reflection while we carried out our projects to promote father involvement, we wished to add a new dimension: that of the father as citizen. Besides the importance of the time fathers spend with their children – thereby participating in the life of their society and transmitting its traditions, practices, and values – the father-as-citizen dimension refers to what fathers do collectively to improve children's health and well-being. The social transformations often referred to in our studies could not have taken place without a struggle and the subsequent articulation of demands. The women's movement, the labour movement, and the associative movement continually remind politicians of their duty to work towards a more egalitarian and equitable society. Although men have been associated with these movements and demands, they clearly have not filled all the space they should occupy as half of humanity and half of the parents of children. Therefore we hope that, in the future, more and more fathers who are involved with their children will pressure the different levels of government to provide father-friendly services for the benefit of children and families.

Continuing In-Depth Participatory Action Research

In Prospère's PAR projects, we have carried out actions in an area that has received little attention until now: the adaptation by services and resources to transformations of the paternal role so that fathers, including those living in specific contexts of vulnerability, are given due attention. As with the health-promotion programs that preceded them, our father involvement initiatives aim to improve life environments in ways that benefit the development of children living in contexts of vulnerability, to support the services providers working with the children's parents, and to treat the latter as citizens with something meaningful to say about their life experiences. Our initiatives also illustrate the flexibility required to respond to the needs and objectives pursued by the different partners, on two levels. First, the collaboration process and the research procedures should be suited to the actors' needs and to ensure their participation in the different stages of the research project. Second, the association of practitioners and fathers with researchers in the knowledge transfer process is not just an effective way to make these projects known in the intervention milieu; it is also a means of strengthening the partners' support and fathers' participation in subsequent actions.

In referring to the ecological perspective, health-promotion strategies and intersectoral action, as well as the triangulation of the research data and the case study method, the PAR projects presented here relied on approaches adapted to social realities, which are complex by nature. The theory of complexity, which is gaining increasing credibility in the scientific community, offers a refreshing and illuminating perspective in participatory action research (Phelps & Hase, 2002) through its recognition that systems possess the competence to face problems that arise. Thus the researcher's role is not so much to understand or to seek solutions, but to activate the process by which the system generates its own solution – the self-solution. In the presentation of Prospère's PAR projects, we have emphasized the importance of allotting enough time for participants to discuss and negotiate their differing points of view so that they can arrive at a common vision that brings everyone together. Time in this context is a structural constraint that sometimes makes it difficult to achieve a working balance among the partners, depending on the mandates and policies of the different organizations or establishments. Within university research groups, institutions, and community-based organizations, each must agree to an investment that is consistent with the desired results, while also guaranteeing the level of participation inherent to this type of research. The successes described in this book should encourage such partners in this sense. As mentioned in Chapter 1, social action is among the expected effects of participatory action research. These effects might not be immediately obvious, depending on the nature, intensity, and duration of a project. Nonetheless it is interesting to note that, when Prospère's PAR projects came to term, some of their effects took on a broader scope in terms of social action. To give one example, the *Grandir sainement avec un père détenu* (Fathers behind Bars) program continues to be offered at several halfway houses. In addition, recommendations concerning needs that emerged in this particular project contributed to the adaptation of the data bank used by Correctional Service Canada, making it possible to better identify fathers among inmates. In another example, the mobilization achieved in the two communities involved in the Prospère project (see Chapter 3) resulted in the establishment of two organizations that continue to support fathers on an everyday basis, thanks to funding obtained following their recognition as not-for-profit organizations. Moreover, the training received by practitioners in Quebec and other parts of Canada in the framework of this same project led many of them to make changes in their practices. On the other hand, policies that would help eliminate the structural barriers hindering father involvement have yet to be put in place.

Researchers who opt for PAR methodology, no matter how hard they strive to achieve a harmonious cohabitation between research knowledge and experiential knowledge, run the risk of finding themselves at a loss if the research process takes an unpredictable turn. When this happens, they should display a measure of humility, a sense of humour, and a certain degree of detachment towards the apparent disorder. As committed actors in close contact with the devastating effects of social exclusion, they acquire tenacity together with a sense of satisfaction that they are working in a concrete – and occasionally successful – way towards a greater measure of social justice.

Continuing Fatherhood Research

To understand the contexts and conditions of the exercise of fatherhood better and to represent the parental component faithfully, we should start with the father's own discourse. Giving a voice to fathers is an integral part of a PAR project, but other sources of information should also transmit fathers' points of view. Government support bodies, however, still tend to omit the realities of fathers in their demographic data.[1] The recommendation that fathers be consulted applies both to longitudinal studies and to more limited studies of the family. Methodological explanations to justify the exclusive use of mothers in samples, such as the non-adaptability of instruments, the fact that instruments have not been validated by fathers, or the difficulty of recruiting fathers, are less and less acceptable given the advancements in knowledge about fatherhood.

The research team quickly became aware of the absence of instruments to measure father involvement and its various dimensions, and therefore developed its own instrument for this purpose. Along with our hope that this instrument will be used in other studies, we believe it is important that researchers continue to develop specific measures of fathers' realities and contexts, following the example of Ohan, Leung, and Johnston (2000) in their validation of the measure of fathers' sense of parental competence.

It seems pertinent in this conclusion to underline the researchers' interest in taking account of the different family members' evaluations of the maternal and paternal roles from a systemic perspective. The differences between these evaluations, which might seem minimal in certain respects but which are often found in fathers' and mothers' representations of their roles, prompted us to document their viewpoints and perceptions in a more precise manner. Regarding this aspect, we lament the fact that children's views of fathers are not taken into consideration, especially since validated methodologies for collecting data from young children are now available. We can only encourage the carrying out of studies that take into account the more cognitive dimensions that are associated with father-child and mother-child relationships.

Despite the expected difficulties of keeping a research team together for almost two decades – as members retire, move away, or leave to take up new challenges – Prospère continued to contribute to the advancement of knowledge on fatherhood with the recent completion of a study and the beginning of a new community impacts evaluation (see Chapter 8).

Final Reflections

Having adopted a constructivist, ecological perspective in our research, we would like to end this volume by justifying a constructivist approach as essential for the advancement of knowledge on fatherhood. This approach oriented all the Prospère projects presented here, particularly in the multiplicity of ways of looking at fathers, which issued from a diverse range of methodologies and which became clearer thanks to the complementary expertise acquired over the course of the projects by actors from both the practice and the research milieus. In accordance with the philosophy underpinning participatory action research, the actors progressively arrived at a better understanding of the study subject by allowing themselves to be mutually influenced. Thus, in a feedback loop, the knowledge acquired in this way was used to develop new perspectives for research and action. The dynamic between researchers and practitioners working with fathers and their families is rich in possibilities, but it implies a investment in time that is often costly in both financial and human terms. Indeed, a common ground should be found where the realities and issues affecting all the actors can be shared among them. This common ground would also be shaped by each person's values and personal and professional experiences. In striving for a necessary degree of consensus among the actors regarding their vision of a problem and its solution, we should remember that certain topics are more contentious, so that achieving a working consensus might require more time and effort by actors and researchers.

The constructivist character is also reflected by the context of social change observed over the past few years, whereby men's relationships with women, with children, and with other men have been transformed. With the evolution of the paternal and the masculine role becoming so closely related to the maternal and the feminine role, an essential dialogue should be fostered between men and women on the importance of the values of gender equality and of power- and task-sharing in the different spheres of public and private life.

The generative approach seems particularly fruitful for fatherhood studies, as it emphasizes fathers' competencies and specificity, instead of focusing on their deficiencies. It also brings out the ways that fathers contribute in their own way to the development of future generations (Hawkins & Dollahite, 1997). The first advantage of this conceptualization of fatherhood is that its focus is on the adult. By bringing attention back to the adult as becoming a parent, the generative approach brings out the various developmental characteristics more clearly, including those related to gender.

The second point of interest in the generative approach to fatherhood concerns the transmission of values, the legacy for future generations – or intergenerational learning, from an educational perspective. Regarding this aspect, it is useful to scrutinize the nature of the values transmitted by the involved father. If, as proposed above, father involvement as a social practice and civic action implies participation in the political process of gender equality, we should ask ourselves if it perpetuates sexual stereotypes or contributes to eliminating them. Indeed, gender socialization of children influences the way they will bring up their own children. The generative approach allows us to understand this phenomenon better, as intergenerational transmission is at the heart of its theoretical and empirical concerns. This is all the more pertinent in that fathers often want to offer their children a different model than the one they were given by their own father when they were growing up. In their various ways, they want to be the model of the "new father" for their children. That the main reference in the generative approach is the adult and his development in no way detracts from concern for the child. On this level, the generative approach agrees with other approaches in which the child's well-being is paramount. The generative adult (the father) is procreator, and is productive, creative, and involved (Houde, 1999), capable of giving the best of himself and helping his child grow and develop.

Without a doubt, the era we are living in is unique, but it is also transitory. Today's children of involved fathers surely will have less difficulty finding a father model than did their fathers. Father models will not only be more available; they will also be much more numerous and diversified. The multiplicity of perspectives on fatherhood reminds us that it is constructed in various contexts and conditions. Thus, decision-makers, practitioners, and researchers are called upon to show imagination so that both parents are always taken into consideration, and to propose new initiatives to ensure that all fathers can contribute to their children's well-being.

NOTE

1 The Father Involvement Research Alliance (FIRA) has submitted recommendations to Statistics Canada in the hope that data collection will better reflect new family realities and fathers' situations.

REFERENCES

Castel, R. (1994). La dynamique des processus de marginalisation: de la vulnérabilité à la désaffiliation. *Cahiers de Recherche Sociologique*, 22(22), 11–25. http://dx.doi.org/10.7202/1002206ar

Devault, A., Gaudet, J., Bolté, C., & St-Denis, M. (2005). A survey and description of projects that support and promote fathering in Canada: Still work to do to reach fathers in their real-life settings. *Canadian Journal of Community Mental Health*, 24(1), 5–17. http://dx.doi.org/10.7870/cjcmh-2005-0001

Dienhart, A., & Daly, K. (1997). Men and women co-creating father involvement in a nongenerative culture. In A. J. Hawkins & D. C. Dollahite (Eds.), *Generative fathering: Beyond deficit perspectives* (pp. 229–259). Thousand Oaks, CA: Sage.

Hawkins, A. J., & Dollahite, D. (Eds.). (1997). *Generative fathering: Beyond deficit perspectives*. Thousand Oaks, CA: Sage.

Houde, R. (1999). *Les temps de la vie: le développement psychosocial de l'adulte.* Montreal, QC: Gaëtan Morin.

Ohan, J. L., Leung, D. W., & Johnston, C. (2000). The parenting sense of competence scale: Evidence of a stable factor structure and validity. *Revue canadienne des sciences du comportement, 32*(4), 251–261. http://dx.doi.org/10.1037/h0087122

Phelps, R., & Hase, S. (2002). Complexity and action research: Exploring the theoretical and methodological connections. *Educational Action Research, 10*(3), 507–524. http://dx.doi.org/10.1080/09650790200200198

Pleck, J. H., & Sawyer, J. (1974). *Men and masculinity.* Englewood Cliffs, NJ: Prentice-Hall.

Silverstein, L. B. (1996). Fathering is a feminist issue. *Psychology of Women Quarterly, 20*(1), 3–37. http://dx.doi.org/10.1111/j.1471-6402.1996.tb00663.x

Appendix A: The Father Involvement Questionnaire

This instrument can be administered as a questionnaire to be filled out, but it may be preferable to use it in an interview context, providing visual support by showing the informant the rating scales. This last approach is encouraged when fathers have low educational levels. The interviewer is invited to start the questionnaire by saying: "Here is a list of activities and tasks that parents do. Your partner takes on more responsibility than you do in certain aspects of family life, and it may be the other way around in other aspects. Can you tell us how often you carry out, by yourself, each the activities I'm going to name? We'll use a scale to help you answer as accurately as possible." (The interviewer shows the father the scale and explains it, making the difference between "Does not apply" and "Never" very clear.)

The father should give answers concerning only one child aged 6 years of age or less (make a random choice if there is more than one). When reading the questions, the interviewer is invited to replace the word "child" by the child's first name, except for the questions on household chores.

1	2	3	4	5	6	7
Never	Once a month	2 or 3 times a month	Once a week	A few times a week	Every day	Does not apply

Appendix A: The Father Involvement Questionnaire

Child's first name: _____ Child's age ___ Child's sex ___

	1. Feed or give something to drink to your child.
	2. Watch a children's TV program with your child.
	3. Hold your child in your arms when he/she asks.
	4. Correct your child's table manners.
	5. Prepare meals.
	6. Include your child in adult activities (cooking, housework, etc.).
	7. Bathe your child.
	8. Cuddle your child.
	9. Tell anecdotes about your child to your friends or work colleagues.
	10. Wash dishes.
	11. Listen to music with your child.
	12. Make your child laugh.
	13. Take care of your child's hair.
	14. Carry your child on your back while playing.
	15. Dress your child.
	16. Tickle your child.
	17. Reprimand your child if he/she is creating a disturbance.
	18. Wash clothes.
	19. Put your child to bed at night.
	20. Praise your child's skill or creativity when playing.
	21. Supervise the morning routine (breakfast, getting dressed, etc.).
	22. Prepare snacks.
	23. Play-wrestle with your child.
	24. Speak sharply to your child if he/she disobeys.
	25. Clean house (sweep, vacuum, dust).

The interviewer continues by saying: "Here is another list of activities and tasks that parents do. Can you tell us how often you carry out, by yourself, each the activities I'm going to name? We'll use a scale to help you answer as accurately as possible." (The interviewer shows the father the scale and explains it, making the difference between "Does not apply" and "Never" very clear.)

Appendix A: The Father Involvement Questionnaire

1	2	3	4	5	7
Never	Occasionally	Regularly	Often	Very often	Does not apply

	26. Reassure your child when he/she is afraid.
	27. Introduce your child to sports (swimming, skating, riding a bicycle, throwing and catching a ball, etc.).
	28. Wash your child's ears.
	29. Comfort your child when he/she cries.
	30. Bring educational games or toys for your child.
	31. Book a doctor's or dentist's appointment when your child needs one.
	32. Give first aid to your child if he/she gets hurt.
	33. Show your child new games or toys.
	34. Encourage your child to accomplish something difficult (e.g., walking).
	35. Take your child on outings.
	36. Talk about your joys and problems as a parent.
	37. Intervene quickly when your child shows signs of distress or pain.
	38. Praise your child when he/she accomplishes something.
	39. Accompany your child to see friends, relatives, or neighbours.
	40. Look after your child when he/she is ill.
	41. Take your child to the park.
	42. Punish your child if he/she does something wrong (breaks something, hurts someone).
	43. Try to get your child to tell you what is wrong when he/she seems upset.
	44. Get out of bed at night for your child.
	45. Soothe your child.
	46. Talk about your child to your friends, neighbours, or colleagues at work.
	47. Keep an eye on your child when he/she plays outside.
	48. Recall what your child was like when he/she was little.
	49. Tell your child you love him/her.
	50. Look at photographs of your child.
	51. Make sure the home is safe for your child.
	52. Think about your child when he/she is not there.

Validation Process for the Father Involvement Questionnaire

Content Validity

The Father Involvement Questionnaire (FIQ) was drawn up based on existing tools, including the Parental Involvement in Child Care Index (PICCI; see Radin, 1981), with the addition of items to evaluate the involvement dimensions established in the definition adopted by Prospère (in particular, items associated with the evocation dimension). The initial version of the questionnaire comprised one hundred items.

After the first period of gathering data from 454 parents (fathers and mothers), we examined the item-by-item distribution according to the children's ages, and subsequently eliminated twenty items that were limited to very young children (such as changing diapers). The eighty remaining items were subjected to a content validation process by ten experts: five parents and five family psychology practitioners, who evaluated the pertinence of each item in the light of Prospère's operational definition of father involvement. To be retained, an item had to be considered relevant by at least eight of the ten experts. The items were also classified by eight other family psychology specialists in nine conceptual categories: basic care-giving, accessibility, planning and arranging, play, evocation, affection, education, discipline, and doing household chores. To be retained, an item had to be classified in the same category by at least six of the eight experts. In all, fourteen items were eliminated in these two stages of content validation.

Finally, an examination of the distribution of the responses, first those of the fathers, then those of the mothers, allowed us to eliminate further items when one of the following three criteria was present: (1) more than half the answers corresponded to the same rating in the scale; (2) a floor or ceiling effect was present (the quasi-totality of the items was at the upper or lower extremes of the scale); or (3) more than 10 per cent of the data was missing. In all, fourteen additional items were eliminated.

Factorial Structure for the Fathers

Using a sample of 850 fathers, we subjected the instrument to factorial analysis. Six principal factors were identified that explained 42.2 percent of the variance. The criteria for withdrawing an item were: (1) the item was not associated with any of the principal factors; and (2) the item could not contribute to the explanation of the variance of another factor. After removing the invalid items, a new factorial analysis was carried out.

Appendix A: The Father Involvement Questionnaire

The final version of the instrument was made up of fifty-two items grouped in six father involvement scales, with an added scale for participation in household chores.

Emotional support (12 items): Behaviour that aims to clearly show the child that he/she is appreciated, loved, supported, and protected
26. Reassure your child when he/she is afraid. 29. Comfort your child when he/she cries. 32. Give first aid to your child if he/she gets hurt. 34. Encourage your child to accomplish something difficult (e.g., walking). 37. Intervene quickly when your child shows signs of distress or pain. 38. Praise your child when he/she accomplishes something. 40. Look after your child when he/she is ill. 43. Try to get your child to tell you what is wrong when he/she seems upset. 45. Soothe your child. 47. Keep an eye on your child when he/she plays outside. 49. Tell your child you love him/her. 51. Make sure the home is safe for your child.
Discipline (4 items): Behaviour that aims to correct aspects of the child's behaviour
4. Correct your child's table manners. 17. Reprimand your child if he/she is creating a disturbance. 24. Speak sharply to your child if he/she disobeys. 42. Punish your child if he/she does something wrong (breaks something, hurts someone).
Physical care (9 items): Behaviour that aims to ensure the child's basic care, health, and hygiene
1. Feed or give something to drink to your child. 7. Bathe your child. 13. Take care of your child's hair. 15. Dress your child. 19. Put your child to bed at night. 21. Supervise the morning routine (breakfast, getting dressed, etc.). 28. Wash your child's ears. 31. Book a doctor's or dentist's appointment when your child needs one. 44. Get out of bed at night for your child.
Openness to the world (9 items): Behaviour that aims to initiate the child to new activities or games
2. Watch a children's TV program with your child. 6. Have your child participate in adult activities (cooking, housework, etc.). 11. Listen to music with your child. 27. Introduce your child to sports (swimming, skating, riding a bicycle, throwing and catching a ball, etc.). 30. Bring home educational games or toys for your child. 33. Show your child new games or toys. 35. Take your child on outings. 39. Accompany your child to see friends, relatives, or neighbours. 41. Take your child to the park.

Physical play (7 items): Behaviour in the form of different kinds of physical contact (including laughter), occurring mostly during play activities with the child.
3. Take your child in your arms when he/she asks. 8. Cuddle your child. 12. Make your child laugh. 14. Carry your child on your back while playing. 16. Tickle your child. 20. Praise your child's skill or creativity when playing. 23. Play-wrestle with your child.
Evocation (6 items): Behaviour that shows the parent thinks of the child when they are not together
9. Tell anecdotes about your child to your friends or work colleagues. 36. Talk about your joys and problems as a parent. 46. Talk about your child to your friends, neighbours, or colleagues at work. 48. Recall what your child was like when he/she was little. 50. Look at photographs of your child. 52. Think about your child when he/she is not there.
Household chores (5 items): Participation in household chores traditionally done by women
5. Prepare meals. 10. Wash dishes. 18. Wash clothes. 22. Prepare snacks. 25. Clean house (sweep, vacuum, dust).

It is interesting to note that the results of the factorial analysis carried out on the sample of mothers regarding their own involvement (data that were available only during the first data-collection period) did not confirm the factorial structure obtained from the fathers.

Metrological Qualities of the FIQ

The instrument was administered twice, with a two-week interval in between, to a sample of thirty-three fathers. The temporal stability indices varied according to the scales between 0.50 and 0.77. The six father involvement scales presented excellent internal consistency (with a Cronbach's Alpha variation between 0.72 and 0.86).

Appendix B: Methodological Parameters of the Effects of the Evaluation

Pre-test and Post-test Design with Comparisons

The effects of the degree of fathers' involvement with their young children between the pre-test and post-test times were compared at the intervention sites and the control sites, using the same criteria as in the selection of the participating sites. Because the ultimate expected outcome of the intervention was father involvement, we felt it important to be able to evaluate this variable using an experimental design that increased the attribution of the effects to the project. The fathers' attitudes towards child rearing and their sense of parental competence were also analysed according to this research design.

Subjects: The Families (Mothers and Fathers)

The data collection of the pre-intervention phase (the pre-test measurements) was carried out in autumn 1995 for site A (and its associated control site) and in autumn 1996 for site B (and its associated control site). The procedure for the post-test (1999 to 2001) was identical. After obtaining authorization from Quebec's Commission d'accès à l'information (Access to Information Commission), nominative information was provided by the Régie de l'assurance maladie du Québec (Quebec Health Insurance Regime) on the households situated in the four territories with at least one child between zero and five years of age. From the total number of children, a stratified representative sample was constituted according the children's age groups (0–1, 1, 2, 3, 4, or 5 years of age). It should be emphasized that the pre-test and post-test measurements were collected from independent samples of families.

Data Collection Methods

Four research assistants at each site introduced themselves at the families' homes; a letter had been previously mailed to each family to inform them of the visit. The two parents were questioned one after the other in one-on-one interviews, beginning with the father figure. To answer, the respondent would point to the appropriate number of the scale on a card placed in front of him/her to offset problems caused by reading difficulties or illiteracy, and to ensure the confidentiality of the answers given by the mothers and fathers. The interviews lasted two hours (seventy-five minutes for the father and forty-five minutes for the mother). Each family first signed a consent form. A minimum of one hundred families per territory (taking the children's age groups into account) was required to arrive at statistically significant differences between the samples, taking account of the 1- and 2-type errors as well as the variation within each sample.

Measurement Instruments

Table B.1 presents the measurement method and instruments used.

The father's sense of parental competence: The Parenting Sense of Competence Scale (PSCS) by Gibaud-Wallston (1977) was translated and adapted by Terrisse and Trudelle, using a Quebec sample (Trudelle,

Table B.1. Measurement Method and Instruments Used to Evaluate the Ultimate Results

Expected effects on the fathers	Objectives	Method
Representation of the paternal role	Sense of parental competence	Questionnaire (translated into French and validated) Gibaud-Wallston (1977) Respondents: Fathers
Exercise of the paternal role	Attitudes towards child rearing	Questionnaire (validated) Sommer et al. (1993); Easterbrooks & Goldberg (1984) Respondents: Fathers
	Father's quantitative involvement	Questionnaire (translated and validated) Prospère team Respondents: Mothers and fathers

1992). It comprised sixteen statements that the parent evaluated according to a rating scale of 6 points. The items were divided into two subscales: (1) the sense of effectiveness (seven items); and (2) satisfaction (nine items). The internal consistency coefficients (Cronbach's Alpha) for the two scales were 0.76 and 0.75, respectively (Johnston & Mash, 1989). The temporal stability over a six-month interval was 0.62.

Attitudes towards child rearing: A questionnaire dealing with the father's parental attitudes regarding empathy, abuse/negligence, strictness, and punishment was used (Sommer et al., 1993). The mean Chronbach's Alpha was 0.74 and the temporal stability was 0.63. A warmth scale was added (Cronbach's Alpha of 0.76; see Easterbrooks & Goldberg, 1984). The instrument comprised thirty-eight items in all. The rating scale varied from 1 to 5.

The father's parental involvement: This questionnaire aimed for a quantitative evaluation of the routine tasks and actions performed by the father (fifty-two items). It was decided *a priori* to evaluate six dimensions of father involvement (forty-seven items): emotional support, discipline, physical play, physical care, openness to the outside world, and evocation. A supplementary scale was added to evaluate participation in household chores (five items). Two rating scales were used: whenever possible, an absolute frequency scale for each parenting activity, ranging from 1 (never) to 6 (every day), and a second scale (forty-three items) to determine a relative frequency ranging from 1 (never) to 5 (very often) for items concerning activities that were more difficult to quantify. The items in the questionnaire were compiled from several existing instruments: the PICCI (Parental Involvement in Child Care Index) by Radin (1981); the Parental Responsibility Questionnaire by Lamb et al. (1988); the Parental Attitudes Scale by De Luccie & Davis (1991); and the Répartition des tâches familiales (Sharing of household chores) questionnaire by Tessier (1983). The internal consistency of the different scales evaluated according to Cronbach's Alpha was satisfactory, varying between 0.67 and 0.82. The temporal stability of the instrument over four weeks was 0.82 (n = 33). The convergence validity of the instrument was established according to the number of hours per week that the father spent alone with his children, carried out household chores, and spent in the workplace.

Social desirability: Since the measurements obtained from the mothers and fathers were mainly self-reported, we added a social desirability questionnaire (Crowne & Marlowe, 1960), made up of fourteen statements with "true" or "false" answers.

Post-test Design with the Control Group (without Pre-test)

A post-test design comparing the participating sites with the control sites was used to evaluate a set of possible effects (intermediary results) closely linked to the activities in the local action plans that aimed to establish more father-friendly environments and practices, to improve the quality and quantity of joint action among services providers, and to change services providers' attitudes towards fatherhood. Although few results presented here issue from this research design, we felt it would be useful to describe briefly its methodology to give the reader a more complete picture of the overall evaluation design adopted.

Subjects

Three principal sources were consulted: the families (mothers and fathers); the services providers and managers; and the inquiries and the regular data collection from practitioners (nurses, daycare workers and teachers) and in the services agencies. With respect to mothers and fathers, we used the sample of parents recruited for the post-test in the framework of the comparative pre-test/post-test design. With respect to practitioners and managers, the resources offered to families with children under age six and services specifically addressed to fathers at the intervention sites and the control sites were identified in advance. For the participating communities, the data from the preliminary field study carried out in 1995 and 1996 were used and updated. These lists of resources were validated by three local practitioners. A list of practitioners and managers associated with these resources was also established. A random sample of some thirty practitioners and managers was made up. These subjects were met in their workplaces for a semi-structured interview approximately one hour long dealing with attitudes and practices regarding fathers.

Observations and Regular Data Gathering

The regular observations and data collection were carried out to obtain, among other things, a description of the physical environments of the Centres locales de services communautaires (CLSCs, Local Community Services Centres) in each territory and to take an inventory of the positive father images disseminated in posters, brochures, magazines, and

266   Appendix B: Methodological Parameters

so on. This type of semiological portrait is frequently used by environmental evaluators and anthropologists.

A report was also done at the beginning of the autumn school term to determine the participation rates of fathers at statutory meetings in the following institutions frequented by their children under age six: Centres de la petite enfance (daycare centres) (three per territory); pre-kindergarten (two per territory); and kindergarten (two per territory). In addition, educators at these establishments were asked to note the participation rates of fathers at parent-teacher meetings concerning report cards and at group outings when parents were invited to accompany the group. Data were also collected by educators during pre-established three-day blocks on the number of fathers who came to drop off or pick up their children at the establishment. Finally, nurses at the vaccination clinic (CLSC) compiled data during a predetermined period on how often fathers accompanied their children to these health care visits.

Measurement Instruments

The collection strategy for each category of expected effects combined several methods (questionnaires, interviews, observations) to obtain both qualitative and quantitative data. Table B.2 presents a synthesis of these instruments, highlighting the measurements that produced the results presented in Chapter 4.

Changes in Services Providers' Attitudes and Practices

The researchers drew up a questionnaire to evaluate the fathers' perceptions of their place in the health, social services, and community organizations in their neighbourhood. The questionnaire consisted of ten items with a Likert scale ranging from 1 to 4 (for example, "In the services offered to the families in the neighbourhood, I feel that my opinion as a father is taken into consideration and can make a difference").

*Perceptions of Parental Roles and the Place Given
to the Father by the Mother*

A questionnaire of ten items was drawn up by the researchers to evaluate (1) the perception of change regarding parental roles (five items – for example, "The way I see my role with respect to my children is changing");

Table B.2. Expected Effects, Methods, and Respondents in the Post-test Research Design, with Comparisons

Expected effects	Method	Respondents
Knowledge of the activities offered, the determinants of father engagement and their effects	Questionnaire 1	Mothers and fathers
Participation of fathers	Evaluation chart of the activities	Person in charge of the activity
	Observation and regular data collection	• Daycare workers • Nurses in vaccination clinics • Teachers
Services for fathers more easily available	Interviews	Mothers and fathers
Dissemination of a positive fathers image	Regular inventories	Visit to the CLSC (by research assistant)
Coordination of services and collaboration	Interviews	Services practitioners
Changes in services providers' attitudes and practices	Interviews	Practitioners Fathers
Perceptions of parental roles and the place given to the father by the mother	Questionnaire 2	Mothers and fathers

and (2) the place given to fathers by mothers (five items – for example, "My partner insists that I do things her way when I take part in family chores"). Both the mothers and the fathers in the comparative post-test sample filled out this questionnaire, whose scale ranged from 1 to 4.

REFERENCES

Crowne, D. P., & Marlowe, D. (1960). A new scale of social desirability independent of psychopathology. *Journal of Consulting Psychology*, 24(4), 349–354. http://dx.doi.org/10.1037/h0047358

De Luccie, M. F., & Davis, A. J. (1991). Father-child relationships from the preschool years through mid-adolescence. *Journal of Genetic Psychology*, 152(2), 225–238. http://dx.doi.org/10.1080/00221325.1991.9914669

Easterbrooks, M. A., & Goldberg, W. A. (1984). Toddler development in the family: Impact of father involvement and parenting characteristics. *Child Development*, 55(3), 740–752. http://dx.doi.org/10.2307/1130126

Gibaud-Wallston, J. (1977). *Self-esteem and situational stress: Factors related to sense of competence in new parents*. (PhD thesis). University of Rhode Island, Kingston.

Johnston, C., & Mash, E. J. (1989). A measure of parenting satisfaction and efficacy. *Journal of Clinical Childhood, 18*(2), 167–175. http://dx.doi.org/10.1207/s15374424jccp1802_8

Lamb, M. E., et al. (1988). The determinants of parental involvement in primiparous Swedish families. *International Journal of Behavioral Development, 11*(4), 433–449. http://dx.doi.org/10.1177/016502548801100403

Radin, N. (1981). Childrearing fathers in intact families: Some antecedents and consequences. *Merrill-Palmer Quarterly, 27*, 489–514.

Sommer, K., et al. (1993). Cognitive readiness and adolescent parenting. *Developmental Psychology, 29*(2), 389–398. http://dx.doi.org/10.1037/0012-1649.29.2.389

Tessier, R. (1983). Étude des conditions écologiques de la qualité et de la cohésion des conduites de contrôle parental. (unpublished doctoral dissertation). Université du Québec à Montréal, Montreal.

Trudelle, D. (1992). *Sentiment de compétence, attitudes et pratiques éducatives chez les parents québécois d'enfants d'âge préscolaire en fonction de leurs caractéristiques socio-économiques* (unpublished doctoral dissertation). Université du Québec à Montréal, Montreal.

Contributors

The Editors

Annie Devault is a professor in the Department of Social Work at the Université du Québec en Outaouais. For the past twenty years, her work has related to father involvement and intervention for fathers. Over the past few years, her work has concentrated more on fathers in vulnerable situations such as social and economical exclusion. She was a member of the Prospère team, and was part of the Father Involvement Research Alliance, a Canadian research coalition on fatherhood. In this group, she was the leader of the Young Fathers cluster. Annie Devault is also engaged in an intervention program aimed at negligent families in collaboration with child protection services. She is a clinical supervisor for the implementation of the program. She has a doctorate in community psychology from the Université du Québec à Montréal, and she completed a post-doctoral internship in health promotion and disease prevention at Stanford University.

Gilles Forget worked for most of his career as a health-promotion officer in public health in Canada. As an associate researcher in the Research and Action Group on Child Victimization, he developed his expertise on father involvement by designing, implementing, and evaluating community-based programs, working with young fathers, and developing new practices to reach vulnerable fathers. He coordinated the First National Symposium on Father Involvement, and was the provincial representative in a national program to support father-inclusive practices and a member of the steering committee of the Father Involvement Research Alliance. He has facilitated a training program on father-inclusive practices in Quebec, elsewhere in Canada, France, and Australia. He is currently a PhD candidate at the School of Public Health and Social Work, Queensland University of Technology, Brisbane.

Diane Dubeau has been a professor in the Psychoeducation and Psychology Department at the Université du Québec en Outaouais since 1991. She has a doctorate in developmental psychology from the Université du Québec à Montréal, and her main research topics are fathering and program evaluation. She was an associate researcher with the Groupe de recherche et d'action sur la victimisation des enfants (Research and Action Group on Child Victimization), and is head of the Centre de recherches évaluatives de programs d'intervention (Centre of evaluative research on intervention). For the past ten years, she has taken on the role of scientific director of the Prospère team. She has developed an expertise in program evaluation and heads a Quebec provincial committee on father involvement.

The Contributors

Jessica Ball is a professor in the School of Child and Youth Care and co-coordinator of First Nations Partnership Programs at the University of Victoria. She has worked extensively in innovative programs to sustain cultural diversity and support community development in the interests of children and families. Dr. Ball completed three post-graduate degrees at the University of California, Berkeley, including a doctorate in developmental-clinical psychology, a Master of Public Health in international health planning, and a Master of Arts in clinical psychology. Her undergraduate degree in Psychology is from the University of British Columbia.

Martine Barrette has a master's degree in criminology from the Université de Montréal. She was the coordinator of the participatory action research project, Fathers behind Bars. Following this project, she worked for many years as a practitioner in the Carpe Diem halfway house. For the past few years, she has been working at the Centre Jeunesse de la Montérégie, where she helps teenagers who suffer from mental health problems. She also supervises master's students at the Université de Sherbrooke.

Dominic Bizot, of the Department of Social Work at the Université du Québec à Chicoutimi, acquired expertise in education, intervention, and research in France from 1994 to 2003 with diverse clienteles, including adolescents, drug addicts, immigrants, families, and prison inmates. Since 2003 he has been developing a teaching and research career in Quebec in adult education and social work. In 2011 he obtained his doctorate in androgogy from the Université de Montréal (Québec). Presently, he is co-researcher for the University Community Research Alliance project, Design and Material Culture (DCM), where he is in charge of evaluating the impact of the DCM on the social development of the First Nations communities targeted by the project. In addition to his expertise in evaluation, his research interests encompass the promotion and development of paternal engagement, intergenerational relations, identity dynamics, community health, First Nations affairs, and gender studies. He is an active member of Masculinity and Society, part of the Centre for Interdisciplinary Research in Family Violence and Violence against Women.

Sylvain Coutu has been a professor in the Department of Psychoeducation and Psychology at the Université du Québec en Outaouais since 1989. His research interests include the study of the social and emotional competence of young children, parents' and teachers' emotion socialization practices, and the evaluation of prevention programs in early childhood educational contexts.

Kerry Daly became dean of the College of Social and Applied Human Sciences at the University of Guelph in July 2010. Prior to becoming dean, he was associate dean (research) for the college between 2008 and 2010. In that role he played a key role in launching the Institute for Community Engaged Scholarship, which now houses the Research Shop within the college. He is also one of the founding directors of the Centre for Families, Work and Well-Being at the University of Guelph.

Jeanne Doré has been the chief executive officer of the Boulot Vers Agency in Montreal since 1995. Since 1983 the Boulot Vers Agency has supported the social and professional inclusion of vulnerable young people ages 16 to 25.

Sandrina de Finney is associate professor in the Department of Child and Youth Care at the University of Victoria. Her primary focus of scholarship is Indigenous and minoritized populations, particularly youth in care and girls/young women. Drawing on over two decades of experience as a community activist, researcher, trainer, and youth worker, Sandrina's academic work documents the impact of (neo) colonial practices and policies and how racialized communities negotiate and disrupt their effects. Her scholarship is rooted in participatory, action-oriented, and arts-based methods, and draws on Indigenous, queer, anti-racist, anti-/post-colonial, and transnational feminist theories and perspectives.

Denis Lafortune, of the School of Criminology, Université de Montréal, has a doctorate in psychology. He is interested in incarcerated people who suffer from mental health problems and in intervention programs developed for them. More recently, he became interested in coping strategies and mentalization as moderating factors in the relationship between child abuse and behaviour problems. In this context, he is also a resident researcher at the Centre jeunesse de Montréal-Institut Universitaire.

Marie-Pierre Milcent, after her receiving her PhD in psychology from the Université de Montréal, has continued her research with the Prospère team. She worked as a research professional on the study Métiers de pères, directed by Annie Devault. For the past ten years, she has taught psychology at Collège Marie-Victorin in Montreal, and has had a private practice as a clinical psychologist. She continues to be active in the research field as a consultant and facilitator and as a member of a research committee on ethics. She is recognized for her expertise in sexual aggression, psychological problems related to a child's birth, and support to parents who are in difficult situations.

Francine Ouellet is a researcher in the Montreal Public Health Department. Throughout her career, she has worked on designing and evaluating health-promotion programs targeting marginalized populations. Inspired by the theoretical perspective of the self-awareness investigation and the empowerment of social outcasts, many of the programs she has coordinated have received both national and international acknowledgment. She has now retired, and pursues her militancy with Centraide of Greater Montreal. A sociologist and demographer, she has a master's degree in public health from the Université de Montréal.

Daniel Paquette is a professor in the Psychology Department at the Université de Montréal, and has been an associate researcher with the Prospère team for fifteen years. He holds qualifications in ethology and primatology. His research work mostly relates to the socialization of aggression in preschool-age children, parenting, father-child and mother-child attachment, and father-child physical play function, and he has developed the activation theory. He has completed a post-doctorate in psychoeducation.

Isabelle Sanchez worked for nine years in the research centre of the Centre jeunesse de Montréal-Institut universitaire. Among other projects, she worked on the evaluation of innovative programs targeting young single mothers and vulnerable fathers. Trained in sociology, Ms Sanchez is currently working at the Université du Québec à Montréal with the Research and Intervention Centre on Suicide and Euthanasia to design, implement, and evaluate a mental health-promotion program for children in primary school.

Geneviève Turcotte is a sociologist with the Centre jeunesse de Montréal-Institut universitaire. Her interest revolves around three poles: child abuse and neglect – in particular, child abandonment and relinquishment; the social insertion of mothers and fathers living in poverty; and the development and evaluation of innovative interventions. She has been involved in the Groupe de recherche et d'action sur la victimisation des enfants since its inception. In her involvement with the Prospère team, she was initially interested in the determining factors of father involvement, and has contributed to the implementation and evaluation of many participatory action research studies.

www.ingramcontent.com/pod-product-compliance
Lightning Source LLC
Chambersburg PA
CBHW020359080526
44584CB00014B/1084